# THE ORPHEAN PASSAGES

OTHER BOOKS BY WALTER WANGERIN, JR.

The Book of the Dun Cow
The Book of Sorrows
Ragman and Other Cries of Faith

# The Orphean Passages
## The Drama of Faith

WALTER WANGERIN, JR.

*1817*

Harper & Row, Publishers, San Francisco

Cambridge, Hagerstown, New York, Philadelphia
London, Mexico City, São Paulo, Singapore, Sydney

*130379*

THE ORPHEAN PASSAGES: *The Drama of Faith.* Copyright © 1986 by Walter Wangerin, Jr. All rights reserved. Printed in the United States of America. No part of this book may be used or reproduced in any manner whatsoever without written permission except in the case of brief quotations embodied in critical articles and reviews. For information address Harper & Row, Publishers, Inc., 10 East 53rd Street, New York, NY 10022. Published simultaneously in Canada by Fitzhenry & Whiteside, Limited, Toronto.

FIRST EDITION

Designed by Donald Hatch

Library of Congress Cataloging-in-Publication Data

Wangerin, Walter.
    The Orphean passages.

    1. Faith.    I. Title.
BV4637.W33    1986              234'.2              85–45725
ISBN 0-06-069256-1

86  87  88  89  90  RRD  10  9  8  7  6  5  4  3  2

*To Cheri, Jon, and John,*
*my sister, my brothers,*
*in ministry together*

I boast and strive with all my strength to be found a Christian. Not because the teachings of Plato are different from those of Christ, but because they are not totally identical. The same applies to the Stoics, poets and historians. For each man spoke well, in proportion to the share that he had of the seminal Word, seeing what was related to it.

Whatever things were rightly said by any man, belong to us Christians.

For those writers were able to see reality darkly, through the seed of the Word implanted within them.

—Justin Martyr, *2 Apology 13*

# Contents

# *Prologue:* Faithing

We desire our nouns to declare the fixedness of things.

We desire nouns *because* they presume the fixedness of things: general categories, particulars in a general category, variations on those particulars, stages in which the variations might be caught and assessed—but always, always at our meeting them, fixed. Named. It comforts us.

A stone's a stone and ever a stone will be. If we return tomorrow and find that stone cracked in two, well, then there are three stones dwelling in our memory, one twice the size of either of the others. And all three participate in the unchanging (Platonic) ideal *Stone.* We will have them solid nouns because we couldn't live forever in the violent moment of the cracking, whose beginning and whose ending are different one from the other, whose ending we cannot know when we are at the beginning—unless, of course, we comprehend the laws that stone-crackings obey, and then we have nouned a process after all, fixing it. We've nouned a verb, as it were. We do that to comfort ourselves; we identify and codify "natural" laws to comfort ourselves: laws are the nouning of terrible verbs.

Likewise, house is house. Even when it's a-building, it is only en route to the thing it ought to be (that which lies fixed within the builder's mind or on the blueprint): house. A-building it is not yet a house, but some other thing, a framework, footings, joists, white pine, and lumber. Wait a while. We will only truly call it "house" when it's reached its ideal, and fixed, condition.

Likewise precisely, faith is "faith" not in the building it, but only in the fixed condition—or so we desire!

And love is not "love," says Shakespeare,

> Which alters when it alteration finds,
> Or bends with the remover to remove:
> O, no! it is an ever-fixed mark,

he says, and then he ends his sonnet with a self-conscious irony which, by its exaggeration, shows the frightfully destructive effect of alteration, verbs, and change: his craft, his fixed place in history thereby, his very being and love itself dissolve:

> If this be error and upon me proved,
> I never writ, nor no man ever loved.

He wrote, all right, despite his protestation (and his error). He wrote as all of us use words: to catch and to fix the things we would not lose, to preserve the subtlest and the loveliest of things, to freeze the fluid.

This is what a sonnet is: it is a cameo, a little stone, a tiny house of the poet's desire containing a thought, an image, love itself, the thing he hopes has not become mere memory but which survives the same *on account of* his expression of the thing. Stop the world!

And that is what nouns are meant to do. Good things we preserve in nouns. Love is a good thing, not to be lost (either the particular experience or the category, thus the possibility), and so we save to savor it in a well-chipped, exquisite, immutable sonnet (and we promise lovers they shall never die, bequeathing eternality)—or else in the word itself, *love.*

Moreover, nouns, like Adam's naming of the animals, give us power over things—if only they will not wrinkle and shift but stay within the confines of that noun. Magics black and white were no more than the naming, the nouning, of spirits otherwise undefined.

Nouns defend us against the terrors by fixing them in time, in space, in the order of the universe, and under our dominance. Why, I am half consoled only to know the *name* of my disease, since it is the not knowing which I suffer; that is a mental anguish to match the physical. And most of the prejudices of the world are, in fact, false, simplistic namings; *we* named the things we feared, and then by those names alone we thought we knew the thing we did not know, and so we consoled ourselves.

Say it again: we desire our nouns to declare the fixedness of things.

And next say why:

If everything flows, we are lost. We have no control in the world; and worse, the world that controls us is, to us, a mystery. Then we are no more than chips spinning in a flood. (Think of the wild, primal waters which in Genesis 1 were defined, confined to boundaries—creation being the divine nouning of things—but which in Genesis 7 were let loose in cataclysm: "On that day all the fountains of the great deep burst forth, and the windows of the heavens were opened—and rain fell.") We are lost, and we lose everything, too: we can keep nothing that we cannot name, not ourselves or our own identities. We cannot speak truth because we can't speak of anything truly if it changes between our seeing and our speaking it. ("Between the idea/ And the reality/ Between the motion/ And the act/ Falls the Shadow.") When our words are meaningless, our hands are powerless;

and the horror is that we cannot even know what crushes us.

Oh, we demand our nouns to declare—or else to effect—the fixedness of things.

Look: even I am pretending fixedness in this very act of writing a book for you, supposing my words still to contain some meaning by the time you come to them to bleed them of that meaning. And I trust the pretense, that not all the blood's run out before your arrival. I would grieve to think that I wrote corpses, or that all I wrote Time turned to lies.

Something must endure. With every significant act attempted, we pray: something must endure.

And now to the point:

As deep as this desire goes in us for the surety of our general existence, so deep and deeper it goes for the certainty of those things dearest unto us: love, loyalties—and faith.

*Faith.*

Faith—defining my apprehension of the deity and the deity's clearer apprehension of my self—faith ought certainly never to change. We desire the noun *faith* to declare a fixed condition, especially when the rest of existence so bewilders us. Let *faith* noun one thing absolutely. *Faith* is, in our wish and Shakespeare's words, "an ever-fixed mark,"

> That looks on tempests and is never shaken;
> It is the star to every wandering bark,
> Whose worth's unknown, although his height be taken....
> [Faith] alters not with his brief hours and weeks,
> But bears it out even to the edge of doom.

What a consoling word that is for the pilgrim, whose wanderings are through this wild world to the city prepared for him by God. When all else flows and therefore fails; when children, husbands, wives, and all their promise, all their spoken promises, river away; when governments go fluid and collapse, and companies liquidate, and jobs evaporate; when all the stars of heaven tumble down and this fair flesh itself shall thaw, resolve itself into a dew—then faith at least, here at the edge of doom, faith, the polar star, faith ought to last unchanged, immutable, serene, and true.

*Panta rhei,* wise Heraclitus? Everything flows? Maybe. But not faith! So plead our souls. Not faith, the God in us and we in him. No, not faith—or nothing at all is left.

And yet—the truths of existence were never founded upon our desiring. Rather, error is, when truth and our desiring are at odds: error, stubbornness, and forfeiture, and blindness.

Whatever we may think we need, whatever we demand, however necessary they may be to jury-rig for us a sense of understanding, in *fact* our nouns are fraudulent, and their security deceptive.

Faith, too, flows. Missing that, we live in Blanding's house. We live a fiction.

Faith alters despite our fine portfolio of nouns and our defining doctrines.

For faith—this mutual apprehension by and of two living beings, both God and us—is *relationship.* And relationship is ever and ever a dramatic thing, subsisting not in definitions which freeze it to objectify it, but in the changing itself. The changing *is* the livelihood of relationship.

I-It is a cold and lonely word, and the function of the noun.

I-Thou may be a perilous word, the dyings of two into one another, one emptying himself to be found in the world, the other one necessarily emptied in order to find the whole world in the first; but I-Thou is union indeed. Relationship. It is *faith,* and the function of the verb. And it cannot be where there is fixedness. If it is named, it is not.

Or, to put it another way: the law, which consists in definings so timelessly fixed that they may be written on stone by Moses or by Hammurabi, kills. The Spirit, the boundless Invisible, the interpenetrating Breath, the Wind which is not if it is not blowing, makes alive. Not in the shaping and the measuring of clay did the *'ādām* come to be, for then it was nothing but a lovelier lump of dust. No, *'ādām* was made alive by an inspiration, by the breathing out-and-in of the divine breath. Life was *living;* living was breathing; and breathing was the single act of two. Relationship is the motion that dissolves boundaries.

"When *Thou* is spoken," says Martin Buber, "the speaker has no thing for his object. For where there is a thing there is another thing. Every *It* is bounded by others; *It* exists only through being bounded by others. But when *Thou* is spoken, there is no thing. *Thou* has no bounds."

Two things happened on the Holy Mountain.

God wrote commandments upon tablets which could, thereafter, be kept in a box as in a noun, and then the people could sinfully suppose that they controlled their God, controlling the box. They needn't trouble any more with fire and fury, risky dealings at the least. Rather, they needed only to return to the box and bear that box wherever they desired—into battle, if they desired—in order to place the power of God against their enemies. This is *faith* as a noun. They lost both the battle and the box to the Philistines.

But two things happened on the Holy Mountain. God did a yet more terrible thing.

God revealed himself to Moses, his glory and the thunder of his speaking—*to Moses.* And the man died at the sight; yet the man continued to live; which paradox is to say, the man was changed, having been called into a relationship with the Holy One. Changed, indeed, and continued to change thereafter, as fire is not a frozen thing; for he continued in conversation with God, says the Torah, "face to face." And the virtue of that relationship was, in Moses, so real, so intense, so otherly (motion always abstracts itself from fixed things and shows itself so dreadfully different), so holy, that the prosaic people of Israel could not bear to look on him. The unnamable terrified them. Fire and fury *are* destructive of securities. So the people pleaded that Moses cover his face in a veil. In other words, Paul's words, they hid the glory, the direct perceiving of God and the free and furious blowing of his Spirit, in the law. In other words yet again, they named the unnamable after all; they nouned it, fixing the unfixable; and though they felt they rose to control it, they did in fact no more than sink their hearts in gloom. But Moses, by whom the Lord performed his signs and wonders, terrors in the sight of Israel; Moses, meekest of men in the presence of the Almighty, lost and living still; Moses, who himself regarded, yea, precipitated changings in the Deity—Moses was a man of faith in deed, in *deed,* in union, in relationship. And his *faith* was a verb.

Faith is relationship. But relationship dies in doctrines about it; at least it hides the while. Neither faith nor love, despite our desire, abides the fixing. It is Shakespeare's sonnet *about* love which is fixed, not the loving itself. His words I may know; but love I must encounter on my own, when I myself breathe *Thou.* Love must be loving. Likewise, it is only our words *about* faith that remain fixed, not the faith itself. Faith is personal and must be faithing. In time our words about faith shall fall nearer our desiring than they do the truth.

This practice of nouning and fixing is, I know, as desperately needful in us as once it was in Israel. We are as easily frightened as they. But it is not an indifferent practice, nor inconsequential. For nouns are fraudulent, and the nouning of our faith quite dangerous in the end.

When we believe in faith's fixedness, then we have come to believe in words, in words, in the nouns and the commission of our nouns—in doctrines, but not in God. We believe (a sad tautology) in the activities of our own minds; we depend upon definitions (but who can rope the Infinite?); and mightily, by our own passionate commitment, we persuade ourselves that these words are not hollow. To the degree that we fear fire and the fury, to that degree we need the nouns. And to the degree that we need them, even to the same extreme degree do we fight for the familiar doctrine. Fight? Why, we rage against the destroyers, those with bright and glorious faces, the verbs. Listen to our condemnations:

*Anathema sit,* the man who says our words are hollow.

*Anathema sit,* the child who cries that the clothes have no king in them.

*Anathema sit,* the Jeremiah in the portico, declaring God alive and no cold, stony temple, announcing God's presence to be greater than his promises.

*Anathema sit,* even him who says our skins are old and patched and leaking wine, unable to contain the new wine that he brings.

*Anathema sit!* Let him be condemned, the one who destroys each well-propounded definition with the proclamation that he is himself the Infinite come seeking a relationship with mortals, he who does so all in the single, detonating word, *Ego Eimi, I AM,* then follows that word with the next, "Do you believe this?"—which is as much as to say: *Thou!*

Stone that man! Cover him in veils! Pall him all over again in the winding-sheets of doctrines. Because, Lord Jesus, to believe you is to leave all nouns, to comet through the void—to verb it! For you give me nothing beside yourself upon which I can stand; nothing, at least, that I can name; nothing, if you are everything and more, that I can comprehend or find the limits of, by which to know you. You whirl me *out* of time and *out* of space, *beyond* all order, *past* the cosmos itself, to glory, Lord, to vast infinitude— and all is changing faster than I can pause to name the change.

You cancel fixedness and my security!

Ah, Lord, a flowing world sea-sickens me. A drunken world is *La Nausée.*

—Listen to us! Even so do we shrink from saying, *Thou.*

And even so it is: faith is a shifting thing, after all.

This is not similar to the world's shift (from which we seek escape in our nouning, our creeds, and the Old Rugged Cross); rather, it *is* the world's shift, is in that shift and with it and under it.

Faith-flux. Faith flows. To be in faith is to be changing— as the wind blows the grass and makes it to bow down, as the sun wakes it and makes it grow, as the grass itself opens tiny flowers to the heavens. To be in faith is ever to be moving through the passages of faith, and to be moved by them. It must be the verb, then: *faithing.*

And three things cry the change of it:

1. That it is *relationship,* as I have said earlier, which

manifests its life in change and which, to be, must also still be changing.

2. That it is relationship—*with the living God,* whose life against our lives mercifully, gracefully, changes.

Faithing is the constant losing of one's balance, the constant falling forward (which is the risk required even for so common a locomotion as walking). It is the constant loss of stability, the denying one's self and dying into God; into God Yahweh; into a Who and not a What; into a God who groans, grows angry, repents himself, returns, does battle, lifts his child on eagles' wings, teaches the child to walk, delights in promising and keeping promises, suffers the disregard of his delinquent child, yet cannot make that child as Admah nor set him as the Zeboiim; into a God who threatens general destruction of his people and then, instead, comes among the people himself as an infant prepared to be destroyed!

Faithing is dying into a living God and not a stone, neither a calf nor an icon, neither a principle nor an ideal, neither a temple nor a tradition nor a statute, neither a memorial nor an objective (not *terminus a quo* nor *terminus ad quem,* both of which may be defined, neither of which is alive, neither of which *is*). The God *autonomous,* the God *a-nomos* altogether, the God eternally the same, this God is, by a paradox, also one who walks the garden in the cool of the evening and then, some years later, announces to the Baptist: "It is fitting for us to fulfill all righteousness." Holy and jealous—yes, he is. But merciful as well. Hidden, yes. Supernal and above all worlds, yes. And silent therefore: so silent that the Psalmist wailed, "Thou hast forsaken me!" So silent and so still that the eerie stillness seemed, to Elijah on Horeb, to make its own sound—a sound of the absence of sounds. Silent, yes. And yet he is a speaker as well, words and sentences and discourse flowing from his mouth, a voice, a speaking voice: the Word!

He, to whom we relate, does in that relationship and for it, on account of it and of his grace, change. He is a living God. He may be the God transcendent; nevertheless, and marvelously, he is also an accommodating God. The relationship itself calls change of his mercy.

To be in faith is to be changing. And three things cry the change of it:

3. That it is a relationship with the living God—*enacted in this world,* this world of the furious swirl, in which all things flow.

This is the forum for our lived relationship. This establishes the conditions of it (yea, though heaven finally provide the alternative to it). And these are the conditions the dear God willingly accepted, in which to whisper, *Thou.* Or what else is the incarnation about?

The incarnation certainly does not mean that God dwelt in the world as a hookworm in a hog—that is, in, but apart from; in, but different from; in, but not *of* created existence nor of the sin that had disfigured it. No, that were a lesser miracle, being the lesser sacrifice, and somewhat parasitical. Other gods, the false gods, came only to be fed and to be praised. This God, at the incarnation, came to feed and to serve. This God, born of a woman, accepted for himself all the conditions of this existence. He was not just in the flesh; he *was* flesh. No foreign matter, he, but matter itself. No *seeming* human, as the Docetists taught; but human, *doulos* to all that jerks us left and right, and obedient even unto the starkest and most signal change, the Change Progenitor, the one that causes terror in every other change we suffer, to which all other changes tend: death.

The world is forever a flowing thing. Until the end of it, when the trumpet shall shock it still, all our lives and our experience are borne upon this flux. It is the unspeakable love of God that he comes to meet us *in the very terms* of this world.

Three things, then—the arena where we meet; and we who meet, a living God and living creatures; and the meeting itself, relationship—three things declare that faithing itself is a verb, a house a-building, yet undone.

Ah, little children! Faith is not yet surcease, nor hiding, nor retreat, nor an island in the waters. Ah, children, you cheapen it by your chatter, judging some to be "in faith" and others "out of faith" as though it were a fixed condition and you, the "faithful" had the right to make distinctions, as though faith, once experienced, were ever thereafter the same. Oh, dear children, "faithing" is neither a stone nor doctrine nor any product of your desiring. It is, rather, the frightful thing: a *drama,* wherein God is the protagonist, the first and greater wrestler, while we are the antagonist, Jacob at Peniel, terribly, terribly deep in the night.

And having said so, I commiserate with you. It is hard, indeed.

For such dark drama as this *does* dissolve our power over anything. No, we cannot keep a thing, not even ourselves nor our identities; and it does insist that something else has power over us, even a thing we cannot fully know nor name (though faithing is finally the process of namings, his and ours together). And so we are afraid, dear children. I know. And sometimes we feel so lost.

*Faith,* if ever it is to be a noun, is properly the whole play, from the first scene to the last, done up and done. But we do not know that last until we are there, until we have come to it both through and by our tribulation. (God knows; but we don't know as we are known.) Therefore, while we are still involved in it, we cannot truly use the fixing noun. "Faithing" allows—appallingly, it presumes—change.

But having heard that, hear too the blessing it implies:

When the relationship between the Lord and us is troubled; when we, like Jeremiah, spit against the Deity; or when we cry, as surely we will in the deep sincerity of our souls, "There is no God!" then, if all we had for definition were the noun *faith,* we would have to judge ourselves faith-less, fallen from the faith, cast out. And that were the worst of deaths to die. On the other hand, if it is faithing which we are experiencing, and if this desolated cry arises from one scene in a long and fluid play, then even the desolation may have its place in the changing relationship, caused by previous action, causing actions subsequent; then despair may be an episode in the drama. And then we are not fallen from the faith, but rather falling within it—and even this, dear child, may be *of* the faith.

For faithing consists in the living relationship. And the whole of the actor's involved: his soul and his body, his eyes and all he sees, his cowlick, his mouth, his ecstasies and his dejections. And when he dies not isolate, but dies from scene to scene, from gesture to gesture, and horror to holiness, why, that were a fruitful death indeed.

◇     ◇     ◇

In speaking of faithing, then, I am bound (if the form is to fit the subject) to present before you a drama, a play, a story. Faithing simply is not a series of propositions, or theses, conceptually joined together; it is a progressive experience. Therefore, we must make an experience of our treatment of it, too. And (propositionally!) we can support the validity of our argument only by pointing to experience. We will do both.

I will tell the story of a particular individual, whom I shall name Reverend (sometimes Pastor) Orpheus; but I will hope that his particulars strike chords in the memories of many people, so that they shall find themselves living in his skin, as he may take up dwelling in their sympathies. He may be the metaphor for our experiences, even as he excites experiences we have not yet had. This is the value of a story, that one soul may cry unto another, deep calling unto deep until more meaning is realized between the two than ever words could individually contain.

My story shall be told in six parts, but this is not to divide one part of faithing from another; there are not divisions. Rather, there are six *passages,* all of them dependent on their others, which the faithing one might pass through, six stages which we isolate for the analysis only. It is an intellectual exercise only. The experience, though cluttered with countless separate details, is always of a linear piece, a flowing continuum.

And, finally, my story of a contemporary Reverend Orpheus finds its archetypal pattern in the Greek myth of Orpheus. This is for several reasons.

In order to comprehend the experience one is living in, he must, by imagination and by intellect, be lifted out of it. He must be given to see it whole; but since he can never wholly gaze upon his own life while he lives it, he gazes upon the life that, in a symbol, comprehends his own. Art presents such lives, such symbols. Myth especially—persisting as a mother of truth through countless generations and for many disparate cultures, coming therefore with the approval not of a single people but of *people*—myth presents, myth *is,* such a symbol, shorn and unadorned, refined and true. And when the one who gazes upon that myth suddenly, in dreadful recognition, cries out, "There I am! That is me!" then the marvelous translation has occurred: he is lifted out of himself to see himself wholly.

Even so does the myth of Orpheus seem suddenly to reveal and make meaning of our experience with the Deity. It is an archetype, a mirror, of our drama; and rising to look carefully into it, we may thus look down upon the sublunary passages of our own faithing, where, in fact, we are.

Can divine truth be discovered by this intermediary of a pagan myth? I think so, truly. The myth, as we've said, is not one storyteller's creation; it has the sanction and the commonality of all peoples; it spoke to yearnings universally suffered; it hinted answers universally satisfying; it crept very close to the universality of God himself. The vital distinction between its word and the word of God, then, is certainly *not* that the myth lies, but rather that it merely images what God performs. It remains forever a story, but God makes history. It asks; God answers. It symbols; but God *is*. It is true; but God is Truth.

"Whatever things were rightly said by any man," says Justin Martyr, "belong to us Christians."

And so we appropriate the myth of Orpheus. How arrogant we would be to scorn the pearl God buried in a dusty field merely because of the dust! (And how impoverished our arrogance would leave us!)

The archetypal myth of Orpheus, then, scene by scene mimicks the sweaty, flesh-and-blood, in-factual progress of our present drama with God. It is an excellent "objective correlative," if you please, by which we can identify the patterns, the sequences, the suffering, the changes of our faithing. It puts a face upon our dark, eclipsed experience, indirectly naming what we cannot name directly—we, who are little in the vastness; we, who when we name the thing divorce that thing.

This particular myth teaches us, being the heart-sufferance of faith. It says that there may be found six turnings in the continuum, though some of us know less than these. It says that of Orphean passages there may be six.

Finally, let me offer an early warning regarding the narrative that threads this book, the story of a contemporary Orpheus: this man is an example of one moving through the passages of faithing, but he is not exemplary. He is drawn fully human, as anyone experiencing the full length of a relationship with God must be fully human: faulty, sinning some sins consciously and others unconsciously, sometimes very clear about his own condition, sometimes fearfully obtuse, yet able, withal, to love sincerely and to believe in the Lord God on many levels.

Surely, I do not enjoin the reader to be like him. Nor ought anyone to seek in him an ideal. Rather, I say: as this Orpheus does, so do we enact a drama with our God. And even as we are, every one of us, complicated individuals of ingenious slights and devisings, baffling even ourselves, so is he. He is not always to be trusted; but his story is. Trust the story. Orpheus, though unique, is at the same time one among a countless throng which includes you and me, each unique as well. We need him in this book. It is absolutely necessary, if I am to *say* that faith is experiential, also to *show* it so—and by my art to trigger experience for the reader. Please, all the weapons of my art are used.

But the fact that this story is a fiction makes it universally true.

# The First Passage: Experience and Language

*Perhaps there were wide green lawns where a man and a woman could walk in the afternoon, and the dark Lombardy poplar standing aside in groves with their gowns wound up around them, gracious, private, kind, allowing lovers quietly to pass. Perhaps the sky was openly, royally, nobly blue, and the floating clouds pure white. Surely, there was the sense that the gods on their mountain possessed the sky. Surely, the sky was clean. Perhaps the city sat at a distance, tumbled on its hills, its houses looking in every direction, their roofs flat, the roads between them winding. And perhaps the man and the woman noticed none of these things, being lost in the souls of one another, and loving. Did they bow their heads when they walked, each to catch the whispering of the other? Did they smile abstractedly? Did one of them play a melody upon his lyre and sing? And just how beautiful were the heels of this delicate woman, footing the grass? How even were the lines of her face? Did they touch? Did they kiss? Did they let drop tears of happiness together?*

*But we don't know any of these things.*

*The story of Orpheus and his Eurydice begins in the mists. It begins with an experience, certainly; but the writers who remember Orpheus do not consider the experience extraordinary, and therefore they spend no words whatsoever upon it. That two should love and, loving, should make commitment unto one another; that two should marry, as these two did, is worthy and real not because it is rare, but rather because it is so natural a move of human life. It is the common experience of many people, however wondrous it may feel to those in the midst of it; and though it must finally come to words if it is to be preserved, it needs no words at the beginning—neither between the lovers two, nor from the writers who remember them to us. We are left to imagine the beginning, in the simple, childlike colors, green and blue and white. We are left to remember the experience for ourselves: in this story it is, but it is mute.*

*As far as the ancient writers are concerned, the beginning doesn't need the attentions of their language; what follows does. They are most interested in the consequences of this love and Orpheus's commitment; but love is the premise that needs no argument.*

*And Orpheus—what of him?*

*Well, he had a divinity in him, though he was as human as you and his heart as full of the running blood. His mother was a goddess, herself a daughter of Zeus and Mnemosyne; she was one of the Nine, the Muse Calliope. Moreover, certain genealogists suppose his father to have been Apollo, though others are satisfied that he was Oeger and mortal, for Orpheus died—murdered, by all accounts, in a manner the immortals could not suffer: not by neglect, but by angry stones, hoes, mattocks,* Sarculaque rastrique graves longique ligones. *But that is for a later time.*

*Orpheus had a divinity in him so persuasive that no one, absolutely nothing, could remain oblivious to it. He could sing. He could put words to his experience; he could clothe his feelings in such sweet language that the feeling itself went forth to grip the heart of the hearer and thence to become that hearer's own experience!*

When Orpheus touched the strings of his lyre, they trembled; when he opened his mouth and allowed the sound its freedom in the ancient air, so sweet and yearning was the music that no created thing could be complete not yet content till it had come to the singer, till the song sang in its soul and the song was its soul. Thou hast seen the oak?—its mighty, knotted branches and the root of it deep in the earth? Thou didst assume that nothing could remove the oak from its place, except the ax and death, for it is a singular tree, independent altogether? Well, the oak, when it heard the song of Orpheus, grew restless. It rustled its buff green leaves as though the wind were whipping it, though there was no wind. Of its own desire the oak drew forth its root and moved with slow, deliberate steps to the stone where Orpheus sat singing, and it sighed. And that stone began to melt, peacefully changing its hardness into softness. And if the stones could turn to pillows, think what power this song would have upon the lion. Why, he mewed, that beast. He laid his great head down in the lap of the sweet musician. He shivered at a human voice.

And all of the people, when Orpheus sang "Ah," said "Ah" in the depths of their souls, and they wept; and how could they hurt each other then? Heavenly harmony Orpheus released—yet Orpheus was only being Orpheus, practicing his own peculiar talent, his gift. It was his character and his birthright, to sing. Almost incidentally his song became the benediction of the world around him, music which made the world love music, concord which caused a willing concord. Orpheus, poet, poiētēs, "maker"—Orpheus had a divinity in him indeed, though *not so much that he was a god as that his gift was godly and could communicate supernal order.*

*What of Orpheus? He was one who sang with godly consequence.*

*And here is something notable: it wasn't his talent that Orpheus loved or cherished, as Narcissus did his own face. Nor did he love or prize the powerful effect of it. These he seemed to regard with a casual acceptance. But neither did he love particularly oaks, stones, lions, or the people, those who loved so breathlessly the thing that he could do. No, Orpheus loved Eurydice. Eurydice he honored with his remarkable talent.*

*And Eurydice he married.*

◊     ◊     ◊

Who can say when, in any child, the dance with God begins? No one. Not even the child can later look back and remember the beginning of it, because it is as natural an experience (as early and as universally received) as the child's relationship with the sun or with his bedroom. And the beginning, specifically, cannot be remembered because in the beginning there are no words for it. The language to name, contain, and to explain the experience comes afterward. The dance, then, the relationship with God, faithing, begins in a mist.

Surely, there may be words *within* the experience, but that is a different use of language altogether: it is the means of participation, of submitting and committing to the encounter. It is dialogue or prayer or sweetly questioning or the declaring of oneself to another. It is the child's sincere confession to the rain that he is sad—to the rain! To the greyness of the day! To the low and frowning cloud. And why shouldn't these things hear him even as he hears them?

Why shouldn't he be able to influence them by his own force of being even as they influence him to make him feel sad? Why not, indeed: they live lives as various and complicated as his own; the sky has a thousand moods; and behind them, within them, something—no, a Someone—commands and cares for them. Someone orders all things, for doesn't the child himself always feel the presence of a greater Other in control of him, too?—and so of all things? The real difference between him and the grey cloud is the difference of mediacy: upon him the Someone works directly, apart from the senses; the child just "knows." But clouds can mediate that Someone to the child, through his senses. He sees something by seeing clouds. In the clouds that Someone is "out there" and wears a face. Someone touches him and affects his feelings *through* the clouds. But because it is the same Someone who knows him, who knows the child, the child can believe that his confessions shall be heard, and maybe he can himself change the day: "Rain, rain, go away. Come again another day." Do you hear me, Cloud? Do you understand me, Dear Almighty? I am so sad today.

In the beginning words talk; they merely talk; and language *is* encounter. Only later does language acquire the secondary function of containing the experience.

And though, at first, the child has no name for this Someone so Significant, this Other, the Dear, or else the Terrible Almighty (*El-Shaddai!*), yet the holiness and glory, the power and even the righteousness of the Other are very real to him—and the love, though kindness and the expression of that love may wax and wane, depending upon the child's own sense of goodness and his health. It is the common lot of all children to encounter and to experience the Deity. And so faithing begins. And because it begins in children, regardless of their cultures, regardless of what languages shall later contain, explain and edit reality for them—because it begins, in fact, *apart from* the interpretive function of language—faithing, we may say, is not unique to a few people: it is at least initiated in all. It is a universal human experience. We all have danced one round with God. But we danced it in the mists.

And then there comes the time when the child awakens to the dance. He becomes *aware* of his experience. And because he takes it so much for granted as a natural part of his experience, he may not yet ask his culture what it means. For a while yet language does not arrive to interpret or to name the thing. Rather, he makes up his own babish explanations, or else he simply uses what he knows in a wordless confidence, just as wordlessly he trusts his bed to keep him through the night. First there is the reality; and then there comes the personal consciousness of that reality; he consciously makes room for it in his existence.

But then—in order for the first passage of faithing to be fully accomplished, effectively to lead thereafter into the second passage—there must occur one more evolvement of the dance. After a while, as the child "matures," as he commits more and more of himself to the daily life of his society, as the Holy Other seems less and less a matter of the senses, neither the reality of the experience nor his own awareness of it are enough. Other authorities arise. His trust in his own perceptions diminishes. His babish names and stories for his experience with the Dear Almighty come under a harsher judgment; they are in peril of becoming fairytales, products of a child's imagination, which one puts away with childish things. Now, finally, language must perform its second function—explaining and containing—in order that the experience be confirmed, preserved: confessed! And so the dance may continue in spite of his maturer world.

First, the experience itself, the reality of it.

Second, consciousness of that experience, that one might truly take one's stand in regard to it.

But third, language must frame the experience that it might be accommodated to the whole, external life of the individual, that it might be affirmed by and in the society that surrounds him, that it might be *acknowledged* as real, approved as good, and preserved. Now the child must needs learn the proper name for God, and how to use it properly, according to traditions and the gathered knowledge of his people. Now the child must be given a more communal ritual for the dance with God, so that it does not die away from him as an aberration peculiar to himself. Now he shall require the received and sacred stories of his people, to retell more harmoniously and historically what had been his babish tales. And now he must be catechized in explanations of what his spirit sensed already.

In other words, though faithing itself began much earlier, now the faither needs religion.

Is this a contradiction? Isn't this the nouning, the fixing, of what in fact is fluid? Yes: catechetics do, in a certain sense, box the experience; they set limits; they intellectualize the life of the relationship; they define faithing, converting it into the faith.

Then won't such fixed doctrines kill the experience of God? Well, it might; but it doesn't have to. Not yet at this point. First, because a kindly catechesis (as opposed to a stern, restrictive one, whose purpose is a legalistic prohibition only) shall allow room in its box for the change and the growth of the child. Its teaching is greater than his knowledge. If it is wise and true, it is larger than the child who enters it, and even its clearest propositions seem yet a mystery unto him. As long as there is mystery, there may be change and growth and the freedom for the dance. And it may not kill his faithing, second, because there may yet come the time when his swelling experience shall burst that box of doctrine and pitch him into a new void—a terrible time, to be sure, but an episode in faithing nonetheless.

But now, right here in the first passage of faithing, the naming and nouning religion has this value, that it consecrates the private experience; this system of language credits its reality, proclaims it, and preserves it. It gives the experience an authentic name and the right to endure. It praises the child in his dance with God. It declares that it has worshiped the same God. And it urges the child himself to use the naming language in a new and potent way: to name his faith in public and aloud; to confess that faith; to vow forever to remain in relationship with God. This *is* a sort of fixing, for it is precisely like a marriage vow. It is the most committed way to say, "I love you." Not only, then, has the child come to love the God that now he can name; not only has he experienced the love; but he has also allowed language—his own language—to confirm it.

Orpheus married Eurydice. The Faithing One loves and then marries the God whom he can name. He marries "Jesus."

All children, we say, experience the Dear Almighty. All people begin, at least, to dance with the Deity. And yet so few continue in the dance. Most do not even accomplish the first passage of faithing, which all have started. And why? Because, when they needed language to name and to save the experience, it was not given unto them. Certainly, in our society, they were not given the language of animism (which would, at this pass, have worked as well as the Christian language). And any myths that might have served (whether Greek or Nordic, that doesn't matter) were as devalued as the term itself: "myth." And for many, many children, neither was the language of Christianity taught. No system came to cradle the truth of their experience. Therefore, the experience fell into discredit, together with their lisps, their nightmares, their summer games, and their conviction that it makes any difference to chant unto the weather: "Rain, rain, go away. Come again another—"

◊    ◊    ◊

When the more contemporary Orpheus was a child, his parents and his friends called him Orphay, a gentle nickname. They would linger tenderly on the second syllable when they loved him: "Orphaaaay." Or they would bark the first when they were angry: "*Or*phay!" His name was changeable; it molded to the hundred moods of a healthy, living household.

And his mother did love him.

She kept a journal of his childhood. In her journal she recorded that he was born with three red birthmarks on his lower left back. This is something that Orphay could verify in the later years, because the birthmarks waited to be found. But she also recorded that his first words were "Mommy" and "Jesus," and this, of course, he could never verify, except that she had written it and she would not lie. What does that mean, that his first words were the names of his nourishers? Nothing, and then again, something. It says nothing about Orpheus himself. He was merely making the sounds his mother made. But of his mother it says very much indeed, for these were the names she taught him, sought from him, and delightedly recorded when she heard them in his mouth. It says that she determined to be significant in the life of her son (but what mother doesn't?); and that significant in her life was the name of Jesus. It says that she furnished her house with the love of Jesus, and that it was in such an atmosphere that little Orphay grew.

And this is the truth, indeed: that sometime in his youth Orpheus began to love Jesus. And finally he confessed that love aloud. But the love first and the confession second evolved from a longer, mistier, and sometimes terrible experience that had nothing to do with his mother as she would have it and less to do with the name of Jesus.

In fact, Orphay was often frightened in his childhood— for he met, and he could not name, Something. What? Well, Something other. Something mighty and unspeakable. *El-Shaddai.* The *Mysterium Tremendum.* Those are the best terms for it, since they would hold no rational meaning for Orpheus, but would be full of terrors. God!

There was, for Orpheus, the night of the snake.

Snakes he knew. Snakes he was, from his earliest memory, not afraid of. He caught garter snakes in the field next to his house, caught them by the tail and drew them backward out of the grass, then dropped them head first into Mason jars where they curled and looked at him with eyes of glass. He knew the rough feel of their scales, the flick of their tongues, the strength of their wrapping muscles, and even the sight of their blood when the tip of a tail would break off and then writhe in his fingers. He thought he understood snakes, though it never occurred to him that they might be thinking about him. He had snapped one once, like a whip, until it did not withdraw into a spiral when he laid it down. It lay loose and long and dead, with its eyes open and blood at the mouth. Well, if he could kill them, certainly he would not be afraid of them.

But then there was the night of the snake, and the whole world changed.

Orpheus was coming home from his grandparents in a far town. He could have been no more than four years old. His aunt accompanied him for the trip, and he was happy. He was, in fact, exquisitely curious because they were riding a train, and he sat by the window on the right side, and there was so much to discover.

The train was traveling south at so fine and furious rate of speed that green fields swept by as quickly as though someone were snatching back a tablecloth. That was marvelous. A great, orange, evening sun sat on the far horizon. The world was simply huge, and all of it focused on Orpheus as if he were its audience of one.

But Orpheus wanted to see the engine of this train. That was his greatest curiosity. Therefore, he kept pressing his cheek against the window, gnawing glass and gazing as far ahead as he could see. But so long as the train went straight, he could see nothing of it. He kneeled on his seat and willed the train to turn. One could say that he prayed to the train that it should turn. And he prayed with such a baby confidence that he was not at all surprised when it did.

Not surprised, but delighted—he started to giggle.

The speeding train began to make a slow bend of itself, curving right, south by southwest, turning, turning. It was a very long train. And the engine that pulled it was black, belching gutfulls of a blacker smoke and plumes of white steam. Orpheus began to applaud the performance and to laugh. Oh, this was a mighty engine!

But all at once the orange sun caught in the window of the engine and flared there, burned there, reflected from there to the child that was staring forward—and little Orpheus was stunned to terror. The laughter died on his face. He froze. He could not even speak or cry out.

For it seemed to him (wordlessly—there were no words

for this) that suddenly the whole train was a living serpent; that the serpent had turned round not to be seen, but to see Orpheus himself; and that out of a flaming eye the snake was glaring at Orpheus—and hating him!

Orpheus had been swallowed by a snake, and he hadn't known it, couldn't remember how or when. All the people around him, his aunt included, were in a snake's belly, but none of them knew the horror of their situation. Only he and the snake knew this. So the snake must hate him, Orpheus, most especially.

The child slumped down in his seat and covered his face with his hand.

His aunt said, "Orphay? Is something the matter?"

But Orphay couldn't answer her. He didn't tell her that he was waiting to die, though this was the truth, because he had no words with which to say it. He had no words at all. And suddenly he had no trust for anything or anyone: either they didn't know the truth, or else they choose to keep him ignorant. The world had changed, and he was lost. The world was not what he thought it was, not when snakes could swell and leap their fields and swallow children down and hate them. The world was laughing at him, at Orpheus, with its trick. And all he could do was to wait to die.

He didn't speak to his aunt. Neither did he greet his mother at the station. Nor did he talk at all that night.

He didn't die (which was a wonder—and a long time, yet, before he went to sleep with the confidence that he'd wake up again). He didn't die; but he had realized a danger, that there was An Other on the other side of all that he could see, not to be dealt with lightly, but to be feared and perhaps to be propitiated: to be worshiped.

He didn't die. But neither did he chase snakes again after that, and he decided to kill nothing that moved. Strangers take no chances. Transgressors have no rights. Children must beware!

But this should be said with wonder, even as it was perceived by him to be a wonder: he did not die, not once throughout his childhood. Several times he should have died. At the very least he should have been abandoned. Yet he did not and he was not, and the Nameless Other, the Terrible Unknown began, though no less aweful, to seem not wholly terrible either. Another principle was active here. Protection. Wardering. Safeguarding. Care and covering—
Love?

When Orphay was six and in the first grade of elementary school, he began to be aware that there was a robber underneath his bed.

He and his brother slept in a double bed in an attic of dim light. The ceiling kept the pitch of the roof. One small window was set at the end of the room, and stairs came up at the other end. The stairs themselves were walled and narrow, allowing the width of one person at a time, and dark. When in the nighttime Orpheus ascended these stairs, his brother coming cheerfully behind, he had the dread conviction that the attic was already inhabited; and the one who lurked therein was evil. He called him the Robber. He hoped with all his heart that the Robber would be under the bed already before he put his head above the bannister.

Orphay kept this knowledge to himself because he was the older; he feared for his brother's safety and he yearned for his peace of mind. Paul should not have to worry as he did. Besides, the single advantage which Orpheus had over the Robber was that the Robber did not know that Orpheus knew that he was there; but this demanded that Orpheus act naturally, show no panic, laugh and talk as though nothing in the world were wrong—and the ruse was exhausting. If Orphay could barely conceal his horror and so his knowledge, surely Paul would fail. And then what? Why, then the Robber would be forced to kill them both. These were the ways of the Evil that could steal into one's bedroom and hide beneath the bed: it kills if it's uncovered.

But Orphay was close to failure himself. For Paul's sake, he told stories in the night. Paul chuckled; Paul listened quietly; and Paul went to sleep. Orphay, on the other hand, taxed himself to tell the story, hoping and hoping that Paul would finally sleep. But when his brother slept, then Orphay could think of nothing but the Robber's face not six inches from his back. He strained his hearing—and he heard. The subtle sounds were there. The man could lie still, but not perfectly: he breathed; his beating heart made the bed tremble. Orphay wanted to, but dared not, cry. Part of him tried desperately to sleep, so that the Robber would be free, released from Orphay's wakefulness, to do whatever he'd come to do—steal, ransack the dressers, slash their clothing, but all in secret, leaving Orpheus and his family alone. Part of him tried to save his family this way from peril. But another part was persuaded that he held the Robber right where he was by staying awake, by moving and coughing to prove that he was still awake. It was a poor pittance of control, but something. It was a dreadful duty he performed night after night; but he loved his family. And it was frightfully confusing, this halting between waking and sleeping.

The boy paled and sickened during the day. His grey eyes grew large. The world was such a dangerous place in which to live, and people were so vulnerable.

Finally it seemed to him he had no strength left for the fight.

His mother said, "Time for bed," but he stayed on the

sofa and did not move. "Orphay?" she said, "did you hear me?" He sat with his legs thrust forward and his face down. He couldn't move.

Paul began cheerfully to trot toward the stairs.

In spite of himself, Orphay cried out, "Don't! No! Wait!"

His mother looked on him with a new attention. "What's the matter?" she said.

Orphay began to breathe very deeply through his nose. He didn't want to cry. "We can't go to bed," he said.

"Can't? Why not?" said his mother.

He shook his head furiously, frowning.

"Orphay, you tell me now what is the matter."

He managed to say, "There's—" But the image of the Robber overwhelmed him, and he burst into tears.

Paul scuttled upstairs. Their mother knelt gently down in front of Orphay. The kindness in her face made him cry all the louder, because he loved her.

"There's a Robber under my bed!" he cried.

She sat back on her heels and gazed at him. Her eyes were so kind, but her mouth pinched itself against a smile. He saw that. "Mama!" he wailed, "he's been there every night, every, every night for a long time."

She put her hand on his leg. That calmed him somewhat; and he was relieved finally to have let the monstrous secret go. His crying softened to sobs. For just a moment he experienced a rush of gratitude.

She said softly, "There's no Robber underneath your bed."

He stared at her. Not once had he expected that response.

"No, but there is, there is!" he said.

"Orphay, how could there be? How does he get in without my knowing?"

"I don't know. He does." Why wouldn't she believe him? And what else could he say to persuade her? "There's a Robber under my bed."

"Orpheus," she said, "you are wrong."

"No, I'm not, Mama. Truly, I'm not. Please! It's a whole man, and if I saw his face it would be wicked. It's a man with a wicked face—a Robber!"

His mother gazed at him a while, considering. Then, with one more pat for his leg, she said, "Right," and stood up, cracking her knee-joints. "Let's go."

"Where?"

"Come with me," she said, and Orphay's eyes widened.

"Where!" No, no, no, he'd done the wrong thing now. Suddenly events were rushing faster than they should, and what he had done was, he had endangered his mother too. She was foolish in her fearlessness. She would not know how to act safely in his bedroom. It urged itself upon him that though he didn't want to die, he'd rather he died than his mother—

But she was already climbing the stairs.

He pressed behind her, wringing his hands, unable to think of a single thing to stop her.

As soon as she had gained the landing of the attic, so had he. But she walked toward his bed, and he shrank backward to the wall. She was so brave. She was so wrong! And poor Paul, who stared at them both, was about to be disfigured now.

His mother bent down and reached to the bedspread where it brushed the floor.

Orpheus began to blink rapidly.

In a single sweep she pulled the entire cover back, making naked the floor beneath the bed, and she said, "See?"

Orpheus squatted down and looked. There was dust

there, and shadow, and space enough to hide a man; but there was no Robber—

—*that* night.

Orpheus did not blame his mother. He didn't blame her, because she did not understand. But she had just now made things much, much worse.

Because, if the Robber wasn't under the bed, then he was still outside, waiting to come in. She had destroyed a delicate routine. Tonight Orpheus had to suffer the further fear that he might actually see the Robber at the window, the shadow of the man—and if that were the case, then the Robber would surely know that he was known.

But worst of all was that she had condemned the boy to perfect loneliness and absolute responsibility. Always before he drew strength from the hope that he could gain an ally by telling her of the Robber. Now that was closed to him. He would have no companion in this contest, none. Hereafter, he was completely alone, his own resources, his own devices—and he was just a child.

No, he did not blame her. He loved her. It was she whom he was saving.

So she became, in the end, his catalyst. Under pressure of no other alternatives but his own strategizing, driven by the anticipation of his own exhaustion, when he could fight no more, Orpheus conceived a new plan. He went on the offensive against the Robber.

In fact, he took artillery from his mother's church. The idea came to him the very next night as he ascended his stairs; it came as a compulsion, or a gift; he knew not the worth of it, but he was desperate against the Evil that had violated his bedroom and threatened his family. The child sang hymns.

He roared them at the top of his lungs.

Stumping slowly, severely, up the stairs he shouted over and over, night after night:

> "ROCK OF AGES, CLEFT FOR ME—
> LET ME HIDE MYSELF IN THEEEE!"

—because he thought that if he converted the Robber to Christianity before he got there, the Robber would be ashamed to kill a little boy.

And it worked. He did not die. No one killed him. The Robber, pounded to nothing by goodness, vanished.

No, say that with wonder: he did not die, but lived. There arose in him a new awe for the Nameless Other who had heard him, and he went about his life with less uncertainty than he had before. Something watched. Something listened. Something inspired, in the breast of a first-grader, confidence. And Something saved him from dying again and again in a dangerous world. His soul was moved unto that Something in a more devotional worship.

How else, except for that Something, could he have made it through the first grade? Max Glettic, twelve years old and unaware of his own strength, would greet Orphay regularly with a friendly punch to the solar plexus. Then Orphay gasped for breath, but tried his best to hide his pain because Max *liked* him after all, and did not know what he had done.

And Orphay was hit by a car and flew, it seemed to him, some twenty feet through the air. He and Paul had been crossing a street. The driver leaped from his car all full of mumbling worries, gathered Orphay in his arms, stood him up behind the front seat, and drove him the four blocks home. Sitting on the back seat were the man's three daughters, staring. Orphay looked out of the window and saw Paul walking home, howling his grief. But Orphay himself, on account of the jolt of the accident, could not restrain his urges; he peed in his pants, right in front of the man's three daughters. The car filled up with tangy odors, and Orpheus closed his eyes, burning with embarrassment. In that hour he sent his knowing to the Unnamed Other—and the hour passed. And he did not die. In fact, he had entered an island of peace before the car stopped and the man withdrew him to carry him to his mother.

Wordlessly he thought, "Thank you—" Wordlessly, because he had no name for whom to thank. Simply, he allowed gratitude both to be in him and to go forth from him. Gratitude was a way of feeling, and then a way of being. "Thanks—"

Perhaps he connected the word "God" with the Other in those days. Truly, it didn't dawn on him to speak of the evolving relationship because it was not so much a thing in his existence as a quality of existing itself; because it was not "a specific point in space and time within the net of the world," but rather "filled his heavens"; and because, though other things surely existed for him, they lived in the light of this relationship. How could he separate such an experience from all other experiences? How could he *speak* of it? If he had, he might have used the word "God"—but with no more meaning than had he used the word *El-Shaddai.* It would have been a mystery-word for a mystery-thing, a sounded sign merely, defining nothing. For if something means everything, it cannot finally mean one thing and seems, therefore, to mean nothing.

Yet—though he could neither name nor truly know the Other—wonderfully, Orpheus began to love it. Most naturally, he began to love it. No, that's not exactly accurate to say, for these things lacking language still were in the mists. It is better to say: Orpheus loved. Love was a way of feeling, a way of being; and love could go forth from him, but it had no object yet that it could name, no heart in which to rest, no hiding place. It went forth and diffused, as it were, into his world. So it increased the tenderness he felt for his mother. And it caused him to hear birdsong with an unspeakable affection (his mother found him smiling and weeping in the backyard, once, on account of a tireless mockingbird) and generally to be moved to his soul by any of the works of nature. But it was a restless love, unhoused and unreceived—

—until he learned a true name for the Other, a name that could single it and give it a visible face, a name wherewith the Other could declare itself unto a child, and two could hug, knowing each other and knowing that each was known:

Jesus.

There came the Sunday which was not unlike a thousand other Sundays, a thousand earlier worships stretching backward as far as the boy could remember, but to which the boy now paid attention as he never had before.

They went to church. Orpheus was quiet, as though a voice said, "Listen! You will hear something today." And, "Watch! You will see something today." In fact, there was no voice; but there was in him a keen awareness and anticipation.

The words of worship droned. The talking was opaque to him, sounds of various pitches and intensities, signifying little; he could not enter the talking.

He liked the singing because he'd always liked to sing. That was satisfying.

But then an awesome drama began to be enacted. People got up and began to move about the room with such solemnity that Orpheus sensed a meaning here, and he felt a twitch of fear. Moreover, everyone except himself seemed to know both the moves and their significance: he was somewhat alien. Now, this dreadfulness of the moment, and his shrinking in humility before it, were feelings familiar to him; this was experience on a higher plane; the Unknown Other was more nearly active than usual and in control. Orpheus, sensing this, got up on his knees in the pew and shot his eyes about the room, trying to see as much of this drama as he could, but afraid. Something was going to happen.

Suddenly it became very personal. His own mother got up and left his side. With her head bowed and her hands folded, she joined a line of people that stretched to the front of this vast room. Step by step, in a slow dance, she went forward. One by one she climbed steps into a raised and Sacred Place; men, dressed in long robes, bowed to her; she bowed back, and kneeled down before them: she had been admitted into a Presence. Orpheus, his heart ramming, craned his neck to see. What were they going to do to his mother?

Now one of these robed men approached his mother, putting his face very close to hers, and his hand to her mouth, a gesture so intimate between the two that Orpheus felt ashamed to see it. And the man mumbled to her, and she nodded; and when he left her, she was chewing. He had given her something to swallow. Why would he feed her? Why would she allow him to treat her like a baby? He hurt for his mother, so weak, so weak upon her knees. No, this was different from the mother he knew.

And then another man came to her and put an enormous cup to her lips, and she drank from it, and she did not argue. Then she bowed her head so deep that it disappeared below her shoulders, and Orpheus had the sudden grisly impression that the head of his mother was gone: it was only her body kneeling there. Who can know what emotions roared through the child on that day? Oh, he could tell himself that she still had her head, and believe it, too. But anything was possible in this world of serpents, or in this moment of unbounded holiness—and so he could suffer the fear that his mother had laid down her head and her life, even while he knew it wasn't so.

She rose; she turned; she traveled the long aisle back to him. She smiled at him—*smiled* at him so genuine and sweet a smile that he almost wanted to cry because she came and did not die, because she looked on him and knew him, because she smiled so otherly and loved him nonetheless. She had gone forward unto mystery, not he. He was alien. And yet she returned to love him in her mystery! He wanted to cry.

She sat beside him and bowed her head and began to pray.

And then he smelled the smell.

His mother moved in a cloud. There flowed from her nose a scent both sweet and penetrating, new and altogether mystic. When he breathed it in, it seemed to suffuse his whole being. It was wonderful. It made his mother wonderful. He gazed at her while she prayed.

He touched her shoulder.

"Mama," he whispered. "What did you eat?"

"A piece of bread," she said, and he smelled the smell more strongly still.

He made strange eyes at her. Not bread. Bread didn't fit the drama. Really? Was it only bread?

She looked a moment on him, then spoke seriously. "I ate the body of Jesus," she said.

Orpheus knew the truth by experience, that when the Other was in control, then no reality could be taken for granted; all realities could melt into other realities; neither names nor habits could keep things as they were. Therefore, that a piece of bread should be a bit of someone's body didn't seem impossible to him. He accepted that.

His mother said, "And I drank his blood."

Solemnly, solemnly Orpheus nodded back to her. Blood. Blood was a strange and terrible thing to drink. It poured from wounds and pain. He had seen snake's blood and his own. It was life. Blood fit the undefined enormity of the drama. The Other was near indeed. The Other was very close to Orpheus now, because it had also seized on his own mother, shattering her common reality, making her to do and then to speak impossible things: "I drank his blood"— and then to smile upon him, Orpheus, her son.

Orpheus whispered, "Is that what I smell?" If he could smell it, then he had been admitted into mystery.

She said, "Yes."

He said, "Whose blood, Mama?"

And she said, "The blood of Jesus."

Jesus.

There he had it, though he had not asked for it, did not even know that he'd been looking for it. By the pure grace of the Other, and in his mother's love for him, Orpheus had been granted a name. He knew at once and instinctively what to call the Nameless Other. Jesus. It was Jesus—though whether Jesus *was* the Other or else somehow shared power with the Other, Orphay didn't know nor care: when he faced the Other, he faced Jesus. When the Other reached to him, it was the hand of Jesus.

Then all at once, but as though it had always been this

way without beginning, the whole of Orpheus's love poured forth from him and streamed to Jesus. He loved Jesus. He loved Jesus with his whole heart—and he was so content.

He'd heard of Jesus before, of course, and knew the stories. But they had been merely stories (even histories) unrelated to the extravagant experiences which otherwise he had in his existence. There had been absolutely no connection between the two—until with his own nose he had *smelled* the blood of Jesus, until his face in fact began to burn in the Presence. Then it was as though all the books with Jesus's words in them, and with pictures, suddenly went blank, white pages merely, because all those words were translated to another plane: they took up dwelling in his, Orpheus's, heart. Or rather, Orpheus took up dwelling in those stories, as though they were houses where he could knock and enter; and Jesus met him there.

Jesus. Jesus. So *that* was his name all along!

"Thank you . . . Jesus." How good to end that with a name.

"Rock of ages, cleft for me, let me hide myself in . . . Jesus."

Orpheus of the grey eyes smiled back upon his mother. And though he could not know it, in his face too was beatitude and a nearly bottomless mystery.

She, in her turn, despite the fact that he said nothing at all, was moved by him and wondered what drama *he* was enacting, privately, inside. His face positively shined for love.

Orphay could do two new things thereafter: he could live consciously in this relationship with the Other, named Jesus, giving himself to it; and he could consciously speak the relationship to other people, confessing it aloud.

That is, he matured in the relationship.

And language came down to frame it, shape it, make it communicable, by which he might himself confirm what already was. One marries another by the spoken vow.

Orpheus, at the age of eleven, had a tooth kicked out of his head. Well, it felt like the whole tooth floating in his mouth, though a stub of it remained rooted in the jaw. He was in the mountains at the time and so for two weeks could not get to a dentist.

At the end of the two weeks, home again, he developed a swelling and a throbbing ache. But he'd had experiences with dentists before, and he hated them. Therefore, he said nothing to his mother. Only when the pain grew unbearable did he mention it—and then he couldn't wait for a regular appointment. On that very day he was sent walking to the dentist. He went in darkness because the dentist would see him after the scheduled patients, six o'clock, the nighttime. It was gloomy weather, and a gloomy Orpheus who walked through it.

He had cried in the dentist's chair before. He was trembling now. But he was growing older, and he determined this time not to cry.

When he entered the dentist's waiting room, he found no secretary to greet him. She had gone home. Instead, there was a single middle-aged woman sitting in that room with wide eyes, gripping the arms of her chair, and staring at him. Noises came out from the other side of clouded glass, swirling waters, the buzzing of a cord drill, the mumble of the man who would be the dentist. Orpheus took off his coat. He meant to hook it on the clothes tree, but that was already covered with garments, and so he sat with his coat on his lap, wondering where all the people were who owned those wraps and jackets and sweaters. What happened to them?

The woman across the room kept staring at him. He blushed.

Suddenly she declared, "That's my daughter in there!" indicating the clouded glass. Orpheus tried to smile and nodded as pleasantly as he could to her; but he was struggling with his own fears and thinking of his plan not to cry.

"She has soft teeth," the woman said, glaring fiercely, as though Orpheus had something to do with soft teeth. He didn't know if this statement also required a nod and a smile. The woman said, "They break off." Orpheus lost nods and smiles altogether. He blinked. "Yessir! Can't never make a clean pull of it," the woman shouted, "but they always break off at the gum." Her eyes continued very wide. Orpheus himself now seemed in pain deeper than a toothache. He reached for a magazine.

All at once there came from the clouded glass a true, extended scream. It was like a dream, where one expects the thing that terrifies him, and it comes. But this was no dream. A woman shrieked till the glass rattled.

Orpheus and the middle-aged woman stared across the room at one another, each frozen in mid-motion, he with his magazine, she clutching the arms of her chair. She had eyeglasses that were going misty.

She whispered, "That's my daughter in there. She's got soft teeth."

Orpheus, prickles going up and down his back, was thinking, *I'm not going to cry. I'm not going to cry.*

Then the door of clouded glass opened up, and a young woman was leaning against the jam, her face pasty-white except for the tiniest pink dots all over it, and her eyes were rolling.

The younger woman moaned, "He broke it off." She took several lurching steps forward, then swayed in the middle of the room, not far from Orpheus, who still had not begun to read his magazine.

The middle-aged woman unlocked her knuckles from the arms of her chair and began to rise. "Do you need me, honey?"

"I—" said her daughter, and began to swoon.

Her mother leaped to catch her, at once producing a piercing sound: *"Robert!"* But the daughter pitched too hard against her mother to be caught, and they both went down in a heap at Orpheus's feet, and the glasses of the middle-aged woman flew across the floor.

All of Orpheus's toothache was gone by now. So was his sense. He stared at the women on the floor before him and pretended to cough.

The outside door opened up, and there stood a very big man. This must have been Robert. With no expression at all, he walked straight up to Orpheus, who swallowed. Robert pushed the boy's feet aside, squatted down, picked up the younger woman in his arms, and walked to the door again. "There's your glasses," he said, and he left.

Orpheus began to point to where the glasses were.

The middle-aged woman pulled herself up to her hands and knees and stayed that way a while, breathing. "Always happens," she said. Orpheus didn't know if she was talking to him, because her head was down. "Always breaks off at the gum." Heavily she rose to her feet. No longer tight, now, but very tired, she reached down for her glasses, and she went out.

Only when the dentist stuck his head into the waiting room and said, "Come, Orphay. Come in. It's late"—only then did Orpheus stop pointing to the place where the glasses had been.

So then, he was sitting in the dentist's chair, upright, two hard pads behind his skull, and the dentist was looking in his mouth and making sounds of dismal disappointment, and Orpheus was repeating to himself, *I will not cry. I will not cry.*

But he did. But in the end he did an extraordinary thing with his tear, and a wondrous goodness flowed into the situation after all, transfiguring it utterly.

The dentist said, "Root canal," and went to get his tools.

Orpheus felt the crying welling up behind his face.

The dentist returned with a needle; and when he put the point of it to the roof of the boy's mouth, the hard palate; and when he pierced the palate and fluid burned above its flesh, Orpheus cried one tear from his right eye.

One single, solitary tear came out. No gasp. No sob. One tear. And this is what Orpheus did with his tear: he gave it to Jesus.

He said in the deep of his soul, "For you," and then it belonged to Jesus; and he meant, too, that his pain and his frights and all his weaknesses were given to Jesus as well. The tear ran down the boy's own cheek. But it had been offered. Therefore, that was the only tear that Orpheus cried that day.

The dentist could not know; neither could his mother record this moment in the journal she kept of her son; but Orpheus willingly enacted his love for Jesus on that day, himself participating in the relationship, giving something important unto it. He matured. He was not only passive. And he realized how mighty and how sweet, how mortally deep was his love for Jesus—and how sustaining. And this: he was someone, too. Not only could Jesus call his name, but he could call the name of Jesus as well. They spoke to one another. Each was significant unto the other. How dear!

One solitary tear.

. . .

First, there was the love for Jesus, the thing itself, alive and real.

And then, with the name of Jesus, came awareness of what was.

And finally language came to frame it. And to confirm it. One marries another by a spoken vow. The vow identifies the relationship; the speaking of the vow is one's willing, conscious, and public submission to that relationship: now one's *own* identity—so one declares—exists only within *its* identity. In this process language is remarkable; it bears into the public air what had been knit in secret, in the womb of the spirits.

Finally, Orpheus spoke his faith in Jesus.

The dramatic moves of faithing which brought him to this point were not in principle unique. The details of the drama were his own because the experience was his alone; the details are always unique, because they are always apprehended by the senses, one child at a time. But the power behind the details, the unfleshed, invisible thing, is the same for all—and that there is a progressive relationship with this tremendous, unnamable power, that too is the same for all.

Children grow up in a relationship with the whole world external to themselves. But when that world is disturbed (as the planet Uranus is disturbed in its logical course by something invisible) the disturbance is comprehensible only if there is a Being, equal at least to the whole world, affecting it. Except for that Being, they dwell in an arbitrary chaos, in perfect meaninglessness, and must suffer the killing conclusion that they are themselves nothing, nothing, less permanent and less identifiable than gross dust. But children by nature do not and cannot live in such non-ness of being. Existentialism is, finally, an intellectual interpretation and an adult's decision, based upon the visible, sensible, evidences alone with the willful denial that these evidences can be signs for anything else, with the restricted premise that nothing *is* but what can be sensed; if it cannot be seen or felt, it cannot be. No, not even the "laws of nature" are anything real in existence or in fact; for, though things seem most often to obey certain invisible laws, one single variance from the "law" proves it to be no law at all (says the existentialist). They see in the disturbances, then, the deeper truth that nothing is constant, that no truth at all lies behind the sensible world, that the sensible world, finally inchoate, is finally all. But children are persuaded of importance, of significance, of value (whether they understand the value or not—that doesn't matter) and of the worth both of existence and of their own existences. This is axiomatic to every step they take in the world, to every risk, to every meal, to every new piece of learning they accomplish. The disturbances of the world, then, immediately announce to them the corollary axiom that Something is responsible beyond the sensible, affecting it: there is An Other, whose being relieves the horror of a world absolutely disordered and dangerous altogether. It may itself terrify them, when they imagine its awesome power; it may even seem to hate them; but it is nevertheless "good" since existence could be nothing without it. And it doesn't even matter whether the disturbance which they experienced could have a rational and adult explanation (sunlight reflected on a train engine's window) because explanations do not speak to the soul, and it is the soul that is reacting. Such explanations ignore relationship, and it is relationship that has the greater reality for children, beings colliding with beings and having feelings for one another. Such explanations require cool time for consideration and assimilation, but it is the immediate terror that wants relief in order just to live now, at this time, in this place. No, the child cannot live in non-ness of being. (Perhaps the child who cannot believe in An Other to order things is the one we call autistic.) Neither can the child wait upon the cool machinery of the intellect. For the child there is An Other, and it is as much in relationship with him as is the whole external and visible world, and it knows him, though he cannot at first know it. That Unnamable Other *is—and is for all children,* not merely for Orpheus.

They all do begin the first passage of faithing.

First, there is *El-Shaddai* and relationship, in which the child may have feelings; and often those feelings, as with Orpheus, turn to love. Why? Because the child fears he might, but does not, die.

And then the child, in various, compulsive forms of dialogue with the Other, comes to awareness of the relationship and takes up his position within it.

But here, now, the common experiences of children divide, and some continue in faithing and others do not.

Unless there is given them, as there was given Orpheus, a language at the right time (this is *kairos!*) and a means whereby to make experience also intellectual; unless words, stories, ritual, and doctrine are available to make space in the rational mind for the heart's conviction of God; unless religion occurs to sustain the personal "religious" conviction, why, then that conviction is lost with their childhood as the opinions of childhood become more and more suspect to their intelligence. That conviction flows into the past *(panta rhei,* indeed); it starves with the host of invisible beings that peopled childhood, some of them merely imagined (the Robber under the bed) but some of them true (the wickedness of the world, Evil Itself, the Fallen Angel being, in fact, that Robber under the bed!), true indeed, but lost now for want of expression, and scorned and wasting and dead.

Faith, *faithing,* begins by nature in children. The relationship is, first, truly there. But it can, in the vast massacre of neglect, die.

Silent parents, parents inpoverished of the language of faith (it doesn't matter, at this point, which religion), parents whose apparatus for explaining experience discounts God as myth (though their own apparatus is only, always, mythic, however sophisticated, scientific, realistic they may please themselves to think it), parents who choose to "let my child choose for himself," these parents are King Herod, and the relationships which their children enjoyed babishly with the Deity—these are the innocents of Bethlehem. It is a slaughter unspeakably sad.

Without the language to affirm it into and within adulthood, the children cease their nascent believing in God. They step forth into the rational, tactile world, seeking other meanings and purposes. And having none other to believe in, but needing nonetheless to believe, they choose to believe in rationality itself and tactility: in this, that they can see a thing and reason from it. No being do they believe in, then; but in matter and a method. And purpose devolves to the self-satisfaction of their own beings, their bodies and their minds. And they become the gods whom they obey and propitiate (for there are always gods) whose desires they fulfill. This is the Slaughter of the Innocents at the strict beginning of the process of salvation, immortally sad.

But some of the children do receive a language. Some are trained in it by a community who trusts its truth. Some are taught to use it, to fill it up with their precedent and undefined experience. For them, faithing has been granted continuance.

Orpheus was among these. In his youth he had come at

sometime to love and to name Lord Jesus. Then, at the age of thirteen, he was given his public day when faithing found expression in The Faith.

This was no beginning, surely, no initiation for him or for any other confessor, since so much preceded and enabled the thing. Orpheus did not at this moment "come" to faith. Altar calls and sudden spontaneous confessions are real, if they are real, not in themselves as though *then* the heavens opened and *then* the Spirit "convicted" the wayward and slew him, as though *then*, abruptly, the sinner met God-Jesus for the first time and *then* was saved. No, they are real, rather, as a proclamation of the thing long growing between God and the child, the thing now ready to bespeak itself, to be delivered into the community. For this we know of a certainty, that faith is only sometimes faith, but it is always faithing: the relationship which is always there and ever changing *sometimes* emerges in a public place to name itself. But that is a most holy moment.

Orpheus loved Eurydice long in the mists of our unmemory; but then, once, publicly, he spoke his love in a vow, and they were married. That was a holy moment.

Thirteen-year-old Orpheus loved Jesus long, even in the mists of his own unremembering; he loved him deeply, as deep as mysteries; and then he, too, named his love in a vow and publicly married himself unto his Jesus. His love rose into view. And the moment was very, very holy. His mother, who had written the word *Jesus* into his journal early, and who had given him the name *Jesus* when he was ready to hear it, now heard the name from his own lips, all full of meaning; and she wept.

Orpheus wanted desperately to be beautiful for the moment.

He had new clothes. That was good, but not good

enough. He had a passable countenance, but he thought it dull and round and senseless, like a plate. And on the back of his lumpish head there always sat a cowlick, an inch or so of willful hair that rose like a row of grass someone missed in mowing. It embarrassed him. He was never quite neat, so he felt always just a tad disheveled, as though he couldn't get creases out of his pants. What good were new clothes if you had a cowlick? You might as well have dirt under your nails, too.

But Orpheus loved Jesus with all his heart. He yearned to *look* lovely and worthy for his Jesus when the time came to say it aloud. He didn't want anyone to patronize him or to smile tolerantly on his words or to judge his love as naive because he looked childish and unkempt. Rather, he wanted the congregation to realize the dignity, the beauty, the transporting goodness of his love, his love and his Jesus.

Orpheus had nothing better to say to them than this, nothing more significant; his appearance should proclaim the glory of his conviction.

But he had a cowlick.

Now, what he did about his cowlick may seem silly, but it wasn't. It was preparation to meet his beloved. It was a sort of anointing. It was a desperate effort to overcome his humility before the face of God—and it revealed the intensity of his commitment.

On the Saturday night before his confirmation, Orpheus washed his hair. Then he combed it into a perfect part, laying every strand against his skull precisely, so that the bathroom light shined from his head as from a polished shoe. Finally, while the hair was still damp, he covered it completely with a nylon stocking, the excess of which he rolled up under his ears, and he went to bed that way. All night long he didn't move, but lay like a saint on his sarcophagus, his hands on his chest, his hair drying, his cowlick being flattened into submission.

Sometimes he slept. Mostly he willed himself to stillness, a sort of sacrifice against the morrow. Truly, he didn't mind the trouble, because he loved Jesus so much.

In the morning Orpheus rose and dressed and went before the bathroom mirror. There, carefully, he removed the nylon stocking from his head.

And straightway there shot up from his skull a whole rooster-tail of hair. A fountain of hair. A nodding tree of soft and happy hair!

"Oh, no!" he cried, and he tried to push it down. It stood up again. He brushed it, but that made no different. "Oh, no!" What would Jesus think of him now? How could Jesus receive him like this? This was ugly and nothing like the sweet, burning love he felt for Jesus. He wanted to be worthy of Jesus.

Orpheus was stricken by unworthiness.

He wet a comb and ran it through the rooster-tail again and again, arguing with it to stay down—and when his head was dripping, it did. And the collar of his shirt, too, was damp. And when he dried his neck, he felt the trickles of water run down it anyway. But the bush was down. And this is how he went to church.

Holding still from the waist up, he sat in the back seat of the car.

Moving stiffly, as though he wore a neck brace, he walked from the car to the church, and he hoped no one was looking.

But when he was positioned in the chancel, facing the congregation with the other confirmands, his hair finished drying. He felt it strand by strand spring up again, like someone uninvited coming to the party; he felt it gladly nodding, gladly waving to the whole congregation, and he felt like crying, but he kept his expression empty, as though he alone did not notice what a glory sprouted from his skull.

Now, here was the measure of his love for Jesus, and here was the blessing of speaking it aloud. When the pastor called his name, when he stood up shocked by the immediacy of the moment and its raw reality, when he began to speak, Orpheus forgot his hair. Orpheus forgot himself altogether.

His grey eyes flashed a perfect delight in the thing that he was doing: the thing consumed him. His face, ignorant of itself, lighted only with the goodness of his love and his Beloved; and then it seemed to his mother that the hair that framed it was a burning nimbus, a radiant fire flaming outward—and Orpheus was beautiful!

"I believe," he said softly—and he meant *believe*: this was the thing he stood upon as verily as the floor of the chancel. "I believe in Jesus Christ, God's only son—my Lord." His heart hammered at the privilege to take such meaning into his mouth and to send it forth clothed in words, his own words. He was saying, *I am,* and, *This is who I am.* But he wasn't saying that at all. He was saying, *This is Jesus,* and, *This is who he is to me.* But he was saying even more than that. He was naming the thing that had been lived, but never had been named this way before. In a sense, he was calling it into being, though it had been before. He was Adam, naming Eve! Or Eve, naming Abel. He was John, who pointed and said, "The Lamb of God." And Paul, who cried, "I am persuaded: neither life nor death—" He was all of these, yet in the exaltation of his soul he was only Orpheus, standing and saying "Lord" of a truth, and of a truth, "My"—truly, truly confessing and confirming a relationship: *He is my Lord!*

And he meant, as in a wedding vow, to say, *Forever.*

When he was done, he grinned and forgot to sit down.

He saw his mother gazing at him and crying, and he was glad, because it seemed to him that she, at least, understood, and that though she was partly grieving the loss of her son, partly she was celebrating, too. It was the loss of her son to Jesus. She, he thought, understood that this declaration and his measureless love committed him to serve Lord Jesus. There was no choice (this vow, in fact, had *been* the choice): his life's work would be to minister, or else there'd be no meaning in his life at all.

A wedding, indeed: Orpheus had devoted his life to Lord Jesus, whom he loved. He was going to be a pastor, preacher, priest.

His mother wept. His hair was a peaceful fire. And the moment was holy. For the boy had said his first word finally, not as a baby mimicks, but as a man means: Jesus.

And so the first passage of faithing prepares for the second.

◇　　◇　　◇

Creatures of the Creator, yet unique among all creatures in this that we have been created in the Creator's image, there is a divinity in us. It is our birthright, even as it was Orpheus's, son of Calliope and the grandson of Zeus; it is a natural property of our natures; it is the faculty and the means whereby faithing may consciously occur; and it may, perhaps, be observed in three separate functions—though in fact the three are often indivisible.

The divinity in us is language.

Of the three functions: it is not altogether wrong to say that animals and humans and God—we three—can practice the first function; that only humans and the Deity can practice the second; and that God alone can purely accomplish the third, though we mimic him in it and recognize this third potency of language as well. Now, these are the three functions.

1. Words work, as we've said, *within* experience. They are a means of personal participation, of submitting and committing to the encounter. They are dialogue, the dynamic process of both separating and also joining those that encounter one another; for when one talks while one listens, there are two roles, two beings; but when one speaks and the other receives *the same thing,* then two act as one. They are prayer or prophecy or "sweetly questioning" one of the other. They may be the impulses of the experience itself.

See how language is the experience in the following dialogue, how language allows the encounter to occur not only on a physical plane, but on an emotional one as well, and then, wonderfully, on a spiritual plane, so that the "Guest" might be comforted and transfigured in his soul before it is done.

> Love bade me welcome: yet my soul drew back,
>    Guiltie of dust and sinne.
> But quick-ey'd Love, observing me grow slack
>    From my first entrance in,
> Drew nearer to me, sweetly questioning,
>    If I lack'd any thing.
>
> A guest, I answer'd, worthy to be here:
>    Love said, You shall be he.
> I the unkinde, ungratefull? Ah my deare,
>    I cannot look on thee.
> Love took my hand, and smiling did reply,
>    Who made the eyes but I?
>
> Truth Lord, but I have marr'd them: let my shame
>    Go where it doth deserve.

And know you not, sayes Love, who bore the blame?
    My deare, then I will serve.
You must sit down, sayes Love, and taste my meat:
    So I did sit and eat.

             George Herbert, "Love (III)"

There might have been a dinner, a guest, and a host without language (though even that is unlikely, given the guest's hesitations); and there might have been the sense of kindness and fond feelings; but there could never have been the transfiguring comfort, the clear presentation of guilt, the gentle abolition of that guilt, and the satisfaction not just of the belly, but of the soul. It took the *speaking* to persuade the guest that he could actually consume the love of the host; and speaking on his own part prepared him, emptied him, in order to make space for that love. Moreover (precisely for our purposes in this study of faithing), it took language to make this encounter a communion on the holiest and most spiritual level. "Who bore the blame" is, to him who understands the words, the careful intrusion of the cross into this conversation; it effects, in fact, forgiveness; forgiveness happens; sins are removed, and a heart is relieved, by the agency of the words: a man is changed in this experience. And the host succeeds in doing what was his desire from the beginning, serving his beloved, persuading his beloved to *be* served.

This first function of language is, perhaps, no great wonder, being so common—until we realize that this is the function Jesus himself performs. He *is* the means of encounter between God and us. He *is* the speaking of God into our ears. He is the Word.

2. But words work, as we've also said, *outside* the experience, to name, to frame, and to explain it. This is the second function of language.

If the first allows divinity among us, the second memorializes the encounter. The first is what happens in Herbert's poem; the second is the poem itself, continuing, so long as it exists, the same, unchanging.

But this second function of language is divine for the further reason that God uses it, too, and we have received it from him. God not only created the world and the things of it; he also named what he created. Light he named "Day." Darkness he named "Night." He called the firmament "Heaven," the dry land "Earth," and the gathered waters, "Seas." In this way he said, "These things are not me, but they are mine." Too, by the name of the thing he expressed the essence of that thing and declared that this is the way that the thing would be forever. Finally, in the name he designated its correspondence to other things and its purpose for being. What God had made, he also fixed, firmed, affirmed, in the midst of all creation, under his clear ownership.

And then God invited Adam to name the animals. Next, Adam took it upon himself to name Eve. And Eve named her children, birth by birth. The authority to name things as God named them—this divinity—was granted unto the whole of humanity. It is dominion over things. We say, "They are not us; that's evident. But they are ours." And *what* they are we are given to know and to express (thus our inquisitiveness and our natural sciences; thus our poems, our paintings, our philosophies; thus the naming of our children, of people, of peoples, races, classes, groups, civilizations). And our naming is meant to preserve these things: to dress, till, and *keep* them—in the best sense, from a senseless death. (This is the good intent of "dominion.") Finally, we are meant to discover the relationship between the things that we name (correspondence), to find their purposes, and to train them into that purpose (whether the thing we train be a vining bean plant or a child).

There is, in this, a divinity within us.

But we have sinned, choosing not only to be in the image of God, choosing also—*demanding*, in fact—the authority of God, to be gods ourselves. And the result is that our naming of things (and of experiences), though it still have a divine value, and though it must still be practiced, can kill.

Earlier I spoke of the deadening effect such naming can have on faithing, fixing it as faith only. Now I add: when sinfully we say of anything, "It is mine!" sin means, "It exists to serve me and my desires," not "I am here to love, to preserve, and to keep it as God made it," and not "My duty is to discover the purpose for which it was created and then to train it up unto that godly purpose." One relationship dominates all the others, that is, our possessiveness of the thing—or the person, or even of our knowledge of God! This relationship brutalizes all others, either using them for our own benefit, or ignoring them altogether, or else sundering them. So the whole earth groans under our self-centered governance, for though we know it well, we've ceased to know how God knew it, and what his purpose was for it. And the peoples and the races are named according to our own self-preservation; we name them for our prejudices; and our sinful names actually justify our cruelty unto them, or kill the chance for true encounter. Adam named Eve for the recognition of himself in her. Now Adam may name Eve for the imposition of himself upon her.

We have a divinity within us. We will persist in using it—as Greek Orpheus persisted in naming his feelings by the song, as thirteen-year-old Orpheus confirmed and confessed the living love 'twixt him and Jesus—often divinely. But often, too, we will misuse it; and when we do, it is no less powerful than when it is well used. Only, the power that should have preserved the life rather embalms the body.

This is what we mean when we say that "nouns are fraudulent, and the nouning of our faith quite dangerous in the end." But the grace of God is that faithing progresses, grows, and explodes the boundaries that faith had set, erupts in new (and terrible) experience, calls the faither into further passages.

3. Finally, words work to cause to be what had not been before. Words create.

Only God performs this function purely—God, who spoke the cosmos into being. For, before he spoke, there was nothing. And when he spoke, the speaking *was* the thing! His word was not a means, no incantation, no magic to body forth a something influenced by, but separate from, the word that called it. No: his imperative "Let there be light" was itself the light. (This is why John later says that the Word is Life and Light; now the person of Jesus, the Word, takes on a mystery too wonderful for words; now we see that when God uses language according to its first function, the means of encounter, he can at the same time create, causing to be what had not been before, speaking into existence the Relationship, the faithing, that the human could not know nor initiate, causing love within that human for himself; now we know why God must act first—first in sending Jesus into the world, and then in whispering unto small Orpheus the stunning word *Thou*—for Orpheus was born muttering the word *mine,* and had no notion whatever of *Thou).*

Only God performs this function purely. Yet dimly, and in a mimic, we too may be poets. Both of our Orpheuses were poets. The poet is *poiētēs:* in Greek, "the maker." Though not from nothing, the poet causes to be what had not been before. He sings, and there gathers under the heart of his hearer the pressure of his music, the swelling of a new word, like an infant. It isn't that the hearer learns a new teaching, but rather that she *has* a new being in her, complete and suddenly. The poet makes a story, peoples the story with characters, sends the characters through twisting histories, and behold: the hearer believes his story to be true—if not historically true, then the *Truth*. And the hearer truly grieves for characters whom the poet merely made. Herbert's poem, when it is read, functions thus; an eating that never was takes place, and the reader says, "It always was." Likewise, Orpheus's hearers, even the trees and the rocks—or Orpheus's hearers, his mother first and then his little congregation, when he became its pastor—discovered, by his mighty words, a love conceived in them that had not been before: for Eurydice. For Jesus. Not that they reflected Orpheus's love for his beloved, moved to know so deep a passion; but rather that they did themselves come to love the beloved. Eurydice was theirs, and Jesus was their own.

This third, creating, function of language is potent—so potent, in fact, that most of the people believe it to be the property only of a few. Yet it is not unique to Orpheus. Perhaps Orpheus had it in a greater degree than others (and so the people regarded him with awe, whispering that he had "charisma"); but even these people used it. Whenever they told a lie so that others believed them, they used it; and when the lie returned to them as the truth on another's lips, and when they too accepted the lie so sincerely that it took up a place in their histories and governed their decisions and their behavior thereafter, they used it. They had created. They had spoken into existence the thing that had not been before, and then they forced existence to take it into account. Now, a lie is always a monstrosity: it has no right to be, and it devours the things that do. But a lie, once believed, *is*. The liar is a poet perverted. He does create, though his creation disturbs good order.

For good or ill, to a greater or lesser degree, people are poets. We all participate in divinity. We have available all three functions of language.

And we are all, in the account before us, Orpheus. (My dear, I would not fear nor hurt with Orpheus if he were not, from the first to the final passage, me.)

The differences among us and in our faithing occur, however, because of our various uses of the functions of language.

No child escapes the first passage of faithing, wherein he experiences, undefined, the Deity; and dialogue takes place within that relationship.

Some children (they may be adults by now) receive the benefit of the naming language at the right time, and the relationship is preserved by a fine and timely confession of faith. At this point many others cease the *passi*, the passages, for lack of language.

But then many of those confessors stop too, right where they are. They presume that this confession, this clear commitment ("I have accepted Jesus in my heart; I am saved!") is the full accomplishment of faith. They have arrived. They have found their place in the bosom of Jesus. They are done. All that is left, they believe, is to go forth boldly with the Gospel, themselves examples of—and witnesses to—its finished product, since for them the heavenly marriage is fixed. For them the fluidity of a living relationship has been boxed in doctrine; dialogue has hardened into litany (or hymns repeated, or repeated prayers), and the creating word would horrify them, could they hear it. Their words from the Creator are laminated on the pages of their Bibles, unchanged, unchanging, unalterable forever.

And when they watch what happens to Orpheus hereafter, they do not understand.

But for Orpheus, faith is faithing.

It began in love and a marriage—a marvelous first passage, as sweet as any spring and lambent as the morning. But time does not stand still at that beginning. It moves. Faith leads, if it doesn't deviate its proper course, to pain and unspeakable pain.

Intensely loving, at the same time intensely honest, Orpheus is in that course.

Grieve for the grey-eyed Orpheus. He will move through hell to that passage where the third function of language shall stun him, finally, with a name—and with being.

# *The Second Passage:* Death and Mourning

*It is always too soon. Death is always a surprise, confounding those who are left alive, no matter how long or carefully they had prepared for it. And it always makes the moments that preceded it seem special, innocent, and dear—and deceitful: the mourner despises those moments, wondering how they blinded him to the catastrophe at hand; yet the mourner longs for them and, sleeping, dreams of them so clearly, of his lover laughing, that when he wakes she dies again, and he cries out, "Eurydice!"*

*Soon after the wedding of Orpheus and Eurydice, while the groom still enjoyed the pain of the love in his heart, still groaned to look on the beauty of his wife, his wife went walking. Lightly she left him at the door. Laughing, he let her go. So young in their love, they were also confident and bolder than they knew. But a walk is a common pleasure, hardly a thing to think about; and it was a good green world; and Eurydice didn't go alone. She went in a company of Naiads, the swirling water-sprites who dwell in the streams and giggle. Why, the woman still wore the wedding chaplet in her hair. Orpheus saw her kick her shoes off for the walk and laughed. How she loved to touch the world! They were too happy to think of harm.*

*Down the lawns she ran, her white feet flashing. Along the stream she wandered. And while the Naiads jumped stones in the water, she paused, tilting her head to one side, smiling.*

*She pondered an innocent thought. Who knows what thought it was that made her smile? No one. It was not an innocent world.*

*Through the roots that clutched the banks of the stream there wound a serpent, steady-eyed, dry-eyed, eyes obsidian, narrow, unblinking, and empty. This serpent saw the white heel of Eurydice. With no passion whatsoever, but in the chilly malice of its nature, the serpent slid like a cable through the grasses, its belly whispering, until it closed behind Eurydice. Then it rose and struck her ankle. Eurydice said, "Oh!" as though startled just an instant. She sighed once, then sank to the ground and stretched her arms upon it and lay still, dead.*

*After a while the Naiads missed her and went looking. When they found her corpse beside the stream, they drew breath and they shrieked, all of them, suddenly. They tore their hair. They took men's voices, and like the waterfall that thunders in the chasm, they roared. They stormed heaven and earth with their lamentation.*

*So the world grew dark in a tempest, and the wind brought down a furious rain—and Orpheus knew.*

*Orpheus knew by the sudden desolation of his soul that Eurydice was dead.* Eurydice! *He burst from his house, his mouth wide open, though the howl he made was soundless:* Eurydice! *The lashing rain became his tears, cold, unsatisfying; the thunder seemed to swell up from his throat; and the wind made whips of his hair. The violent gloom of the afternoon seemed perfectly right to him. Eurydice was dead.*

*In the days that followed, Orpheus learned a wracking*

*loneliness, and none in the world could help or comfort him. He took his instrument and sang as he never had before. By the stream, now swollen with its own grief and turbulent in guilt because it had not protected Eurydice, he sang.*

*In deserts, on the precipice, the jawbone of the mountain, the sad man sang his sorrow and called with all his cunning the name of his wife: "Eurydice!" The deserts broke in rain and wept. The mountain could hardly bear the sound of the song and trembled. The song was powerful. His hurt hurt all creation. But it was futile in the end, and for him there was no answer nor Eurydice. Eurydice was dead.*

*Everyone—the oak, the stone, the lion, and every human heart—was moved by the desolated beauty and the yearning of the poet's song. So passionate, so pleading, and so sad, it seemed a sorcery; it brought a winter to the world.*

*But what is beauty if it has no purpose? What good is the song that is void? What worth has the talent that's lost its reason to be—or the love that has lost its beloved? Vain exercises, however much it move the people. An empty, empty genius.*

*Orpheus, poiētēs, had come to the limit of his poetic craft, his "making" ability. He could cause sorrow in the oak, and that loyal tree shed all its leaves. He could wring tears from the rock. But he could not sing Eurydice to life again. Not life. He couldn't make life. What he was, that he could sing. What he wanted, even that he could sing about—but he couldn't sing it into being. Therefore, his grief was real indeed in the ears of the world. And his desire pierced painfully all who heard him.*

*But, though they might by the skill of his song imagine Eurydice and seem to see her still by the stream with the chaplet in her hair, in fact she was not. She was only, still, the poet's desire, breath and words and yearning, nothing more.*

*And Orpheus, because of the twin intensities of his love and his honesty, knew that she was not. So the art that astounded the world, drawing its worship and its reverence, blessing everyone else, to him was nothing.*

*Eurydice was dead.*

◊     ◊     ◊

As long as death, however many words we spend on the subject, remains an indistinct eventuality, so long will resurrection from the dead seem nothing more than mild insurance—however many words we spent on *it.* Resurrection is only as good as death is bad, as easily believed, as easily dismissed. We call it a miracle, but we don't really mean that, because we don't really need it. We call it a miracle, but in fact—until death is experienced and proves it otherwise—we don't think resurrection all that impossible or even unlikely, and this is because life itself is so persuasive: we can hardly conceive of there *not* being life. So resurrection is simply life's extension. What should be, what *should* survive the nuisance Death, is no wonder nor miracle. Miracles are things that simply cannot be.

All this changes when death truly comes, and I experience it.

When I find my child dead in her bed, and the cold and the heat rush through my body, so that sometimes I am stunned to silence while other times I pace and wring my hands and cry and cannot sit down; when I look out through her bedroom window at the street and grow angry at what I see, unable to conceive of the world continuing the same, of people mindlessly accomplishing their daily lives, and I hate them; when death is an ending absolute, and when I learn this by lifting my child's body in my own arms, and her head hangs down, and I demand aloud, "Why should a dog, a horse, a rat have life, and you no breath at all," and I howl, "You'll come no more, never, never, never, never, never"—*then* things change. Then, when there is in fact no life, and cannot be, resurrection from the dead is the greatest desire of all. Then there is no good in all the world without it. But—God help us!—then and only then is resurrection revealed as impossible. As life persuades us of life, so death persuades us of death. Its ending is, when we experience it, the ending absolute.

When life cannot be, then its being were miraculous indeed.

But I will not be convinced of the impossibility of resurrection until I have suffered the fact of death.

And I will not completely suffer that fact until it is someone I completely love who dies and whom I desire to come again. It must be my heart that dies. All other deaths I can file away in some corner of my understanding, because they are lesser than me. But this death kills me because her life had been so necessary for my own.

There must first be love.

And then there must follow truly the death of the beloved, and the grief, and the grief.

Or else the hope of resurrection remains a formality and its fact a pious doctrine.

In this way does one experience depend upon another, even in the drama of faithing: death upon love, the marvel of life again upon a death indeed.

. . .

Now, see how a nouning theology can sometimes sub-
vert the proper process of our relationship with Jesus, our
faithing.

In the beginning we love the Lord Jesus above all things.
It is a good beginning. Then we learn to declare the death
of this Jesus, and that too is right. It is the core of our
preaching, whose theology is Christocentric, whose Christ
is centered upon the cross. We *should* move step by step,
dramatically, to Jerusalem from Galilee and to the cross. But
so long as his death is theology, a proposition in a system
of propositions, it is a pallid declaration after all since we
do not experience the thing we speak about. Oh, it may
move the more sentimental among us to sweet tears; but
these are suspect, theology being a matter of the mind. And
whether we are sentimental or coolly mental, this death
too—this most momentous of deaths—we can file in some
corner of our systematic understanding, and so it is lesser
than us. We consume it; it does not consume us; therefore,
it is never truly perceived by the heart as an ending absolute. What wonder, then? What sort of miracle can the resurrection be when next we come to declare that too? It is
only words.

Or, to put it another way:

We preach, today, the death of our Beloved (even truly
loving him!) in the pluperfect: it is, for us, an act completed
in the past. We look backward toward it from this present
time. Therefore, though it may indeed be real for us, an
historical memory and no mere exercise, yet we see it
through the window of that other event which stands historically *between* us and the death. We see it through the
resurrection, also complete in the past, completing the
death. Defining the death. Bounding that death of Jesus into

a little space and a little time, neither of which is *our* space or time. Because we always know the death together with its resurrection, resurrection never seems nor is impossible. Never, never, in the case of Jesus, do we feel his death as absolute and infinite, forever. Never do we stand, then, with the corpse in our arms, weeping, "Thou'lt come no more, never, never, never—" Never the desolation. Never utter hopelessness.

Look: because of the resurrection, we do not know this death *as death.*

And because his death is diminished, so, by a paradox, is the resurrection itself diminished. There cannot be the shock of it, the speechless wonder at the grace of God, who gives what could not be. Our minds say that it is a gift of the Almighty. Our theologies declare it so, spending many words on it. But our souls are not drowned in delight, because our souls had never first despaired.

Or so it goes if faith's a noun, a catechesis, the confession of a thirteen-year-old Orpheus, a body of doctrine from which to deviate (to move, to move at all) is to be judged heretical—

—if faith is not the verb, faithing.

We preach, "Jesus died," and we preach truly.

But might we not also, in an agony of grief, in a present and immediate relationship with the Lord, weep, "Jesus is dead. Dead now. Dead indeed"—and still weep truly?

To preach, and then again to be (when being is always, dramatically, becoming)—these are two different things.

We preach, "Jesus was crucified, dead, and buried. On the third day he rose again from the dead," and we preach the past tense truly.

But might we not also find ourselves *in mediis rebus,* in

fact on the road to Emmaus, sad and stumbling, you and me and Cleopas, with no other word for the stranger who approaches us than, "They crucified him—but we had hoped that he was the one to redeem Israel," no other word, no reference to nor knowledge of a "third day" because we haven't yet lived through the third day? Might we not so much doubt but be ignorant of a resurrection? In other words, may we not experience the complete despair of the disciples, live now the drama they lived then, suffer in fact the death of the Beloved (even while he stands alive beside us, but our eyes today as yesterday kept from recognizing him), three days seeming all our days, since death is the death of hope as well, and death is an ending absolute?

I think so. Or else our hearts would never burn within us at the miracle of the resurrection.

For the latter depends upon the former. And both are experience (not emotion merely, nor sentimental imaginings and tears, but the dramatic totality of our beings). And experience occurs in relationship. And that is faithing: the passages, the changings of relationship with God.

I think so. I think we travel with the disciples in more than a paradigm.

I think we run all innocently (even we of training and much knowledge) upon a present, unexpected death, and grieve, and grieve indeed: for the event of the crucifixion, as historical as it is, does also slip its moorings in time, not to repeat itself but simply to *be* for each antagonist of the Deity, for you and me and Orpheus, to be experiential now as it is historical then, to be real in the sequential events of our personal lives, real in the clutter of palpable details, dreadfully real.

"Once for all," this crucifixion. Once—but for all. It was

through a tent not of this creation that he entered, once for all, into the Holy Place; but it was also within this creation that this High Priest died: but in time and out of time, that he might redeem all times! Once in time—that he might draw all times into the holiness of that one time, and our time too, yours and mine and Orpheus's. Through the "eternal" Spirit, all our times and all our persons were spattered by that blood which flowed but once.

Look:

Old Moses stands before the second generation of the Israelite nation, the first having fallen in the wilderness. He stands at the Jordan on the east side and assumes a past event to be present as well: not because it did not conclude in the past; it concluded. Not because it was being repeated; it happened only once. Not because it had never taken its root in time, affecting the people then; why, it had been calendared, and the days of it were counted. What then? What could Moses mean—except that the relationship with God, enacted within the arena of our histories, is nevertheless a relationship with One who gathers all history into himself. He enters history, truly. That is his merciful love and his humiliation, thus to invert his authority. But he is God: he is the vortex into which all histories whirl, not only for their meaning, but also for their being. History centers in him. In him all tenses are one tense, being found in the indivisible Now—though he himself may choose to say "was" and "is" and "will be." In him the past is brought into the present. And when we stand before him, in marvelous relationship with him, we stand now before the living past— at once both past and efficaciously present for us. We stand before the Was-and-Is-and-Is-To-Come!

Therefore old Moses cries unto the second generation of Israel that time is ruptured—or rather that times are patched together in God; that the impossible not only is possible in him, but has occurred; that the covenant (relationship!) is with those who were not there at its making— but that because it is with them, they were there at the making after all, there in fact, there in the full experience of fire and smoke and horror and holiness.

Old Moses says, "The Lord our God made a covenant with us in Horeb. Not with our fathers did the Lord make this covenant, but with us who are all of us here alive this day—"

It is a complete and present identification with a past, completed event. What was, is—because both *is* and *was* are found in God, in whom both are one, in whom Israel lives as well, and moves, and has its being.

Likewise, even as Israel feared the fire on Horeb, though they lived a generation afterward, so we do grieve the cross on Golgotha; we suffer the death as an absolute death, though we live some scant millennia afterward.

I am aware of the questions raised by exegetes concerning Deuteronomy 5:2–5. They try to make reasonable and historic sense of the Mosaic conundrum. They wonder whether the Deuteronomic editor was ignorant of the tradition that the first generation of Israel perished in the wilderness (since it's never again mentioned after the second chapter)—and so they make their historic sense by placing the writings themselves more tightly into history, history effecting the division between the tradition and the editor, history being a final and most reasonable authority here. Others conjecture that the writer simply bunches all the wandering, conquering Israelites into a single generation, setting that body as a whole in contrast to the earlier patriarchal generation ("Not with *our fathers* did the Lord make this covenant—"), in which case the loss of some in transit is incidental to his point. Both explanations dismiss the paradox of Moses's assertion ("You were there, where you were not"), and time is in order again, clean, sequential, rational. Past is past, present present, both divided from the other—safe! And Moses was no fool.

But even if we must assert another meaning in Moses's mouth (the second solution); and even if (with the first solution) we must admit another setting and speaker for these words than Deuteronomy presents—that is, Moses himself on the edge of the promised land, the edge of entering, the edge of death; even so, I find in here the collision of the times, the interpenetration of past and present within the eternal. For in either case, the final setting of these words is likely to be ceremonial and regularly repeated through the centuries. The Hebrew words of the second verse sound singingly liturgical:

> *Not with our fathers the Lord this covenant established,*
> *With us,*
> *Yea, us,*
> *These here,*
> *And all of us alive today.*

If such words were repeated in a ceremony of covenant renewal, then it isn't an editor mistaking the song, and it isn't old Moses opposing nation Israel to patriarchal Jacob, neither is it just the second generation any more, standing before Horeb, in a mystery, and trembling. Why, it is generations upon generations of Jews remembering personally—and stating in rhythms most emphatic—that they who are alive are also the ones with whom the covenant was established, each generation participant, each one caught again in the holy warp of time and face to face with God then, God now, God forever.

So then: whether we find this truth, this unifying of the times, in Moses or in the received text or else in the ceremonies contained in Scripture, we do nonetheless find it in Scripture.

Moreover, it is among us today. We, too, assume in our sacred ceremonies that the times might be conjoined, peopling a past event with ourselves. This was one of the premises Luther wanted preserved when he demanded that Christ's blood be recognized in the wine; he feared to lose the reality of a bloody Jesus to mere memorialization. And even those who shrink from such words as "real presence" make so much of "symbol" that it becomes, in their practice, more than metaphoric action—for they do die in their baptisms, even when they do not die, and the death they die is Golgotha's, and their tomb is Joseph's, the man from Arimathea. For they repeat Paul's words as fact: "All of us who have been baptized into Christ Jesus were baptized into his death. We were buried therefore with him by baptism into death." Surely they understand that to enter Christ's death is to know it intimately, and that to know it is to grieve it. And at the meal, again, however they interpret it theologically, few discount the violent contrarities, the mystery, of Paul's other words: "The cup of blessing which we bless, is it not a participation in the blood of Christ?" And "As often as you drink this cup you proclaim the Lord's death until he comes." In ceremony we cross the times; we participate in what was as though it is; we proclaim by our very participation that indeed it is. Death now. Death present. The death that was—is!

Like old Moses, like the temple priest, like Luther, like the Catholic celebrant at Eucharist or the Baptist minister in the baptistry, all of us confess the collapsing of the times together into Christ. The notion is certainly among us.

"Might we not find ourselves in fact on the road to Emmaus with Cleopas?" Christendom has been repeating, "I think so" for some time now. And Christendom has meant more than a doctrine, since its assent has been preserved in an action: "Take, eat," and "Believe, and be baptized."

And yet, as far as individual Christians are concerned, here is an irony: the very ceremonies which would translate us to the day of the death of Jesus, and into that death, the very sacraments which would *un*define defining times, we do ourselves regulate. We dominate them, instead of allowing their dominance over us, and so forestall the threatful, consuming experience of bereavement. We do not want to be on the road to Emmaus! Let us, rather, consider grief without truly grieving.

Ceremonies are controlled experiences. They occur at ecclesiastical choosings, despite the agency of the Divine. They obey a rubric. Their gestures are fiercely ritualized. And we participants have often been more passionate about our interpretations of the event (distancing ourselves by committing ourselves to a strictly, safely, human dialogue), have been more passionate in arguments regarding the practice (sprinkling? submersion? wine? juice? close? closed? doctrinal agreement?) than passionate in and for and by the event itself, than passionate a-practicing it.

No, we fear to lose control. We fear fluidity. And we would not want to find ourselves on the road to Emmaus, desolated by the death of Jesus.

Yet, that is precisely what happens in faithing—which the pure, unsullied sacrament reflects in small. Faithing happens; to us; but not by our control. Faithing happens; but not through a few separated and identifiable elements only, the humble bread and the red, red wine. We are prepared for those things and forewarned. But faithing bushwhacks

us. And faithing embraces all the natural junk of this historical existence, spills outside the ceremonial, shocks us on
the streets, by the angry honk of a car horn, by the sudden
passing of one beautiful woman. It enacts the same wonder
as would the sacrament: times collide in the Timeless. But
it has a vagrant quality and is ungovernable because it is not,
like the sacrament, restricted to sacred places, clarified commandments, consecrated elements, and the presence of a
visible, familiar, trusted cleric.

It terrifies us.

It is Jesus Christ, authoring our passages on his own
terms.

Jesus Christ, who in himself contains the times, although
he dwelt within a time. (This miracle, this is grace!)

It is Jesus Christ, whose presence and whose person disturbs the times. "Your father Abraham," he says to the Jews,
"rejoiced that he was to see my day. He saw it and was glad."
But "the Jews" are as bewildered by Jesus' saying as the
critics are by the Deuteronomist's. It is not reasonable. And,
like the critics, they would make historical, sequential sense
of it, putting the past back into the past: "But you are not
yet fifty years old," the protest, "and have you seen Abraham?" (Even so they confuse Jesus' declaration, since he
didn't speak of his seeing Abraham, but of Abraham's seeing
*him,* by which there could be both revelation and divine
relationship.) Now Jesus shatters their logic, their nouning
language, and the security of a stable, predictable world. He
announces to them the very quality of his being: that he is,
even as he stands before them, the vortex of all the times;
that in him all the past is present; and that those who are
found in him may participate in the past indeed—as well as
in the future. He does all this in a single word, applying to
himself the divine name: his deity, fulfilled in itself, does this

thing. "Truly, truly, I say to you, before Abraham was, *I AM.*" Our father's past is our Savior's present.

It is terrible to be in relationship with such a Jesus. How can we abide the maelstrom he releases around us? Why, we take up stones to throw at him. We assert our own authority. We grasp at personal control over our own lives and damn the dizzy horror of time let loose. This is what we do: we explain, interpret, theologize, create systems of balanced rationality in which there must be no ambiguity, each word meaning but one thing. We name, we name, we noun the thing until it is subject to our intelligences once again and teachable, until it is fixed in a writ, inert, and dead. Safe! We retire safely into our doctrines—

—or else we let it be.

We gaze humbly at the Christ and see the living Abraham.

Then all the protecting structures vanish. Understanding dies in us, and nothing, nothing is left but to trust.

We gaze childlike upon the Son of God and see both Moses and Elijah discussing with him the second Exodus. And a cloud comes.

Then the centuries implode. Behold: the cloud that blackens our American sky is the same cloud that rolled around Mount Sinai, that smoked the Temple before a terrified Isaiah, that darkened noonday at a glorious death.

We gaze, abased, upon the Lord, and this is what happens:

We find ourselves companions of the first disciples, experiencing with them the worst that any could imagine, the death of the One beloved above all others, in whom our lives had meaning, in whom *was* our life: he had been our hope! This is in fact what happens: we run suddenly against death absolute, and we grieve now, now, a real, consuming grief. But we are the ones who grieve especially, since nothing prepared us in our twentieth century to suffer the death of the *risen* Christ. We'd thought that the logical sequence of the times had preserved us from that. Nevertheless, in an astonished misery, there we are, here we are, stumbling toward Emmaus.

Death is real.

Because he is dead.

They have killed him. Everything is altered by that single stroke. The face of the world has fallen.

"Are you the only visitor to Jerusalem who does not know the things that have happened there in these days?"

This, in the second passage of faithing, is what happens: the dear Lord Jesus dies.

◇　◇　◇

Reverend Orpheus turned from the altar to the communion rail, holding the paten in his left hand and one wafer in his right. Six members of his congregation filed into the tiny chancel. One by one they knelt before him, filling the rail from wall to wall, bowing shoulder to shoulder. The rest of the people were singing: "—drink wine together on our knees, / Let us drink—" They were singing from memory, rocking unconsciously left and right in their pews, sixty, seventy of them, a goodly number in a sanctuary which could hold a hundred comfortably. It was a small congregation. It was a celebration in the colors of human complexion, since the parish was black and situated in the inner city and "black" meant walnut and chocolate and umber and sepia and cream and ash and parchment and gold and coal. "When I fall on my knees / With my face to the rising sun—"

they sang, their faces forward, watching the familiar ceremony, waiting their turns to line the aisle and to move into
the chancel and to kneel.

In two brief steps Reverend Orpheus approached the
first woman on his left. "Take," he said, "and eat."

This was Mrs. Allouise Story, a retired teacher of a stern
and schoolish disposition, fiercely dignified, fiercely private.
Yet she closed her eyes and opened her mouth and allowed
her tongue to creep out on her lower lip. The gesture was
so intimate, and his own response so personal, that the
young man felt a tingle when he touched the wafer to her
tongue. Normal decorum was suspended in this ceremony;
folks came as close as kissing, and old women didn't shrink
to show their souls. Orpheus never ceased to wonder at the
evidences that his dear Lord Jesus was present, causing the
trust that caused such closeness in his people.

He loved this service to his Jesus. He loved deeply the
administration of the sacrament.

And so, to each of the six bowed down in front of him:
"Take and eat." With each of them the sweetly private moment of murmuring, "Take, drink," when they allowed his
face to hover next to theirs, when they allowed him to tip
the cup to their lips, and he smelled their various scents,
the human below the cosmetic, and he served them as
though they were helpless infants, and they were not offended. For all of them, then, these signs that Jesus embraced
them all as one and freed them from their isolations, from
their self-protective fears, for he had become their protection and their safety: he was their Savior. They could look
and act and *be* weak. Jesus was their strength—

—and Jesus, so the heart of Reverend Orpheus exalted
silently, was here!

It was with a nearly painful gratitude that the young man

returned once more to each of the six communicants, dismissing them, now, and touching every head with the palm of his hand in blessing. He wanted them to feel him personally; and he wanted to receive their feeling—stiff hair, soft hair, a mattress of the curly hair, bald skin, a woman's cheek: *Bless this one, O Lord,* he thought; and he thought to each, *Do you know how much I love you? Do you see how good the dear Lord is, to inspire and strengthen such a love?*

So grateful was he to his Jesus, that his heart would pound and he would hum and chuckle in his nose while six returned to their pews and six more came to kneel. Orpheus loved Jesus with all his heart. To serve Jesus, then, to have been entrusted with these people of Jesus, was purely a gift from the dear Lord Jesus which kept perpetually the face of his Jesus before him and for which he could not find words enough to cry his thanks.

Orpheus was a pastor. He could not think of a better, more honorable thing to be.

"When I fall on my knees / With my face to the rising sun, / O Lord, have mercy on me!" So sang his little congregation.

Once, while he was preaching (he stood in the aisle to preach, feeling too separated from the people by the pulpit, feeling too official underneath his God within a pulpit), he caught up a restless child in his arms and continued to speak while he rocked this child. And what did she do? She curled against his breast. She clung to his neck. And what did the people do? First they smiled; but then they dropped warm tears at the sight.

Reverend Orpheus was not surprised by their tears, though he had not intended such a reaction. Rather, he thought to himself, *The dear Lord Jesus is here. They see that, too.* So their tears were his tears, because the gentle presence of Jesus always caused a joy that overflowed in tears. He understood.

Often, thereafter, he forgot formalities and acted in a manner most familiar. Close to Jesus, close to the people: the first permitted the second; the second revealed the first.

And the consequences of both was that the people grew very close to Reverend Orpheus. They loved him much.

Orpheus was not unaware of their love for him. He saw it and received it and was glad. But he didn't depend on it, nor did he grow proud on account of it. This wasn't because of personal virtue in the man. Simply, he was thoroughly satisfied by the love of Jesus. That love alone contented him and made him proof against the lesser dependencies. The protective value of the love of the Lord was that he did not hunger another's love nor any other God nor even the praise or the estimate of any human whosoever. He was fulfilled and therefore unaffected either by vainglory or by scorn. If he thought anything of the people's affection, he thought, *Signs! These are signs of the dear Lord Jesus' love for me.*

These, then were the good days, the very early days of marriage, Orpheus and his Jesus—days nearly unreal in their goodness. The young man still groaned to see the beauty of his beloved, and he saw it everywhere; all things still were possible. Young love smiles upon the whole world, believes itself unconquerable, no task too great, because *its* love is a mighty charm and its marriage shall last forever. Young love, consumed with itself, sees the whole world in its own image. Young love is so innocent.

Orpheus lived in the parsonage next to the church. Both buildings sat in a weedy, deteriorating neighborhood.

One day, as he walked between them, a car passing in the street hit its brakes, and the driver, cried, "Hey! Hey, come'ere!"

Orpheus went to the man, who stared steadily ahead, through his windshield.

"What's goin' on?" the man said, as though it were a statement, a harsh greeting.

"Nothing," Orpheus said. "How are you?" He didn't recognize the man.

The man said, "What's happ'nen," but still did not look at him, and Orpheus didn't know how to answer.

"Look!" snapped the man, as though suddenly making a decision. He threw the car into reverse. "Look. Wait. I wanna talk." He squealed backward to the curb, flung open his door, and arose slowly, a very huge man with his jaw set. He leaned against the car until Orpheus came near.

"What you doin' here?" the man said, gazing away.

Orpheus said, "I'm the pastor. I live here."

"Um-hum," said the man. And he said, "Been a slew of robberies here-abouts. Take for instance that house—" indicating one three doors down from the parsonage "—where my lady stays. Her stereo was stole. Twicet. Second time it happened, I says, 'I'm gonna patrol this street. Me an' my menace.' Did you know 'bout her stereo?"

Orpheus said, "No."

"Um-hum," said the giant, staring off. He said, "You white, ain't'cha."

It was a statement, not a question. But Orpheus could agree and did. "Yes," he said.

"Um-hum. Well. Me an' my menace, we gonna enforce order, that's a fack. Folk nosin' here is liable to lose noses."

Suddenly the man stepped away from the car and commanded, "Look there. Look down there!" He gestured to the floorboards under the dash. "See down there? See it?" Wrapped in cellophane was the most enormous pistol that Orpheus had ever seen. "My menace," said the giant.

Orpheus didn't know what to say.

The man reached a long arm into his car and pulled the gun into street-sight. He said, "Now s'pose you tell me what a white man wants round here—" still not looking at Orpheus.

Orpheus said, "Maybe you don't live here, and that's why you don't know. I've been pastor over a year at this church—"

But the man cut him off. "I come and I go, man. Maybe I don' live here, but I b'long. Don'chu be tellin' me where I am an' where I ain't. You! This ain't a place for you, an' I don't yet hear the excuse I'm lookin' for. Preacher!" He spat the word.

Now, here was the marvelous discovery that Orpheus made: he was altogether unafraid. Innocent. In fact, he was *not* terribly aware of menace about. The world that could not turn his head with praise could hardly threaten him.

It was the most natural conclusion to this episode, then, that Arabelle Lee came driving down the streeet in her car and, seeing the two of them talking, slowed to a stop. "Hey, Bill," she said.

The man muttered, " 'S'appenin'?"

Then Arabelle said, "Pastor, can I talk to you today? I got somethin' to talk about." She was a member of Orpheus's church.

He said, "Come this afternoon," and she waved and drove away.

Then the giant started to say, "Hoo! Hoo! Hoo, man, you don't know how close you come. Hoo! I thought you's the thief creepin' these streets. Oh, man, I was ready to teach you a thing. Hoo!"

But Orpheus felt neither relief nor superiority since he hadn't felt fear in the first place. This was the measure of his contentment in the dear Lord Jesus. So sufficient was his love, so complete was his life these days, so consumed by the presence of his beloved, that he was somewhat oblivious to the realities and the dangers of his world. Orpheus, in the good days, was not bold nor virtuous, neither intrepid or wise or eminent. He was simply, sweetly, innocent.

And when the big man humbled himself to beg ten dollars of the Preacher, Orpheus took that change too for granted and loaned the man the money and knew he'd see neither the man nor the money again.

Gladly, gladly Reverend Orpheus ministered for his Jesus, gratefully and well.

He assumed it would go on forever. Why not? Life persuades of life—

But this is what happened.

On Good Friday, wearing no other liturgical garment than a black cassock, Reverend Orpheus stood in front of the congregation, stood solitary in the chancel, and spoke in quiet tones of the death of Jesus.

He had a gift for speaking. His words had power in the second and the third degree; he knew this instinctively, for hadn't he convinced these people of much of the things he saw in his heart? Hadn't they seen them as well, merely because he'd spoken them? Well, they should certainly see this thing as well, the passion, the suffering and death of their Lord. It was the event at the core of their faith. Yes, they should see it.

For that reason he would narrate it only. He would not "preach" it. He would not interpret its meaning nor seek a moral in the event nor call the people to do anything whatever with it except to hear it.

And so it was: in the mouth of Reverend Orpheus that night the story did not become a paradigm or a lesson or even the object of faith, any one of which would have allowed the people a measure of control, since they would have remained separated from it to handle, manipulate, or apply it as they would. In his mouth the story was told merely, delivered living, as the single irrefutable truth of the moment.

The lights were low and yellow in the sanctuary. The stained glass windows were black when he did this brave thing. Night was on the outside, canceling color. Night was in his somber grey eyes. Night was in the softness of his voice, and the music of his speaking was a dirge.

It was a brave thing that he did; but Orpheus was not brave. He was innocent. He did not know that a serpent lurked in such an exercise, and that as real as the story was, so real would the serpent and that serpent's murder be.

Lean Orpheus whispered to the people, "Do you see where Jesus stands?"

They screwed their eyes to see.

Good Friday was a thoughtful time. They would be patient.

Reverend Orpheus said, "He stands in a black, black night outside the city. Can you see him? Torches light his face in orange and shadows. One torch, the torch that Judas carries, comes very close so that his two eyes flash. Jesus whispers, 'Judas, with a kiss?' We hear the whisper. So does Judas, but he leans to him and kisses him nonetheless. Now the soldiers step forward, surrounding Jesus with their fire. The dry grass crunches. They pull the arms of the Lord behind him and bind them. Jesus does not resist but glances, rather, at the bewildered faces of his disciples and tries to ease them. He says to the soldiers, 'I'm the only one you want. Let these go.' They go. The disciples scatter into the night, and he is alone with his captors."

Reverend Orpheus fell silent a moment. The congregation stared steadfastly at his face, listening, seeing. He whispered again, "Do you see where Jesus stands?"

They nodded.

He said, "He stands in a room of the High Priest's house, and it is still the night. There is an audience of his accusers crowded round the walls. The guttering lamps make hideous shapes of everyone; and the High Priest sits at a table in front while Jesus stands singular in the center of that room. Do you see him? He is on trial. The Priest is determined. He knows the verdict that he wants, but he grows impatient with the stupid witnesses who step forth, who cannot even lie well. Suddenly the High Priest strikes the table and rises and assumes the judgment himself. 'Talk!' he demands of Jesus. 'Defend yourself!' But Jesus stands silent and still. Can you? Can you see him? The High Priest can. The sight infuriates him. All at once he throws the game aside and cries out the only true question. 'Are you—' He hunches over the table. The light makes a cave of his mouth. 'Are you the Christ, the Son of the Blessed?' Finally the dear Lord answers. He says, 'I am.' At once the High Priest grabs his robe at the breast and rips it apart. 'You hear his blasphemy,' he roars to the room. 'What is your decision?' All along the walls the accusers come to life, muttering, 'Death.' They hear themselves and grow the bolder. Louder, they cry out, 'Death!' They close in upon the dear Lord. They slap his face. Oh, people, they slap his face—because he is guilty and they are free and he's the one to die. They slap Jesus' face, but Jesus only bows his head. Do you see him?"

A second time the pastor fell silent. He wasn't looking at the people any more, but down to the floor at a point between them. Above the black cassock his face had turned pale. His lips were chalk. The people saw this and were moved. It is impossible to say how much they came to love Reverend Orpheus then. They held their breath and listened intently to his voice—which was music, and the music was an elegy.

Reverend Orpheus said, quietly, "Do you see where Jesus stands?"

Still bowing his head to the floor, he said, "He stands before the Roman governor, whose authority it is to kill a man. This is the state. This is the brute, collective power of all the people. This is Rome. Rome bends down and sneers, 'So you are the king of the Jews.' And Jesus speaks one final time. 'So you say,' he says, and he says no more. The dear Lord Jesus is silent thereafter. But his eyes are open, and he watches the horror and the hurt of this world. Does he cry out?" murmured Reverend Orpheus. "I don't know. I don't know if Jesus ever cries out underneath his pain, until— I don't know. Perhaps he goes as quietly as a lamb, I don't know."

All at once Reverend Orpheus raised his head and thundered, *"Do you see?"* The people flinched. The pastor's eyes were haunted, burning them, distressing them; but they could not look away from him, and he drove the question like a dagger into the air: "Do you *see* where Jesus is standing?"

He said, "He is standing on the porch of the praetorium—silently, but he is bleeding; silently, but he is draped in a soldier's mantle soaked with blood; silently, but the

Roman governor is demanding that the people choose between him and a criminal, one for death and one for life. Jesus is standing silently, regarding the people massed before him, while these people scream their violent, manic desire. They scream, 'Crucify!' Can't you hear it? They scream, 'Crucify him!' and they mean our Jesus!"

Until this moment, Reverend Orpheus had been speaking from the dead center of the chancel; but now he seemed to shrink. His shoulders bent into a sort of privacy, and he moved. He stole toward the wall—for support, it seemed, since he leaned against it as though the act of standing were too difficult for him.

His voice fell into a meditation most personal. Yet the congregation gave him such an acute attention that they heard the words however quietly they came; and the greater their straining, the deeper went their emotion. Someone began to cry.

The pastor's voice sounded like one low note on the organ, held incessantly.

Reverend Orpheus murmured, "Do you see where Jesus hangs?" and the people yearned to answer, *Yes,* but no one said a word. He said, "Do you see *how* Jesus hangs from the wood?"

Now, this is what was happening in fact: Reverend Orpheus was himself seeing Jesus, him whom he had loved his life long. No longer was Orpheus telling the historical story. Neither was it his perfervid imagination nor a seeming: he was in no trance. He was in fact at the cross, and his stunned murmuring merely reported events as they happened before him.

"It sounds like burlap," he whispered. "The tearing of flesh and tendons in his arms sounds like the tearing of burlap. *O Lord, why don't you cry out?"*

To the little congregation, Orpheus whispered again, "His bones and the weight of his body grind on the spikes. The lower he slumps, the tighter goes his chest. It closes on his lungs. He can't breathe. Look! Look! He is raising himself on the nails, shivering; his mouth gapes; he sucks air; his stomach's a convulsion while he heaves against the nails—and this is how he breathes! Why do I breathe so easily, but he has to fight for breath? Now he sinks again and the wind is expelled in a sigh; but the sigh is a prayer. Do you hear him? Jesus says, 'Father, forgive them.' Do you hear him? The whistle in his chest is love. Is that how love sounds? He says, 'They know not what they do.' I want to touch him, but he's so far away from me, because he's on the cross and I am not. He's—dying. I am not.

"There's such a crowd around me that I can't get closer, but neither can I separate myself from them and run. When Jesus looks down, he sees us all together. Does he know that I am different from them? Does he know how much I love him? They are laughing to protect themselves from his pain. They're making a beast of him, a fool, to protect themselves from sympathy and from guilt—catcalls, leers, and mockery. They jeer the God in him, and they slap me on the back, including me in their—*Not me, Jesus! I'm not one of them! Don't look at me now!*"

Suddenly Reverend Orpheus closed his eyes and wrapped his arms around his chest as though against a bitter cold. He groaned.

"It's dark," he whispered. The congregation swallowed and shivered. No one was crying now.

"Darkness at noon," he said. "All at once a wind is up, and the scorn of this mob is turned to horror. They are scattering, but I can't leave here. Jesus' hair snaps and whips in the wind. There is a writhing in his face. The lines go deep, like carvings in wood. He is staring into the black skies. He rolls his eyes from the left to the right. Now he rounds his mouth. Now he thrusts his body from the cross, and he shrieks still louder than the wind. He is shrieking to the heavens, oblivious of me. He doesn't know me any more. I am nothing, all my calling lost to him. He is wailing past the spheres, crying, crying, *Eli, Eli, lama sabachthani!* O you merciful God, what a loneliness is there! Answer him! Answer him! Make some sign for him—or what is left for me?

"In all of heaven, there is no answer.

"Jesus' lips draw back, like grinning. I can see his hemispheres of teeth. The wind claws at his beard. His eyes are dying coals, burning in the blackness, awaiting an answer.

"But there is no answer. Not even my crying is an answer for him.

"No, nothing is left for me. I look to Jesus. Jesus looks to the heavens. The heavens are void. Nothing is left for me.

"But in the time that follows, while Jesus' body sags mortally upon the wood, I think over and over again: *One thing is left, that I love you.* With my eyes I search all the cavities of his flesh and bone. I touch his temples and the corners of his eyes; I caress the separation of his ribs—he is being pulled apart—and I think: *even if you see me as one of your enemies, yet I love you.* In the wild gloom of the storm I think: *even if you close your eyes and cease to see me at all, yet there is this for me, that I love you—*"

Reverend Orpheus's voice sank lower and lower, down to nothing. The congregation sat immobile, fixed on his black form against the wall, seeing but not seeing the things he spoke about.

For them it was a story of incredible force, told with such fateful conviction that time and space were revoked for the moment, and the Story was all, the Story possessed its own time and space. Yet for them it remained a seeming and a story—potent, to be sure, causing cold and darkness and the trouble of mortality upon their hearts; a violent, binding story; but a story nonetheless.

But for the teller of the tale, it was the truth. What between Orpheus and the people was a story, between Orpheus and Jesus became an event. It was the single real event of his existence. Tellers make tales of what they do in fact encounter. And the power of the tale is precisely the reality of the encounter.

This is what was happening in fact: Reverend Orpheus was seeing Jesus, whom he had loved his life long, and Jesus was dying.

Appalled by the thing he saw, Orpheus whispered, "He turns his head to the left shoulder. There is no comfort. He turns his head to the right, but there is no comfort. His breaths are as weak as wrens fluttering at his lips. Oh, see! He opens his mouth like yawning. He stretches his bones. He twists his face to the skies—blind eyes! Blind eyes, O my Lord Jesus! And he utters an agonized cry, cosmic, long and desolated—

"Oh!" gasped Reverend Orpheus. "Oh, no!"

For in that tormented posture the Lord Jesus suddenly petrified. Before the seeing of Orpheus, Jesus ceased to move, still straining away from the cross, the mouth and eyes still gaping, the chest and all his muscles in a spasm. But the flesh changed: it hardened and shrank and cracked, exactly like old wood. The blood dried to paint. The cross turned stone. His teeth became a whittling, his wounds five etchings, and his tendons cords of polished wood. This was the Jesus whom Orpheus loved with all his heart—a carving.

In that moment, on the dark night of a late Good Friday,

Jesus died. Not again. No, not *again.* This was the once-for-all-time death of the Lord, except that Orpheus was there to see and to experience it.

Yet, it was the true death sifted by the ages, preserved and bequeathed from age to age, from the faithful to the faithful, by Mass to the masses, and by gravid ceremony to the single soul; so that the dear Lord Jesus, suddenly dead, was no more for Orpheus than a medieval Spanish crucifix. Christ's tomb was the woodenness of a piece of art; and the cry was there, but the cry was silenced; and this was all, now this was *all* that was left to the lover of Jesus: the worn treasure of the church.

"Oh!" said Reverend Orpheus. "Oh, no!"

And then he said no more. He was stunned by the sadness of this ending, and within him was a speechless emptiness. He had never expected to feel such an impact of despair. The despair was real. *This death was real!* His beloved was gone, suddenly, upon a painful cry. And search he never so desperately, he could find nothing left except that cold carving of an agony.

Jesus was dead. There was absolutely nothing left to say. He felt like crying.

Therefore, the silence lengthened in the little church which could seat a hundred comfortably. The congregation grew embarrassed for him. He was leaning sideways against the chancel wall, his face buried in his hands; they didn't know what to do for him or with themselves. Here and there a man cleared his throat, a woman coughed.

But Reverend Orpheus had only a wooden image on a sculptured cross, no text, no lesson, no litany, nothing next. He was trying not to cry.

It was Mrs. Allouise Story, finally, who took matters into her own hands. She was the organist for the evening and always strict about good order. Finding no acceptable reason for Reverend Orpheus's failure to continue, she began to play and to sing the next scheduled hymn—in a clear soprano: "Were you there when they crucified my Lord?"

Women joined her. Men muttered into rhythm. Generally, the people began to be reassured, and the song swelled: "Were you there when they nailed him to the tree—"

For his own part, Reverend Orpheus heard the music gratefully. It drew him outside of himself for just an instant, and he thought that the change might abolish the agonized figure before him. So he went to the altar and faced it. He took a breath, and he too tried to sing: "Were you there when they laid him in the tomb—"

Then his voice caught. After all, the music had the opposite effect of soothing. It broke him down. It released his feelings. He bowed his head all the way down to the linen, and now—while the congregation moaned, "Oh, oh, sometimes it causes me to tremble"—he wept. Not one solitary tear, but a rolling stream of tears and sobs that shook his shoulders. No, melody didn't cover the trouble. Melody melted his sensible defenses, and he cried.

So the hymn died before its ending, in spite of Mrs. Story's efforts. And some in the pews were crying with their pastor, though they couldn't understand the circumstance; and they loved him profoundly now: *See how he loves Jesus?*

Mr. Arthur Williams, an elder, began to speak the Lord's Prayer. The people got raggedly to their feet and prayed with him. They were astonished, when the petition came, how loudly Reverend Orpheus prayed, "Deliver us from evil!" But when they said, "Amen," they bowed their heads and quietly departed the church into the night.

Then Reverend Orpheus thought that he was alone with

his wooden image, his frozen Jesus screaming. He nearly knelt before the altar, nearly crumpled there—but a hand touched his shoulder.

"Pastor?" It was Dolores, young and gentle, sympathetic. Orpheus moved his head to indicate listening.

"It always rains Good Friday," she said. "Always has, as long as I remember. Good Friday is a moody day." She patted his back a moment, then said, "But on Easter the sun always shines. That's the truth."

She said, "Good night, Pastor," and he heard her steps brush the carpet. He heard the door complain when she opened it, and then bump shut.

Orpheus had never felt so lonely.

The serpent had slid through the centuries as though through stands of daffodils, had come to the cross that stood within one time, above all times, and had bitten Jesus in the sight of his faithful Orpheus.

Orpheus spent Saturday sitting at a card table in the dining room of the parsonage. He lived spare; there was no other furniture in the room but three folding chairs from the church basement. Books lay on the hardwood floor. Before him was a yellow pad of paper. He was writing an Easter sermon.

He was ashamed of his performance last night. He wished he could apologize to the people, and this sermon, if God gave him the grace, would be that—not that he would say, "I'm sorry," but that he'd smile again with confidence.

But another thought both sustained him for the work and intensified the work: that he had himself created the image of the crucified Christ. He hoped that the strain of his office and the exhaustion of the season had made him vulnerable to dark moods, that it was his weariness which

reacted to the Passion Narrative and made him cry. Therefore, he intended to recount the resurrection story as skill-
fully as he had the crucifixion. If he had preached the dear
Lord Jesus dead, why then he'd preach him living again.

Orpheus had a gift. He knew that. Language was a potent
tool. He knew that. He wrote and he wrote for the sake of
his Savior and his own salvation, and the card table trembled
underneath his writing.

He frowned severely over the yellow paper. His soul was
crying in a wilderness, *Jesus? Jesus?* His mind was demanding of the Scriptures, *Show me Jesus!* And his writing was
his way of listening for an answer. *Jesus?*

Orpheus did not, that Saturday, consider that the power
in his words might belie autonomous power in the Jesus
whom he loved, making himself both killer and creator. The
notion was too dreadful and his heart already too lonely. He
did not consider that, should he be successful in restoring
the wooden image to life again, then Jesus were no more
than the chimera of words, or else the pale reflection of a
human soul, the fine effect of finer language.

No—throughout that Holy Saturday, at least, Orpheus
ignored any possibility of weakness in his Lord and chose
to believe it was weakness in himself. This was, in fact, the
easier way to go and less dangerous than admitting such a
horror as that Jesus was truly dead. He thought that his trust
in Jesus was the fault, that he was guilty of doubt, that his
own faith was not proof against a battering wind of words.
It was not power that he saw in himself, but infirmity—and
that frightened him. He felt that he, not Jesus, had changed,
had turned a tiny epicycle away. And if this were the case,
then words could most righteously strengthen a slumping
faith and once again encourage trust. In fact, his words
would be evidence of the faith. Therefore, he marshaled all

his skill for this sole sermon. He meant to preach the life into him*self* again.

But he did not, either on that day or in any other, love the dear Lord Jesus less. Know that! Rather, he loved him more fervently than ever before, painfully, bleedingly loved the Lord entombed. The degree of his love was the very degree of his passion to find the Lord again, of the panic that wrote a glorious sermon, and of his grief.

Oh, no! Never suppose that the death of Jesus is the death of love for Jesus. Or else the soul would not be so disconsolate; nor the face so strained, as though crying out from a precipice, the jawbone of the mountain; nor the writing so intense: *Jesus! Jesus! Jesus!*


"See?" said Dolores, catching the pastor at the front door of the church.

Orpheus looked at her and saw a woman of a rich, mocha complexion, deep red under the brown as if fires burned in her flesh. She was smiling over pure white teeth.

He smiled in return, but distractedly. "See what?" he said.

"The sun," she said. "The sun, Pastor. It always shines on Easter."

She was right. He hadn't noticed. It was a bright day, yellow and green and flooded with a morning light. Inside, lilies jungled the chancel, and the stained-glass windows patterned the people in primary colors, and the people themselves sang black and boldly without provocation. The sanctuary was shoulder and shoulder, a sea of cheerful folk; and all their smells flowed forward in waves, coconut and French perfume, Old Spice and candy and ham. "Jesus Christ is risen today!" they sang. And on this particular Sunday, more than any other, when Reverend Orpheus preached to them, they said, "Amen!" He preached like a keening violin, sweeter than the angels' song. They said, "Amen!"

"Why do you seeking the living among the dead?"

Under this preacher's tongue, the cemetery burst into fountains of flowers and became a garden. So he spoke it, so it was. Human grief resolved itself in streams of living waters; dark souls took flesh again—and the hopeless Mary Magdalene, when confronted by Jesus and *"Mary"-ed* by him, flew up on wings of hope. Her tears turned to laughter in the mere speaking of her name. She leaped to him, *"Rabboni!"* face to face, the woman and her Lord.

So the preacher spoke it. So it was.

"Why do you seek the living among the dead?" All the savage sorrows of the people's lives the Reverend Orpheus transfigured in the resurrection of their Jesus. Each became a ruptured tomb, each a hurt that had an ending and a purpose, each the ground of a brighter flower, a thing of God. Seeds! Their troubles were seeds after all, dead in the earth of their experience to rise and blow new faces, all of them the face of Jesus. Sunflowers! "Why do you seek the living among the dead?" Behold, the Lord of all did not abide in death below, so low and under all, but rose on his own glory to reign above all and in all and through all. He split the rind of the tomb. He stunned the enemy. He strode into the empyrean and his laughter went forth like the comet!

"Amen!" said the people. "Amen!"

And "Why do you seek," preached Reverend Orpheus, "the living among the dead?" A foolish enterprise, when death itself is dead. It is seeking something in a nothing. Can that be done? It is to retire into yourself alone. Should that be done? It is to search through no place at all for that which lives in every place. Can you make yourself so small, as to be nowhere at all? Why, that's a joke, and the joke of the universe! His laughter goes forth like the comet, catching you back to life as well. For who can hear the Lord's loud laugh at our own silliness and *not* be moved to laugh along? And when we laugh, why, then we are children laughing at childishness, free of ourselves, free and riding the tail of the comet, forgiven and flying at once: alive!

So he said, and so it was.

"Amen!" the people chorused, nodding, frowning as though the meat were sweet indeed, grinning helplessly, flying! "Preach!" they cried, and Orpheus preached.

"Why do you seek the living," he said, "among the dead?" For the sin that killed you, the sin that hid the sunlight of God, the sin that made of this whole world a graveyard and a nation of the dead, that penumbral sin is burned in a fire, and the fire is bright. The snake that bit the Savior, *it* is dead. The sin that took his life was taken in his resurrection. Listen to me!

"Amen!"

Then it isn't that life is gone and must be sought. Oh, no! The dead are raised to life—but their eyes are blinded by the light, and they do not know. The sudden light of a burning life makes but a passing darkness—in your eyes. Do you understand? It isn't that the dead must seek life, but that the blind must seek sight.

"Amen!"

For life *is.* And life is everywhere. Blindness only makes a seeming of "the dead."

"Amen!"

And those who do not know their blindness *seem* to seek "among the dead." Oh, what a sad distraction! Seek the living? No! No, but seek sight.

"Amen!"

Seek only to see, and you shall most certainly see the living.

"Amen! Amen!"

*Why,* cried Orpheus unto his own particular soul, *do you seek the living among the dead?*

And when he was done, this is what occurred: the people in the little sanctuary clapped. They applauded, standing, the things that he had said. They saw. They saw indeed some things they'd never seen before, and the spontaneous reaction was to clap.

Reverend Orpheus, Reverend Orpheus—he had the gift!

But when he was done, this too is what occurred: the pastor looked on the people with bewilderment, and then he shrank from them as though the clapping slapped and wounded him. Something in him withdrew from their gladness and even from their community, and it seemed to one or two that he was about to cry. His chin trembled. He looked like a child, lost, frightened, and defenseless.

But then the reverend hardened his face into the ghastly mask of a smile as white and scabrous as the collar at his throat. No, he wasn't going to cry. He determined not to cry. He set his face to no emotion at all.

And this was the reason for his fierce behavior: Jesus was dead. The Christ was still the wooden figure fixed in agony. The silent scream and the crucified corpse still hung in the air before him, uncanceled, unresurrected, persistent in its death, real.

Jesus was dead, the dear Lord Jesus. Not all the dazzling language of the preacher had changed that truth. Then neither had his language caused it in the first place. On Orpheus's Good Friday, Jesus had bled and died indeed. There had been no frenzy nor the delusion of an exhausted spirit. There had happened the fact and an experience too bulking still to be denied. This was the grief that fixed the preacher's face in its mask of smiling: that on Easter Sunday morning, the dear Lord Jesus had not arisen again.

Orpheus, Orpheus! How do you preach so well? You preach the pain of your heart's desire. You preach your yearning. And so it is your skill to cause the stones to cry, and the people say "Amen" because they imagine the thing that you would see. But there is the end of your "making" ability, and your limit. You cannot sing your Lord to life again. Not life. You can't make life. What you desire, that you can sing; but though you can entice an entire parish to its feet by crying forth the name of Jesus, yet that passion comes not of the presence of the Lord, but of his absence. It is a beauty born of anguish.

The preacher held a secret in his heart that day, that he was mourning. In secret he wandered the graveyards and he wailed.

Jesus was dead.

◊     ◊     ◊

First, love and a declared commitment, with the conviction that these will last forever.

Then the faithing one is vulnerable to the death, when Jesus dies within the language that had framed the experience in order to keep it—when all that is left to the faithing one *is* the framework, structures of language, the nouns; and these, too, are lifeless, like the shell of the chambered nautilus. (In fact, the experienced drama has burst its defining boundaries. Namings fail for a while.)

For Orpheus it came in the telling of the tale.

For others it may come less clearly, less climactically and, perhaps, with no intensity at all. It could happen at leavetaking, when the child enters the world on her own.

A new philosophy, a book, an acquaintance can precipitate it. So could sexual awakening. So could marital divorce. Or it may occur as indistinctly as a tumor, unnoticed until long afterward when the symptoms appear—and even then they are not easy to diagnose. In any case, the intensity of the grief measures the intensity of the love. Great love collapses in great grief. A forced, affected love has hardly the energy or the interest to affect grief. Yet, in all these cases the second passage of faithing does come:

The object of our loving—but not the loving—dies.

Death is death and shall be known as Death.

It's shocking in its brutality, indifference, finality.

We can't believe, until we meet it, that anything would be so utterly void of mercy or kindness or care, so powerful, so deaf to the goodness or the weakness in us. With no malice whatsoever, it dashes its victim against stone walls, breaking her until she slumps and utters nothing, not a groan; and then it neither smiles nor sneers, but grabs another, and that one a child. No matter: it was a child at hand. No appeal either: death is Death.

And talk we never so much, prepare we never so much, pretend we never so much that we understand what is to come—when it comes in fact, we understand nothing. The encounter with Death takes our breath away. The experience hits like a wrecking-ball against our breasts, stunning us with grief. Who can believe the pain it causes? None, until she hurts with it. Who truly believes that Death is today? Very few, until one puts her hand upon the chalk cheek of her beloved and finds it cold.

We say, "Jesus died."

We *say* that he was crucified.

We confess repeatedly that he humbled himself unto

death, even death on a cross. The words. We confess the words, which is to say: we repeat the words, believing that we believe them. But there is only one word among these words that we believe; that word is *Jesus,* which we believe because we conceive him living and have experienced him. We love him. But *death* is a fiction in our hearts, his death a metaphor at most, a sentiment causing tears, perhaps, as we imagine the sweetness of his sacrifice, but the sacrifice was endurable after all. He survived it, didn't he? We surely do.

For us, Jesus always was, is, and will be—with a curious lacuna somewhere in that series, which fondly we call his crucifixion. He was, when we were stumbling children. He is, now that we continue as adults. He will be, forever and forever, *saecula saeculorum,* ever present, ever helping us.

But suddenly and without warning the words *He died* seize the meaning of experience; and then his humbling himself unto death on a cross hammers hard against our innocence: died the Death! And when finally it takes its place in the experience of the faithing one—in her life and not her mind—it does with violent force change the tense. No! No, not died: *dies.* Jesus Christ *is* dead. Dear people, at that moment of terrible recognition, it isn't Jesus who suffers, whose suffering was accomplished millennia ago. (Now we look at the thing through the eyes of personal experience and find that we, too, are much responsible for the collapsing of the times: Christ folds the times together; our grieving keeps the fold in place a while.) Rather, it is we ourselves who suffer an astonishing bereavement—and our suffering cries *Now!* to the event. Pain knows nothing of the past. So long as something of the hurt remains, it holds its cause in the present, and it keeps our attention totally upon the present, conscious only of this present moment when we hurt, fearful that the future will be no different. So the cause is not past and the future, by our apprehension, not future.

Death—even the death of our dear Lord Jesus—is death and shall be known as Death, felt as Death, brutal and indifferent and final.

But this, at its beginning, is what our grief will look like: because it comes precisely at that pass when we were content in the presumption that the process was finished, that faith, the noun, was sized to us like a suit of clothes to be worn the rest of our lives, we deny the death of Jesus.

Denial. We know nothing of the word *dead.* We qualify the horror of the thing.

We say, "I just don't feel it any more." We mute the loss by thinking of Christ as "absent" or "gone." We blame, perhaps, our own "weak faith," our "backsliding," our failure to *keep* faith, to pray as we should, to study. We blame, perhaps, our worldly ways, our impiety, our sin. It is easier to bear a fault in us than a fault in God; it is acceptable that he should turn away from the sinner and so be gone because this is a loss with a cause and an explanation, and thus we salvage sanity, if not gladness. On the other hand, it is unacceptable, it is unthinkable—it destroys the cosmos—that the God and foundation of our lives, that Life Itself, should die. (But what must Peter have felt, who called him Christ before he died, and Son of the living God?) No, this is a paradox impossible and treacherous. That's why, for our own sakes, we accept responsibility. Or else we intellectualize the thing, naming it with terms bland and blind and faceless, terms conceptual, not experiential: *Deus Absconditus*—the nature of God's holiness is transcendence; Jesus is hidden; "I don't got the joy in my heart any more." *Deus*

*Incognitus*—Jesus unknowable after all; he dwells in a cloud of unknowing; "I'm a poor fool" and "Such knowledge is too wonderful for me; it is high, I cannot attain it." We talk this way. We teach this stuff—despite the incarnation when human eyes were given to *see* his glory, glory as of the only Son from the Father.

No, but cast down those eyes, you who grieve. And you who travel to Emmaus, stand still and seem the thing you are: sad! Jesus of Nazareth, the one you believed to be redeemer, he is dead.

There comes to the faithers the Easter without joy. There comes the Gospel without substance. There comes that morning when the Son and the sun don't rise again. This is not uncommon. These things are the tomb, suddenly, palpably cold because the body within is dead—and the faither knows this because she has not, in fact, ceased to believe that they are true. No, she believes the material of the Gospel, and the Bible, and its Holy History, and its teachings; she believes them. And she loves Jesus. Or, she *would* love Jesus, if she could find the warm Lord to be the receiver of that love. But she can't. So all these things grow cold and stony and more hollow than the tomb of Joseph of Arimathea. There comes the Gospel without life. There occurs the extended night, the endless night—

And what then? Then our grief grows angry, and that looks very different than denial. Denial blamed ourselves, if it blamed anyone. Anger accuses other things, other people.

All of the hymns and all of the ritual which used to make us glad now hurt us; we become impatient with them. The stories, the statutes, the teachings, the whole language of religion which once had been security for us now hectors and mocks us—exactly like old shoes: when the widow cleaned her closet and found the old shoes of her husband, they mocked her; the shoes themselves said, *He is dead;* she threw them crashing through the window, and then she fell on her bed and wept bitter tears. Scriptures themselves may be the old shoes of Jesus, and religion the persistent evidence of death. All that had been right is wrong. All that had been nourishing is now corruption; and there lingers, could we admit it, the odor of putrifaction.

How suffocating are the traditions of the Church! How arrogant and heartless! So: blame the Church. Hasn't the Church betrayed us? (But death is always betrayal!) Pick, pick at the petty inconsistencies of the Church, both to satisfy and to justify our anger. Or, when we have grown bold enough—because neither crying nor condemning can relieve our anger—then wash our hands of it. In a rage we may reject everything implied by the title *religion.* With Simon Peter we may pitch ourselves into the life that has nothing to do with Jesus: "I'm going fishing," forget the rest. I'll make money; money can't betray me.

But so much rage is ineffectual after all. Death remains. Grief remains. And the terrible void remains, despite our shouting efforts to fill it with ourselves. And the church remains untroubled. We've only succeeded in finding our own limits; how tiny and how helpless we are in the universe! And what is left, then, but to cry? Not cry out; merely to cry. To stand still on the road to Emmaus, looking sad. To despair: that is the third face of grief, when the mourning has arisen, honestly to be acknowledged and experienced. No more willful denials of the thing. No more ragings by which to control the thing. Finally the thing itself is real before us, consuming every other thing in its significance, consuming us:

The dear Lord Jesus is dead.

And grief has found its proper face.

. . .

And yet, all these convulsions of grief are a passage within the drama of faithing, very much a part *of* faith and not apart from it.

Be very clear about this, you who are discouraged by your suffering sister, you who would condemn her careless attitude as sloth, her anger as hard-hearted impudence, or her morbid depressions as signs of apostasy and a fall from faith. No, she has not left the faith. Job hadn't left the faith either, ye comforters. Rather, your sister is performing certain intensely necessary and painful acts *within* the faith. This is faith. This is faithing.

Therefore, do not cease to love her now; and surely never separate yourself from her.

She hasn't stopped loving Jesus. That is precisely the conflict and the anguish in her. Loving is the pain in her, because her loving's unrequited. Soon enough this difficult knowledge will surface; soon she will admit both the love and the death of her beloved; and then like Orpheus she will cease her wanderings and all her futile forms of grief; then a certain hope, though hapless and grim, will spring up in her; and then she will enter the third passage of the drama, wherein there is something to do. And she shall change again.

Until then, love her. Honor her for the depth of her suffering, if for nothing else.

And salt your love with wisdom. Know that nothing of her happier faith is to be suspected or else judged "false" on account of this present sadness. It was as true as childhood; no one discredits the value of childhood just because the child grows older; no one calls its truth illusion just because it had to be put away. Her sunnier faith was, in its day, valid and good.

Salt your love with wisdom. Know that now she's *not* believing that there is no God or that the universe is godless altogether. Neither (mercifully!) has God resolved himself into a proposition or a principle. He is not for her a myth, a fantasy of cultures. And surely it is clear that she's not become an atheist. It is different from all of these—because she is still wrestling in the drama with the Deity, still experiencing the changings of that relationship, and these alternatives imply no relationship at all. No, God is not suddenly nonexistent for her. Rather, Jesus, whom she loves still, from whom she received grace upon grace, is dead. Jesus was alive. That is not doubted. Now he's dead. And *that* is not nothing.

Salt, I say, your love with wisdom.

Be silent, as you are with all who mourn.

But be near.

# The Third Passage:
# Mortification,
# Supplication

*Now, this is the reason why the ancients remembered the story of Orpheus: not that he loved so deeply, nor that his beloved died, nor that he mourned, even though his mourning made a haunting music. Many people have done and suffered these things. But Orpheus did more. Driven by his agony, he did what mortals do not dare to do, could they even believe it possible. Alive, he sought the dead.*

*It isn't that he sought death, that he should die and be released from sorrow. He sought the dead, to see and speak with them. That journey, taken with his eyes wide open to all death's mordant forces, is the more terrible. This is why the ancients revered him and remembered.*

*Orpheus hung his lyre on his back and traveled alone through a wild country. He walked an uninhabited land, frightening the smaller creatures as he went. He climbed a frowning immensity of rock until he came to the promontory of Taenarus. And there he found a cave, a portal to the dark tunnels. This cave he entered without hesitation, and he descended.*

*His love alone persuaded him to crawl down stones into so black a Stygian night. His love for Eurydice. Because no one freely chooses the horrors of the Kingdom of Death. Suicides think they choose oblivion; when they ar-*

*rive in this place they would willingly endure the poverty, the labor, and all the afflictions of life again. No one comes here freely, not even the queen of the region herself, Proserpine, who was abducted from the sunlight and forced to reign beside her abductor, Pluto. No one freely descended—except Orpheus, because he loved and could not live without his love.*

*For a long time downward, he heard nothing but himself, and he could see just nothing at all. But then the sounds of the kingdom arose to him, and then he was passing them, level by level, and the oppression nearly broke his heart.*

*First he heard the wails of infants, children dead in their innocence. He paused near those he couldn't see. It's one thing to suffer in sunlight the loss of a baby; it is quite another thing to hear the bewildered loneliness of the baby itself.*

*Down he descended. Then came to him the ceaseless groanings of those who had been falsely accused and innocently executed. Unrighteousness has a voice! It cries out from the ground. It is the victim, still unsilenced.*

*But down Orpheus descended. And he heard the shocked cries of the suicides. Lower still he heard the perpetual sighing of those who died of an unsatisfied love, and again he paused, filled to tears with sympathy.* I know you, I know you, *he thought.* This is my misery, and does it last forever?

*And down, and down, and a great noise swelled around him like a storm. He heard the shrieks of warriors, the howling of troops, the whimpers and pleadings of the soldiers wounded and left to die. Voices roared through the caverns like a wind. He couldn't see them, but their number was countless and their clamor hideous. So then: not only the dead, but all the treachery of humankind gathered*

*in this realm, and here it found its voice, so that Orpheus
could not be deaf to the outrageous enormity:* This is what
humanity can do! *Worse, this is what it has routinely done
throughout the ages, justifying itself in the sunlight but
stowing the truth of its doings in hell. And what then? Why,
then this is the soul of the race. Who can bear the revelation? Who can endure to know this people not by its
smiling face, but here, in the depths, at the core, according
to its nature and its truth?*

*This is why the ancients remembered Orpheus and told
his tale: no one chooses the horrors of the Kingdom of the
Dead, its bitter revelations, the cold accusation it lays
against the living. How could one trust even the living
thereafter? To enter hell is to learn that hell has entered
life above and is the darkness not only under the earth,
but in the human heart. No one chooses such knowledge—
except Orpheus alone, because he loved.*

*And down. Orpheus climbed all the way down—until,
through the shadows of the condemned and past their personal and appropriate torments, he came at last to the
thrones of the lord and the lady of horrible Tartarus.*

*Their glory was a lurid light, like pale smoke; and he
could see.*

"O positi sub terra numina mundi!"

*Orpheus sang a song. The living among the dead, made
heavy with his flesh, this poet sang a song.*

*With all his art, with all his heart and soul and
strength, he sang for Eurydice. He struck from his lyre a
music sweet and foreign in the lower air. On that music
his voice rose up as if on wings, gracefully; and in that
song he made his supplication.*

*He sang, "O positi sub terra"—and immediately Queen*

*Proserpine covered her face with her hands. She couldn't help it: she was remembering! This living, lovely voice recalled life to her and love again. She was overwhelmed with memories.*

*Orpheus sang this song:*

> *"I haven't come to spy on you;*
> *I have not come in pride to you,*
> > *Deriding death with life*
> *Or scorning those who cry in you—*
> > *But for my wife.*
>
> *"I've come because the pain in me*
> *Humiliates, remains in me,*
> > *And makes a death of life;*
> *The sun himself is slain for me—*
> > *Without my wife.*
>
> *"The woman, sweet Eurydice,*
> *The laughing, light Eurydice*
> > *Was poisoned of her life;*
> *The serpent murdered hideously*
> > *My wife, my wife.*
>
> *"By hell, by this vast emptiness,*
> *Its sorrows and its silences,*
> > *I plead for life from death;*
> *Unwind the fatal wool. Lord, bless*
> > *My wife with breath.*
>
> *"Oh, give her but a season, Lord!*
> *The world, its creatures, all its store*
> > *Pours down from life to death:*
> *All ends are your forevermore*
> > *And in your debt.*
>
> *"Then you shall have my wife again.*
> *Full of her years my wife, my friend*
> > *Shall fall from life to death—*

> "Or else you have me now!
> I'll *shear the thread.*
> I'll *break the bough:*
> *So flesh and spirit, friend and friend,*
> *My wife, her husband, sister, brother,*
> Two *shall drop to death,*
> *Choked of our breath,*
> *Choked of our breath*
> *Together!"*

*So sang Orpheus. The last words, the most passionate words, shot like arrows through all the dark caverns and struck and were still. He lifted his fingers, and the lyre trembled and died as well. He bowed his head. He did not know what to expect.*

*But all around him, like a water stirring, a wonderful thing began, a thing which had never before occurred in the Land of Iron Law: the spirits wept! The ghosts were weeping!*

*His plaintive song had done this thing.*

*As thick as starlings when they circle and crowd a single tree, ten thousand souls came whirling around the singer. They were sighing. They were crying. They made a rain in hell.*

*And those who were being punished knew a moment of peace from their punishments. Ixion's wheel, which turned him over a pit of fire, ceased turning. He leaned and listened.*

*Tityos's liver was allowed like a flower to grow, because the vultures that fed on it were distracted a while; and he wept for gratitude.*

*Sisyphus paused and sat upon his stone and bowed his head and did not labor, but listened.*

*And the officers and the executioners of the kingdom*

*wept. The Furies wept. Tisiphone, who is rage—she wept. Megaera and Alecto, who are slaughter and envy—they wept.*

*But more grievously than any other, the queen of the region herself, half living, half holding to the sunlight even in this darkness—Proserpine dissolved in tears. He sang the thing she yearned for. He loved as she would herself be loved. She kept her face within her hands and cried longer than the others. The human hurt in her.*

*So then: what could not happen when the iron laws relaxed and the kingdom suffered the skill and the love of this singer, suffered his song and altered?*

*Proserpine raised her face and gazed at Orpheus. "Peace," she said. Then she fixed her eyes on the distance and whispered, "Behold."*

*Orpheus turned and looked—and saw Eurydice.*

*She was walking toward him with her eyes cast down. And though she had been light before she died, and though she was a weightless phantom still, yet she limped on one foot because of the bite of the serpent.*

*But to Orpheus that little stumble, that delicate fall on every other step, was exquisitely beautiful. This was his Eurydice.*

◊     ◊     ◊

*Follow me.* Jesus appropriated the rabbinic custom of teacher-student relationship and made it his own. "Follow me," he said, and those who did became his disciples. But "Follow me," he repeated even then, intensifying the call, urging further meaning into it, ever deepening the relationship—until, in the end, there can be discerned four degrees of meaning, four stages of the following, four evolvements in the relationships. Well, the *Vocatio* in the mouth of Jesus was always more than mere beginnings; it was relationship whole. But since it had, whenever he spoke it, the effect of beginnings, it insisted on the relationship's changing, being made new. This is the characteristic of a living relationship, that it changes.

And this is the relationship we, too, experience with Jesus. The four meanings of the *Follow me,* then, may illuminate various passages in our own drama of faithing.

In the beginning, "Follow me" was a delightful if difficult invitation: "Come unto me." *Come* not yet unto what Jesus would perform, but *come* unto who he was, a teacher above the picayunish teachers of the Pharisees, a rabbi whose laws were few, supernal and comprehensive, the which he would himself accomplish. To *come* was therefore to be relieved of a hurly-burly of responsibility, of heavy burdens hard to bear, weighing on our shoulders. To *come* was a manumission: no longer need we be slaves to the fierce cacophony of societal demands, religious expectations, familial pride, personal resolutions, civic duties, professional obligations, mores mute but biting nonetheless. Then our masters had numbered in the thousands, all of them crying in their own tongues, "Measure up! Measure up!" not one of them observing what they asked. But *come,* and our Master was one. And he was righteous. And he was loving. And what he asked was that we love him alone (oh, sweet simplification!), and that we learn from him alone. And since *come* meant not only that we gave ourselves to him, but also that he gave himself to us (a giving which none of our worldly masters would promise or else perform), then *come* was *covenant.* It was founded upon a relationship which embraced two beings entirely, nothing withheld from the other. When we took his yoke, why, he took it too: it was a double yoke, and we were yoked together. And love was not only allowed, but empowered: we loved him with his own love back again. Likewise, he loved us unto the full flowering of our own beings and not to the flattering of his own. Certainly he sought to see his image in ourselves; but behold: his image *was* our personal selves made perfect, the *imago dei,* clean as at creation!

Therefore, *come* was "rest for our souls," and easy and light.

And *come* was Jesus, breathing *Thou* to us who, when we answered, breathed *Thou* in return.

This was the meaning of his "Follow me" when he spoke it at the seashore to Peter and Andrew, to James and John. It was the beginning, even as it was the end of their bondage to (and their security in) their identities as fishermen, their father and families, Capernaum and its ordered existence. Now there would be no homes and no pillows, but Jesus only. Now there would be no lands, no worldly prospects, no transactable reputations, no time to bury kin, no kin at all, not even a pleasant farewell: "Lo, we have left everything and followed you." Jesus only. Nevertheless, with what alacrity they left the boats to follow him! It was very good. And it was *him:* they joined themselves to Jesus, who he was, the person that he was, not yet to what he came to do. *Thou,* they said, still ignorant of the baptism that awaited him. Perhaps we may point to that ignorance as evidence of their innocent trust in him, and praise it. But it is also, perhaps, the cause of their quickness to "follow," and the reason why "Follow me" is at first delightful and easy and light.

Love in the beginning is so lovely that one persuades oneself it must go on forever. "O dear God, let faith be the noun, we beseech thee!"

But faithing is a verb, after all.

And this first meaning of the call to follow Jesus illu-
minates the first passage of faith—but the first passage only.

Of the third meaning, and of the fourth, which is the
profoundest and the most fearful, we shall speak hereafter.

The second meaning stands before us now. It is disclosed
when he, whom we have come to love, does what he has
come to do. Now, it is true that the person and the work
of Christ cannot be divided; one defines the other. But it is
also true that we are dim of wit and slow to know, that our
knowledge, not our Christ, progresses from stage to stage
of wakening. We, therefore, by the divisions in ourselves,
divide our Jesus, loving the He before we know the Deed.
Moreover, we are appalled by the Deed and therefore resist
believing it so long as we can. It is not a thing we can be
taught by the speaking; rather, it is urged upon us in experience, and only when we have no choice but to bow and
suffer the outrageous fortune do we admit that such is our
fortune indeed. Oh, children! That admission comes only in
submission.

And what is it that Jesus came to do?

Why, to die.

Which is to say in our untutored ears, to defraud us,
inviting our love only to amputate the object of our love,
leaving our love a bleeding stump. But that's not possible,
not of him who also truly loves us. Therefore, we cannot
believe it by the speaking only—

We are Peter.

"Who do you say that I am?" asks Jesus. And Simon Peter
cheerfully answers in terms of the person alone, still ignorant of that person's work: "You are the Christ." All would
be well if we and Peter could together abide in that narrow,
static and comforting name alone—the title only; and faith
would be a noun.

But Jesus begins to teach them (as we are taught as well)

"that the Son of man must suffer many things, and be re-jected by the elders and the chief priests and the scribes, and be killed, and after three days rise again. And he said this plainly.

"And Peter took him, and began to rebuke him—"

God forbid, Lord! This shall never happen to you!

We are Peter, but with the logic of the tenses on our side—

What has been cannot be *yet to be!* This cannot happen to you again.

Even so we resist till what was—what was to be—*is*; until we suffer the death truly; until we have experienced the second passage of faithing, the death, and truly begin to mourn.

But then (and here starts the third passage) with new motivation on account of our mourning, with eyes made mature by weeping, and with a perceiving deeper than the surface person of the Christ, deep to see the working of our dear Jesus, we return to that first call, "Follow me," and find therein a second meaning, one which gives us hope.

It is as though we wailed in our grief, by the pure ir-rationality that love allows, "O dear Jesus, where *are* you now?"

And he answered with perfect rationality, "Among the dead."

And we: "Then I am lost without you. How shall I find you any more?"

And he: "Why, follow me."

And we: "What? Seek the living among the dead?"

And he: "No, seek the dead among the dead. Have ears, child; I said, 'Follow me.'"

And we: "But how can I follow you to such a place?"

And he: "No, not a place; a state. Follow me: be like me."

And we: "How, Lord? How? Already I've left everything—"

And he: "Die a little." And again he, to our confusion,
saying what he'd said before but what, before his death, we
could not understand: "If anyone would come after me, let
him deny himself and take up his cross and follow me—"

Ah, denial! By the *cross* we follow him!

"—for whoever would save his life will lose it, and
whoever loses his life for my sake will find it."

*Follow me,* its second meaning, allows a sudden, outrageous hope: that there is something we can do! We can
do as he has done, and so be with him. We are not totally
helpless.

He: "Are you able to drink the cup that I drink, or to be
baptized with the baptism with which I am baptized?"

And we, with James and John—a little less ignorant than
they (since by now we have a notion that the wine and the
water are death), though not so wise as we shall be (since
as yet we do not realize by experience the most fearful quality of that death)—we, nearly silly in the boast: "Yes! We
are able."

And finally he, delighting our souls, for it sounds not like
a warning but like a promise: "The cup that I drink you will
drink."

Suffer—there's the meaning! Deny ourselves and die a
little—that's the method! Why, we may suffer to good
effect!

We are Peter again: "Since therefore Christ suffered in
the flesh, arm yourselves with the same thought, for
whoever has suffered in the flesh has ceased from sin, so as
to live for the rest of the time in the flesh no longer by
human passions, but by the will of God."

Oh, we are so bold at the beginning of the third passage,

and confident, and a perfect conundrum unto the world: the world never took such joy in pain.

We will, like him, die a little. We will mortify this flesh, killing it by degrees, our souls set on Jesus, following Jesus in order to find him again.

We will fast, for that is the sacrifice of our personal desires; that is the affliction of ourselves, even as the Israelites afflicted themselves on the days when their oneness with God was renewed. And didn't Moses fast before he met the mighty God, to receive the law of him, and Daniel before his visions, both preparing themselves by submitting themselves? Then so shall we. *Thy will be done.* And didn't our dear Jesus fast between his baptisms, the river water and the bitter cup, signifying the emptying of his will both before his ministry and before his death? Then so, following him, shall we.

We will deny ourselves. We will divest ourselves of the things of this world and even of the desire for them. In rags ourselves, we will clothe the naked. In danger of our own disease, we will visit the sick, and to our own humiliation visit those in prison. Our possessions we will turn to alms and so learn the mercy of Jesus because we cannot ourselves remain unafflicted when we serve those who are. Mercy *is* the sacrifice required of our Lord, and by him: it is a personal sacrifice, to eat with the sinners and those cast out by the rest of society. Then we will more than eat with them; we will live in, with, and for them; and our houses shall be houses of mercy.

These are the pieties. They are, in this passage, very good. And there is suffering in such acts because we deny our natures thereby. And down to hell, down to hell we go by descending into the detritus of humanity, by walking among the stinking consequences of human wickedness (that there should be poor; that they should suffer), by living hungry with the hungry and befriending those rejected.

But we follow Jesus, and there shall we find him again.

And if it comes to this that we must die the death indeed, we will. No, we shall not be surprised by the fiery ordeal that comes to prove us, as though something strange were happening to us. We will be hated and reviled by this world. Well, and we invite such contempt as evidence that we are doing well and that the genuineness of our faith has passed the test. Moreover, we will rejoice to share Christ's sufferings in order to find our Christ again.

Follow thee? Yea, we will follow thee, in love for thee, even unto death.

And when we have reached a measure of holiness, when perfection sanctifies us for the endeavor, then we will also pray for thee, for thy life in this life once again, that thou mightest dwell beside us as thou didst before, full of grace and truth, when we were innocent and children. We will pray to see thee, and for thy resurrection.

And so, with commitment, vigor, true devotion and with confidence, begins the third passage of faithing.

This is the passage of good works. This is the period when the faithing one is convinced that his good works also cause good consequences. Is he wrong to believe in the value of good works? Is he deluded to think them effectual and that his relationship with Jesus depends upon them, upon his own pieties? Shouldn't someone quote him Paul: "By grace you have been saved through faith; and this is not your own doing, it is the gift of God—not because of works, lest anyone should boast"?

No, no, of course not. Here, at this pass in the drama whole, works are perfectly right. And they must have the faither's full conviction. And they do accomplish a significant move from this passage to the next. Something, certainly, is achieved by them (though that something is not, in the end, what she had expected, is not so much a revealing of Jesus as of herself).

For several reasons these pieties are in no way to be condemned.

First, because they are born of love for Jesus: their intent is not the salvation of one's self but—as ridiculous as this may seem—the purchase of one's beloved back from death, from the Nowhere to which he has gone, the reviving of Jesus. Despite all the language of "making oneself worthy for Jesus," the process of piety is in fact the opposite. It isn't the self but Jesus who is the object of this labor, even as he is the object of true loving; the preservation of one's soul is beside the point, for the promise to die for Jesus was truly and faithfully made; it was no ploy, nor strategy for salvation (so long as the loving of Jesus is itself no ploy, but true indeed); no, death was the anticipated end of humility and holiness, both. Martyrs have existed in the Church. They are no fiction. Saints have gone this way before, by good works achieving remarkable things, revealing Jesus gloriously. Do not blame the boldly young who believe all selflessly that their decreasing can benefit their beloved, increasing him. Do not devalue their devotions or else speak of them with a haughty condescension. The whole Church was young and bold once.

And this is the second reason why pieties are appropriate: they do not, finally, characterize the whole drama of faithing, but have a proper place *within* it. Their sequence must come, even if it must then be left behind.

Again: doctrines fix things. Doctrines noun the verbs. Then doctrines—because *we* cannot tolerate the hazard, the dizziness, or the foreboding of the flow—are set up as standards against which we judge the rightness and wrongness of this act or that attitude, as though acts and attitudes could freeze to abide the judgment. But such use of doctrine is a dreary winter, freezing the life of faithing at its very heart.

On the other hand, when doctrine returns to its humble service, interpreting the acts of God unto our little intellects, both to explain what is and has been, and to prepare for what shall be, embracing the drama whole, though standing aside from it, as it were, the way a viewer humbly stands aside from the play, then doctrine will not issue condemnations upon a part as though that part were the whole, nor will it damn the young man simply because he is not wiser yet, nor criticize the older merely because he hasn't the energy of the young. In fact, doctrine will cease to sit in judgment at all. Even doctrine will say, "There is a glad, good time when it is right to believe in the holy effectuality of good works, disciplines, and acts of mortification."

Even doctrine will declare, "Pieties, unqualified and free of apologetics, do have their place and purpose, to be a means indeed for drawing the lover closer to his beloved, the faithful to his Jesus; they must be played through, with committed innocence, even unto their end without the destructive challenge of a 'truer' or 'more valid' revelation—as though, in their time, there is no other way in all the world for finding Jesus *except* the pieties; or else that truer, deeper revelation itself shall be jeopardized."

Oh, let the good works be, and do not blame them. We teachers do not teach. We merely name, accompany, and encourage. Instead, it is the good works which are the teachers. They are grave masters indeed, and shall, if given wholeness and scope, deliver a lesson more dreadful than our soft hearts could ever lay upon the young, if we love them.

The relationship itself was ever the instructor.

◊      ◊      ◊

Pastor Orpheus hated the county jail. When he went in to visit prisoners, it was with no sense of personal importance. He went powerless and uncomfortable. When he came out again, there was no satisfaction in him for the work accomplished; there was the relief only that he was outside, on the street, free of a nasty obligation.

The jail caused in him a miserable confusion of emotions, and he hated it.

He confessed his feelings of relief as one confesses a sin. He prayed for a holier, happier attitude. At nine and noon and three in the afternoon (since these were the hours of prayer that he now observed absolutely), he prayed, "God, make me hungry to serve. Make me content in service." He prayed his prayer passionately because he truly suffered the sharpness of his conscience. But the prayer was never answered. He loathed the jail until the end, suspecting that his loathing came of pride. He hated what it did to him, because he was a near nonentity within its walls, subject to the moods of the guard. He hated what it did to the prisoners whom he visited (which hatred he counted worthy, since it indicated human sympathy). But he also sometimes hated the prisoners themselves and feared them (which hatred was clearly unworthy and caused him Davidic spasms of contrition: shouldn't he feel tenderness for those he served?) Harder and harder he prayed the prayer which God refused to answer. The turbulence persisted in his spirit—

—but he persisted in his work. Pastor Orpheus visited the jail with a devout regularity, spending no less than an hour behind the doors each time he went.

. . .

This was the change that the people of his church saw in Reverend Orpheus: suddenly as they put it, he "got down to work."

Sometime between spring and summer he began to spend long hours and an inexhaustible energy working on behalf of the whole inner-city neighborhood. He smiled less than he used to; but then, he was busier than he had ever been before.

Stella Johnson had a theory. She was an old woman who trusted the sanctity of tears. She said, "God touched that man," and she raised her finger to prove the solemnity of her point. "He cried Good Friday. Remember? Remember? Couldn't help hisself, but broke right down in mumblin' tears. Well, that was when God put his Spirit in the man. I mark the change from that minute on."

Not everyone was as convinced of the cause as Stella was; but everyone admitted the difference, and they were moved by it. "See what a pastor we have?" they said. "He practices what he preaches." It became a badge of the congregation.

Throughout that summer, that autumn and that winter they, too, changed in respect to Orpheus; a certain watchfulness developed in them, and they ceased to call him "Reverend." They called him "Pastor," and they wondered concerning his health.

Pastor Orpheus was unaware of their praise. He was too intent on the labor, and the labor was increasing. Neither did he notice that the inner city as a whole was watching him, beginning to trust him. The trust of the poor is not expressed in praise but in demanding. So the demands on his ministry multiplied—spontaneously, it seemed to him, or else by the grace of God; but he was encouraged by that, because he took it as God's approval of his new commitment to service.

He answered his telephone scores of times a day, each call a need he felt bound to fulfill. As the need grew greater, he became creative. He established a relationship with a grocery store in the city, whereby mothers might get milk on his written order, and families fresh vegetables, and old men meat; and he raised a fund of money from which to cover the bills incurred.

He dialed the phone daily, persuading the utility company to be merciful and to wait a day before they cut off gas or water or electricity to homes where children lived. And then he dialed other churches and agencies, persuading them to help him pay the overdue account. In this way his voice became known not only to the poor, but also to the systems of the city.

And who could predict any single need before it came?

One Saturday night, midnight and later, he spent two hours on the telephone, talking and talking to keep the young man on the other end awake. The young man cried and sang songs and apologized pathetically and kept slipping toward sleep, toward death. He had overdosed in a Holiday Inn and had called the pastor when the panic seized him. Throughout the crisis, while he waited for the young man's sister to find him, Orpheus was nagged by a practical problem: "I have to preach tomorrow," he thought. "When will I sleep?" But then he did the same as he had done so long ago in the dentist's chair; he gave his weariness to God. He made a sacrifice of sleep.

And who can know, before he goes down into them, what depths of sinful suffering the city encloses? There is a darkness there; and in that darkness people wail their sorrows in a thousand minor keys. It is a strident hell of noise. There is a darkness there, because spirits are invisible, and it is the human spirit crying out. There is a darkness there, because evil complicates these lives impossibly: this is the confusion of the blind, who cannot see to free themselves.

Into that darkness, down into that gloom of confusion, Orpheus chose willingly to descend—to serve.

"Do you remember," said Arabelle Lee, "that I wanted to talk to you last spring?"

Pastor Orpheus nodded. He remembered. It had been the day when her arrival saved his life—according to the giant man who meant to patrol the neighborhood with "my menace" against robbers and white folk. She had not returned after all to speak with him, and he had not been surprised.

"I remember," he said.

"Well," she said, "that was 'cause John beats me. I wanted to tell you that John, he beats me. And that's part of the reason why I came today."

They were sitting in Pastor Orpheus's tiny study. Arabelle kept running her hands between her knees, terrified. She had high cheekbones, which intensified the fright in her eyes. John was a very big man. Orpheus did not think that he could protect this woman from John—not physically, anyway.

Arabelle said, "I think I got the VD," and she sighed.

"Is that the problem, then?" asked Pastor Orpheus. He didn't know how he could relieve VD either, but he asked.

"Naw, that ain't the problem," said Arabelle. She told him that she had been examined by the health department, which gave her a tentative positive reading. They could give her shots, she said. No problem. But they also wanted the names of all the men with whom she'd had intercourse in the last three months. She had fine, long fingers—beautiful fingers, really; gifts of God for slender delicacy. She ran those fingers constantly through her knees.

"Is that the problem?" Pastor Orpheus asked.

"Naw, that ain't no problem at all," said Arabelle. She could name the men, she said. She remembered them all—no problem. But one of them, of course, was John, with whom she lived, she and her daughter by another man. The fact that she and John were not married was no problem either. Orpheus didn't even ask after that; wearily, he did not ask. Arabelle was twenty-two years old.

But the health department wanted these names in order to contact the men. They would order each to appear for a personal checkup. They wanted to chase down the network of the disease. Arabelle understood all that, she said. But if she gave them John's name, then they would call John—and that *was* a problem, definitely.

She began to cry.

"I know for a fack," she said, "John ain't been to bed wit' no one but me goin' on six months now. He get that call, an' he goin' to know it's me put them on to him. So he goin' to know I'm worried I got VD. An' he surely goin' to know he ain't the one that give it to me." She leaned forward to Pastor Orpheus with a pitiful pleading in her white eyes. Her spilling tears wounded the man; he hurt with her. In peaceful times Arabelle laughed, laughed often and lightly like a child.

"Pastor," she said. "If it wa'n't him that give it to me, then it had to be someone else. Don't you see? He goin' to know that I been slummin' on him."

She broke into sobbing.

"That's the problem, then," said Pastor Orpheus. He wanted to still her nervous fingers and to hear her laugh again. At the same time he wanted to give her iron diapers, to lay John low—to blow a clean wind through the city—

She nodded and sobbed.

What was the problem? Remorse? Contrition? Hardly. The slender, high-boned, beautiful woman in front of him was scared for her life. John could kill her—or Tulip, which was her daughter's name. In a fury over his offended manhood, he could hammer her with his fists until she stopped protesting. This was no exaggeration. This was the cold truth—despite the fact that he held down a good industrial job and had never once been late to work.

"So," she said. "Pastor," she said, while she wiped her eyes. "What I want to know—can I lie to the health department? Would God mind?"

Even so did Pastor Orpheus sink into the sour soil of the city. He descended with his eyes wide open, and he did not sleep nights, thinking of the puzzled, painful lives of the people. They lived in a cruel darkness.

"The man's gone tired," said Stella Johnson of Pastor Orpheus. "Does he got to push hisself so hard?" She cleaned the church building and saw him often, even when he, passing through, didn't see her. She put knit stockings over her shoes in the winter for traction, so that she wouldn't slip on the snow and break old bones. Mr. Arthur Williams, who stopped by the church regularly in his capacity as head elder—checking things out—blew on his coffee. "He got a pasty look about him now," said Stella, "and his eyes look sunken."

"There's no doubt," Mr. Williams agreed, "but that the man should get some rest. Don't know why he doesn't."

"Ain' nobody sick, but he picks up and goes to them," said Stella. "Ain' nobody troubled, but he comes through here blowin' sighs and heavin' sorrow. Ain' nobody had their gas shut off, but he goes stompin' to the utilities to fuss an' fight. I seen it. An' I seen it drain him. An' this is what I think, Mr. Williams. I think it's killin' him."

Mr. Arthur Williams considered her opinion a moment then said, "He needs a wife."

"Needs somethin'," said Stella.

Williams said, "But it makes the other churches round here sit up and take notice, don't it?"

Stella snorted. "It's killin' him," she said.

Pastor Orpheus heard nothing of such conversations. He was oblivious to good assessments, to concerns regarding his health, and to remedies, all three. This wasn't humility in him; it was preoccupation. He was obsessed with his service.

He was seeking Jesus.

Orpheus was seeking to be worthy of Jesus. He was, in fact, seeking to breathe life into that carven figure of agony which hung ever before his eyes. He wanted desperately to raise his beloved Jesus from the dead; that is why he did all that he was doing, and why he took the city to his heart. It was his mortification. It was discipleship, but solitary and unexplained. By obeying the commands that the Scripture contained, obeying them with every fiber of his body and his spirit—making his mind the mind of the Lord, and every waking hour the Lord's—he sought to call his dear Lord Jesus from death to life again. He was barren without Jesus, forlorn. Therefore he sacrificed himself. He would gladly exchange his life for Christ's, so much did he love the Lord. He prayed six times a day that Christ increase at his own decrease; he prayed this with white knuckles and tears, that Jesus come to his dedication, that Jesus arise within his own emptied life: *Where are you now? Will this mean something to you?*

And in the same spirit he did what he despised to do: Pastor Orpheus continued to visit the county jail.

There were three stories in the jail building. The sheriff's desk and offices were on the first floor; prisoners were on the second and the third. A visitor went up in an elevator he did not control; the guards did that from the second floor; one was at their mercy.

To go up in the county jail was, in fact, to go down into the world and to enter the region of the dead.

"Reverend Orpheus to see Corie Jones," said Orpheus into a black phone, first floor.

"What? Who? What?"

"Coral Jones," the Pastor repeated. "You're holding him somewhere on Three. I'm his pastor, and I'd like to see him."

"Wait," said the voice and disconnected.

This meant neither no nor yes. The guards seemed incapable of granting their supplicants a simple answer, nor did they mess with explanations. Civilians had no rights. Preachers in particular were kept in the dark. Orpheus hated it. The phone at his elbow could ring again, and the voice could say, "Come back tomorrow" then click off without waiting an answer.

But on this day he heard the elevator whine in the wall, coming to get him. Permission had been granted after all.

The ride in that tight box was always slow and claustrophobic. Abandon rank and freedom and all your personal schedules, ye who enter here!

Except that the anteroom would be dead-lit by a ceiling full of fluorescent tubes, and cold, and cinder-blocked on three sides, Orpheus had no idea what he would find. Human souls took terrible postures in prison.

He remembered Dolly, as the elevator labored upward. Dolly was a baby. She had three babies of her own, but she was no more than a baby herself, a thin stick of a woman, terrified about her future. She had been waiting to be transferred to the state penitentiary when Orpheus visited her. He had brought a Bible, which the guards gave back to him, prohibiting the gift.

"They gone and th'ew they Kotex at one 'nother," Dolly had told him, gripping her side of a wire-mesh screen, her eyes beseeching him, because if this happened in the county jail, what would she find in the state prison?

Orpheus remembered Dolly. "They was screamin'," Dolly had said, "blacks at whites and whites at blacks, an' I shut my ears, y'know, like this; but it's a stone wall in there, Pastor, an' I could hear them screamin' *m. f.* an' evil things, an' they shoved they faces th'ough the bars, 'cause cain't get at one 'nother—but they could do this, an' they did: they took the bloody Kotex off and slap *th'ew* them! An' it ain't so wide between the tanks that somebody 'ud miss somebody else, oh—"

Dolly was an infant, a baby. It's one thing to suffer in the sunlight the personal loss of a baby; it is quite another to hear the bewildered loneliness of the baby herself.

But Jesus loved the little children.

*Do you see me, Jesus?* thought Orpheus as he stepped from the elevator into the bright anteroom. There was a bank of lockers for his pocket possessions. There was a metal detector, a door frame from nowhere to nowhere—and at the far end, thick glass punctured by a speaking hole. Guards chatted amiably on the other side of the glass, ignoring Orpheus's arrival until it suited them to summon him; and even then they wouldn't look into his eyes. They'd screw a meaningless sheet of paper into a typewriter while they talked to him, cracking gum. *Do you see me? Is this what you went through?*

Orpheus was tired of it all.

He went to the glass and put his mouth to the speaking hole.

"Reverend Orpheus," he said, the hole swallowing up his voice, "to see Corie—Coral—Jones."

And then he was surprised by the guards' reaction. They all looked at him together, and one went out a little door to reappear at another in the ante-room. He held this door open with his foot.

"You come to talk to Corie?" he said.

"I hope to," said Orpheus.

"And he gon' talk back at you?" asked the guard.

Curious question. "If he doesn't mind," said Orpheus.

"Well, good, good," mused the guard. "That boy surely needs to do some talkin'."

"You mean, someone needs to give him a talking?"

"Naw, I mean he ain't talking 'tall. He ain' spoke, he ain' et; he laid him down when we put him in the cell, and he ain't even moved since. No good. No good for a man to be doin' nothin'. He go to your church?"

"He's a member, yes."

"I figgered. Well, maybe it's a preacher can shake him loose. Come on."

No metal detector. Orpheus went through the steel door with all his possessions still in his pockets.

The guard preceded him down a long hallway; the walls were painted white, the light fixtures recessed—and sound: there is always sound in the jail; the distant muttering of men echoes on cinder-block like chanting, wheels rolling in wheels. They made a hard right turn. They passed a trustee in slippers pushing a cart of books. Now the hallway was made up of cells in series on their right. Side by side, with stone dividers, each cell duplicated the next, each a dark lair eight foot deep and five wide, and windowless; half the space was a bunk, half was the cold floor and a lidless toilet. Each had its pupa, its prisoner.

The guard stopped. "Jones," he said as though tacking up a sign. The doors of these cells were bars only. Nothing was hidden.

Jones.

Pastor Orpheus looked down to find young Corie Jones belly-flat on the floor, wearing nothing but his underpants, his head on his forearms at the bars, his beautiful hair squashed and nappy, his black eyes closed.

Oh, you, Jones. Oh, Corie, what are you doing in there?

The guard bent down and shouted, "It's your preacher!" as if Corie were deaf. "Pay him heed, Jones. Do ya good." And to Orpheus he said, "He's your'n," and left, the milk of human goodness.

Orpheus squatted. Corie hadn't so much as opened his eyes.

Can I touch you, Corie Jones? Do I have the right?

"Corie? This is Reverend Jones, Corie. Remember me? We met at your Mama's often enough. I shook your hand when you came through the living room. Remember me?"

Oh, Corie had a midnight skin, velvet of a shining pile. Now he did a wonderful thing: he raised his head an inch. His eyes slid open and found the face of the pastor one fleeting second, then they rolled closed again, and his head sank. It was something.

"Do you mind if I talk to you?"

Corie didn't mind. Corie signaled absolutely nothing. He was himself a prison within the prison, deep inside himself.

When he'd opened his eyes, he had allowed Orpheus a glance down twin chimneys into the abyss.

Pastor Orpheus shivered at the sight, and in that same instant determined to go down the hole for Corie, after Corie—though he didn't know the way nor what was wrong.

He talked. He sat on the floor with his back to the bars; and in a low, comforting voice, he talked. And if Corie wouldn't answer, Orpheus would answer for him. And if Corie wouldn't even appear, why, Orpheus would (he had the gift!) fashion a ghost for Corie and speak to that.

He talked. He talked *of* Coral Jones as well as to him. He tried to call a Corie into being:

"Corie, you joined the Navy after high school and spent four years in the service," Orpheus said, glancing at the young man. "They made a cook of you, and things were not so bad. But you felt the mildly mutinous spirit of men not altogether free, and when your hitch was up, you took the discharge. You came home. That's when I met you, remember? I remember. It was your eyes," said Orpheus, "your eyes, Corie Jones, that struck me. As soft as doe's eyes, large and brown, and always moist—and I thought, when we shook hands, that these eyes are vulnerable. Be careful, I thought: they can be wounded.

"Well, and you were lazy, that's the truth. You didn't try hard for a job. You thought you'd earned a rest. You drifted to the streets. You did that, Corie Jones. Then, when you did begin to look for work, you couldn't find it. No cooks needed in the city. So then you prowled the streets not by choice but by the sentence of society, and you were unhappy. Am I right, Corie Jones? I'm right. I met you there. You hardly saw me. But I saw your eyes, and they were doe's eyes, miserable. They didn't belong on concrete—"

Through all this talk, Corie did not move. Pastor Orpheus had no notion whether he was being heard or whether his insights were accurate. The facts were right; but the interpretation was holy and faithful guessing.

Neither did he speak all this at a single sitting. Orpheus returned again and again to Corie's cell, now wearing his clerical collar, now carrying a Bible, giving every visible sign of who he was, praying. He was ignorant of the dangers of descending into another human soul. He pleaded righteousness. But he persisted.

There came the day when he touched Corie. And since the young man didn't protest, he touched him continually after that, stroking his neck and shoulders, the beautiful skin, by every means available to work his way inside.

He did not yet understand Corie's distress, nor what was the best thing to do. The cell stank fearfully. Guards flushed the toilet for the prisoner. The man was growing thinner.

But, growing tired on account of the effort and the mystery, and stroking Corie's skin, he kept coming, and he kept on talking.

"So you re-upped. Nothing at home with your mama, I know. Nothing on the streets for you, so you looked to the Navy again to build a house around you, to fill your need. Back to the boats went Corie, seeking order for his life, and a little meaning, too. And the Navy is ordered, that's a fact. But the Navy didn't love you, did it, Corie Jones? What did you do? I don't know. You committed some crime. Free spirits are criminal spirits; hungry spirits are undisciplined. They put you in the brig, and that was worse—worse than the concrete streets, where you could kick a stone if you wanted to. Are there bars on the brig, like these bars here? And did your eyes roll in restlessness?"

He stroked and stroked poor Corie's skin, and he developed a true affection for the man. Touching causes love.

"Then the Navy gave you a choice. To save their money they offered you a dishonorable discharge: get out of our sight, civilian Jones! Don't ever come back again! You took the discharge, and you fled.

"Where, Corie? Where did you flee?

"Home again, Corie Jones. But there was no welcome for you. None. And now, though you looked immediately and desperately for work, no jobs for you either. No, not for one dishonorably turned out and poor besides and black: an ex-con, Corie Jones.

"So where did you flee? Nowhere. You fled to a nowhere. And who were you then, Corie Jones? Nothing."

Stroking, petting the poor man's skin, Pastor Orpheus came three and four times a week, the mechanical elevator, the anteroom, the guards gone taciturn again because he seemed a useless, mumblin' preacher after all and they were sorry they'd relaxed the regulations in the first place. Grimly they led him down the whited hallways to the cell: "Jones! Your preacher! Jones, flush the damn toilet, will you?"

But Pastor Orpheus talked and talked and touched his child. He was looking for Jesus! He had remarkable reserves for such a quest, a mighty store of spiritual energy; and he endured—he *desired* to endure—the humiliation it caused him to love the poor, the black, the foul, debased and worthless Corie Jones. But who *was* Corie Jones, and what was he to him? Why, he was the cold, carven figure of agony, the wooden Christ upon his cross, dead!

Sometimes Corie made a purring sound while Orpheus stroked him, and that was purely a blessing.

Like a monk in the oratory, Orpheus kept on talking.

"So you looked to fill your emptiness your own self, Corie Jones," he said. "But you filled one emptiness with another. You smoked the reefer. You snorted the little lines of coke. All your money was dusted with that coke. You spent a dusty money. You spent all the money. You shot up and laid back and floated and crashed, Corie Jones, O Corie Jones, my Corie Jones. And what did you do when you crashed? Well, you were no more than an animal, then, and there was no worth in you, and all you knew was that you didn't like to hurt—even the animals don't like to hurt. So what did you do? Ah, Corie Jones, in a fog, but the fog was inside of you, you rolled a man. You beat him down on a downtown street, and you took his little money; and you did this on Seventh Avenue, across from the police depart-ment; and when they came out in the night after you, you swung at them, too, so it was two cops on your back, and they brought you down, Corie Jones; they brought you down to the ground itself; they brought you down, your teeth in the dirt, and the dirt stuffed your mouth, and you chewed on the dirt, grinding it like the animal that only doesn't want to hurt, but hurting. You swallowed the dirt, and you never got up again, Corie, because you were noth-ing, not even the animal. Not even the animal. Nothing, and couldn't hide it any more. Corie Jones, he's in jail where he belongs, not arguing nobody the shame, but lying on his face, 'cause he is nothing, nothing, no one any more. Let even God forget him. Corie is dead."

It was a dreadful prayer.

But Pastor Orpheus looked at Corie underneath his hand and saw a wonder; the man was weeping. Tears had pooled at the root of his nose on his sideways head; and tears ran onto his arm, then onto the floor. Corie Jones was crying!

"Oh, Corie!" whispered Pastor Orpheus, his own nostrils

flaring. "Will you talk with me now? Can we sit up like humans and talk with one another?"

Corie raised his head a fraction and opened his wet, brown eyes and looked at Pastor Orpheus and, ever so slightly, nodded.

Well, the pastor leaped to his feet.

*"Guard!"* he cried. "We need a room. Can we have a room to ourselves?" He was trembling. Slowly, painfully, Corie Jones was rising to his feet until he stood in underwear behind the bars.

A guard appeared and granted a certain mean admiration for this triumph.

"Follow me," he said, unlocking the cell. "You got fifteen minutes."

He led them to a tiny room, totally white and windowless: two chairs, a metal door with a small wire-meshed window in it. He admitted them, stood back, locked that door, and walked away, his hard shoes clopping.

Corie Jones and Pastor Orpheus took chairs facing one another. Pastor Orpheus leaned forward, gazing, so he thought, at fields of possibility, at his bony black child. But Corie only drooped his head on his chest and sighed—and that, in the moment, was frightening, because he was disappearing again.

"Corie, you cried," said Pastor Orpheus. "I saw the tears, Corie. I saw your soft eyes wet. Do you know what that means?"

Corie didn't answer, didn't so much as shrug. He was sinking into himself.

"It means you talked to me. Your soul said something, and I heard it. It means you welcomed me a little way in. It means you got feelings. It means you're not nothing, because sadness is something. And it means you let me to see that something, therefore you called me 'friend.' We're friends, and you said so. Corie? Corie?"

Corie's chin was on his chest. His arms hung straight down on either side of him. His thighs came out of his shorts like skinny tree limbs. He did not move. He seemed so naked, black in a bare white room.

"Oh, Corie, don't leave me now," pleaded Pastor Orpheus, whispering, but unable to mute the panic in his voice. "We're so close, so close. Let me see your eyes again. Let me see those eyes of the doe, so soft and startled and gentle and wrong for the streets. They're such good eyes, Corie. We have so little time."

But the man answered him nothing.

So Pastor Orpheus prayed aloud: "Dear God, I'm begging you for Corie Jones. *I have the right!* You must hear me, because of the need, because he is dying, because he shouldn't die, because I have done everything you asked of me, because I am not praying for myself, but for him, and he is your child after all. Tell him you love him! Prove your mercy for him. Let him be at peace, and talk with me, and live. O God almighty, let Corie Jones live again. Do you see that I pray out of my suffering? Is that nothing to you? And do you see that I suffer because of my love for you and for Corie Jones, both? *I have earned the right!* You must, by expressions of your own love, persuade my Corie Jones that he is worth something in your sight, and that he can live —"

In these and other words Pastor Orpheus prayed a desperate prayer, all his ministry balanced on the scaffold—nay, ministry itself thrown into the wager, and waiting the hand of the mighty God.

But Corie Jones seemed oblivious of the drama near and for him. He was a stick-man, collapsed upon his chair. His eyes were closed.

And so the handful of little minutes passed away. And finally Pastor Orpheus heard the clop-clop of the shoes of the guard returning down the hall, and he began to despair.

But God himself said, *Peace.* God said, *Behold.*

And then, in the very next moment, the dazzling miracle took place, and Orpheus was granted insight, and he knew precisely what to do, and he did it.

The guard rapped the door three times.

That sound horrified Corie Jones. All at once he sprang to his feet, knocking the chair backward, waving his arms and throwing his head from side to side. His eyes! His eyes looked like the rolling eyes of a stallion when its face is being lashed, and he himself, his whole body, was rearing away from pain.

Pastor Orpheus recognized those eyes: they were of someone falling, someone perfectly lost with nothing familiar around him, nothing whatever to cling to, an alien in strange air, falling. Corie hardly knew where he was. Corie was bewildered by the guard's knock, because he did not know what it was. He had no name even for a knock. It was threat, and he was imperiled!

"Oh, Corie!" cried Orpheus. And this is what he did: he flew to the man. He gathered him bodily into his own arms and hugged him as fiercely as he could. He, Pastor Orpheus, *became* the world around Corie, a total, enveloping womb for him. He pressed his face to Corie's face, and he whispered, "I love you, I love you," over and over again. "God loves you. All along God has been loving you. He never didn't love you, not even when you didn't love yourself. He's been waiting, Corie. He's been waiting every day of your life for you to come so that he could hold you just like this, so that he could call you his child, his guest, his son: 'Corie Jones, you are my son, lost and found and dead and alive.'

Oh, Corie, and he will put rings on your fingers. And he will put clothes on your back, a holy coat they made in heaven. And he will dress you fine, Corie, fine, and laugh beside you, and then you never *seen* such a party as he will give for you, for you, O Corie Jones—"

The black man subsided. The naked man relaxed. The frightened man went soft in Orpheus's arms. And on that day he said nothing. The guard frowned at the shining joy in Orpheus's face while he hugged his Corie; but how could the guard know that Orpheus had just seen a spirit, the spirit of Corie Jones come walking toward him through the mists?

On that day the man said nothing. He went to sleep— no, not on the floor, but on the bunk in his cell.

Ten days later Pastor Orpheus answered his telephone to hear the operator ask, "Will you accept a call from Mister Coral Jones?"

He shouted, "Yes!"

Calls from the jail, even local calls, are always collect calls because the authorities make sure that they will get their money. Prisoners must reverse the charges.

But Orpheus hollered, "Yes!"

And the operator said, "Go ahead."

And then there was a silence in the line, but a breathing silence.

"Corie?" said Orpheus. "Corie Jones, is that you?"

Silence. Breathing. Orpheus stood up and pressed the receiver to his ear.

"Corie," he cried, "did you call me up? Did you do that? Did you dial this phone with your own finger?"

Silence still.

"Did you tell the woman my name? Did you tell her *your* name, Corie? Oh what a marvelous thing you have done!"

Then a low voice said, "Well," and Orpheus was beside himself.

"Well!" he shouted. "Yes, yes, well. Well, what? You going to talk to me?"

"Well," said Coral Jones, so low and sweet and distant. "Well," he said slowly. And then he said, "I love you."

Corie hung up.

But Pastor Orpheus, the receiver still against his ear, burst into tears. He cried as helplessly as he had Good Friday long ago, but with gladness. He had just seen Jesus. It was as though he saw a phantom, the shadow of a little wind. Jesus was black, with great brown eyes like those of a doe.

And the sight was beautiful.

◊     ◊     ◊

There is such a thing as effective lustration. It has its time and its right and its desired consequence. The drama of faithing comes, by a devout and loving process of personal consecration, to its climax: the votary is sanctified for prayer; he prays; and his prayer proves good. *My will be done* is done indeed. It is not wrong, in its place. It is not wrong, though the faither has in fact inverted the holy order of obedience, presuming that he can gain the celestial station to command the Deity himself.

How arrogant he may then seem to others both religious and worldly! How untouchable in his convictions! How obstinate, impervious, dogmatic, hard, and bound to his pieties—or else how supernal and how saintly he may seem ("O Thomas Archbishop, save us, save us, save yourself that we may be saved; destroy yourself and we are destroyed"). Yet it is not wrong: he acts in zealous love for the Lord Jesus. And it is not wrong: it *is*. It just isn't *all* there is.

And though the unrolling of the scroll will show the

achievement chimeral in the end, yet the chimera is not nothing, and the faithing one is not deceived. He has seen Jesus. The vision is of a phantom, bodiless and unsubstantial, yes. To all the scornful analysts, it is outrageously unprovable. Nevertheless, it is real. Nor is it a subjective reality, born of the vision itself; it is objectively real, apprehended *by* the vision: he has seen a something. He has seen the phantom of the spirit of Jesus. Or, more precisely, he has seen the *promise* of the spirit of Jesus. He has placed himself into the cleft of the rock. He has endured the hand of God across his sight, until the Almighty had passed by occluded. And then, in a trice, he saw the back of the Lord—not the face of the Lord, nor yet the glory of that face, but the back; and all this as in a cloud. He saw the thing that is (though it takes its existence only from a greater thing, which itself proceeds from the thing yet greater still): he saw the Promise—of the Spirit—of the dear Lord Jesus. He saw, and his love was quickened even beyond the finitude of human flesh.

After such a benefaction, what could he *not* accomplish? He is a Knight of Faith triumphant.

So then, there are three episodes in this third passage of faithing, and the first may be of long duration, while the last is as fleeting as the time it takes to realize that it has been.

1. The lover of Jesus himself shoulders the whole burden of the relationship, since Jesus has died; intentionally he mortifies his flesh—a kind of a death, though not yet the same death, being the willful choice of the living, a choice which can persist only so long as life persists *to* choose. The lover of Jesus sanctifies his person, body and soul, seeking the same emptiness which the Lord Jesus exemplified by descending from God, by humbling himself to death and death on the cross. ("The same" we say, meaning by that only so much as the faither is able to understand of Christ's

humiliation at this particular Passage.) In the faither this is, at present, a paradox, for volitional humility, practiced with an eye cast forward to reward, is a proud sort of humility, though we must not impugn it too greatly, since it is humiliation nevertheless, and the world can never understand it. It truly suffers its sacrifice.

The lover of Jesus *goes out,* crawls out, departs the motives and the patterns and the spiritual precincts of this world. That is to say, he seeks to make himself holy, by dint of his own effort to be found righteous in the sight of God. All this he does in order to gain approval for the supplication that he shall make before the (impersonal, transcendent) God-That-Is on behalf of the (personal, once immanent) Jesus. He prepares himself for prayer. For *the* prayer.

Does he realize what he is doing? It doesn't matter.

Does he know that this is but a median passage and not the end? Likely not, for it has its own end, its burning objective, and right now requires the totality of his commitment.

The faither is the monk, by vow beholden to the asceses, painfully practicing, gladly believing in the efficacy of several austerities.

He is the psalmist who sings in confidence, "Vindicate me! I have walked in my integrity!" He is the psalmist who sings for the vast hosts of the self-denying and the pious: "I do not sit with false men, nor do I consort with dissemblers; I hate the company of evildoers, and I will not sit with the wicked."

He is the humorless young man, so fiercely committed to justice that his very presence seems a judgment on the world.

He is the little brother, the mendicant Francis of Assisi, sweetly laughing among the lepers.

She is the woman-child brutalized by men in her own home, able, by an ineffable, incomprehensive love, to transfigure her suffering into a sacrifice offered in behalf of her beloved Jesus. Or else she is Teresa of Avila, who did the same with her physical afflictions.

He is young Martin Luther, thrown to the ground by a bolt of lightning.

He is St. Julian, Hospitator, who shuttles travelers back and forth across the wide river in his little bark, who, one violent night, is asked to stretch his naked body skin for skin upon the cold body of a stinking leper to warm him—and does.

He is the social worker who enters the habitations of the poor, seeking the riches of the kingdom.

He has a hundred faces, past and present, sanctified or vilified; but always the divine hunger is stamped upon his brow, the alien light is in his eye; and always he is persuaded of success.

He does indeed approach a holiness. . . .

2. And in that state, the faither prays.

This is the second episode, performed in the utter conviction that he must be heard, not only for the righteousness of his formal self-preparation, but for the sheer rightness of his suit, and also for the passion wherewith it is made. The passion is so consuming that it *must* blast to nothing any reservations which the Deity, the God-That-Is, might have. So: this prayer is, as it were, a focusing of heat. Its form (that is, the furnace in which the fire is, and the ductwork upward to the Deity) is constructed of a careful and devout self-mortification, external works, a shaping behavior. Its energy (that is, the fire within the furnace and the heat blowing upward through these ducts) is the roaring love of the supplicant for Jesus. And its purpose (the warming of the Deity himself) is what? Is nothing less than to change his mind, to melt him by love into loving, to persuade him to repent himself and thence to raise his son from the dead, even into the life of the supplicant again: the faither's supplication is for the resurrection of Jesus.

Unspeakably audacious is such a venture, by any standard.

Yet Abraham had the boldness to plead with the Lord on behalf of his nephew's life.

And Moses more than once, in the face of divine decision and despite the wrath, propitiated Yahweh for Israel, the son whom he called out of Egypt.

And Hosea cried, in the name of the Lord, "My heart recoils within me, my compassion grows warm and tender. I will not execute my fierce anger—"

And what Moses heard in the cleft of the rock was "The Lord, the Lord, a God merciful and gracious, slow to anger, abounding in steadfast love—"

And there is the enigmatic record of Jesus's own prayer, passionate, painful, priestly, a prayer for (it seems) the saving of his own life, a prayer which does not remember *"Thy will be done"*: "In the days of his flesh, Jesus offered up prayers and supplications, with loud cries and tears, to him who was able to save him from death, and he was heard for his godly fear." And he was heard. Who knows what that means?—except that God did not dismiss him, cut him off, condemn or curse him for such rash, audacious praying, but received the godly fear as good and godly fear. And as cryptic as this description is, it befits the faithing one at this passage, for he is about a paradox: he is acting *like* Jesus (the Jesus fixed in time past) *for* Jesus (the Jesus penetrating all time, past and present); *like* the Jesus that lived (offering prayers with cries and tears) *for* the Jesus now dead (needing prayers of cries and tears). And God shall hear him, too, for his godly fear, his good and godly fear.

The God-That-Is relents.

Do not devalue it. As presumptive and foolish as it may seem, the prayer for life in the face of death—life from the rule of the dead, in the midst of the Kingdom of Death—is efficacious!

*Here is a dead one. I seek a sign. Restore this dead one to life agian, and in that life reveal my Jesus. I seek a miracle: not that Jesus rise to raise the dead, but that in the rising of the dead, Christ may be raised for me.*

3. And the God-That-Is relents. Does he weep tears? This God does not weep tears, this *Elohim,* the imponderable, the faceless, the infinite, whom only the Son has ever seen, who, but for the Son, would not be known by anyone, save as Mighty and Righteous, whose righteousness is perilous unto the people since it is, simply, his Being—what he is, is righteousness—which cannot finally be known apart from the Son. And the Son is dead.

It is with darkness, then, that the faithing one has pleaded. Into the impenetrable cloud he has sent his cry. Hoping and without hope he has wailed for the life of his beloved Jesus.

And the God-That-Is relents.

In a sharp, sweet stab of pain, the shadow of the ghost of Jesus appears—there, *there,* so lovely as to take our breath away. Oh, but he is beautiful!

But in the instant when we become aware that we are seeing him, awareness itself beclouds the moment, and sight straightway becomes a memory. But it is a burning and tenacious memory. "Didn't our hearts burn within us?" Our love has been touched from without, and the tingling of that touch persists to remind us: *it was real.* It was exquisite, delightful, and real. "Yes! Our hearts did burn within us. We *have* seen light and life." But the vision and its vanishing happen at once. They are one thing and the same thing; that's how fleeting the triumph is. "And their eyes were opened and they recognized him; and he vanished out of their sight." So quick. Only then, in remembering, do they ask, "Didn't our hearts burn?—"

Having seen him this once, and cherishing the picture, we are a thousand times hungrier to see him again. So what? So the darkness we had endured seems darker still because of the brilliance of the sight.

Please know this—be courageous enough to accept it: it is the sight of the living Jesus, so long besought; it is the very reality of that vision; it is the face of our Beloved *precisely* which darkens the darkness for us thereafter.

And then this is the melancholy state into which we must next pass: into a darkness commanded.

Into a darkness divinely intentional.

Into darkness absolute and unrelieved by any light or evidence that God is love, or near, or God at all.

The fourth passage of faithing *is* darkness.

# The Fourth Passage: Faith, Conviction, and Not Seeing

*There was no help for it.*

*When Orpheus saw Eurydice limping out of the fogs of Tartarus and when he recognized her slender tread and saw her bare feet on the stones, his face brightened as if he would laugh, but he broke into tears. Like a child he cried, "Eurydice!" because he loved her. And she returned his gaze, though she was not crying.*

*But there was no help for it: he could not touch her. He could not greet her with a kiss or by touching her lily face. No command restrained him; this was merely the nature of things, that he was living and she was not, that she was an unsubstantial phantom brought forth by the pity of the gods. His finger wouldn't find what his eye could see.*

*Thick with human love, he whispered, "Eurydice," and the queen of the region herself leaned forward, drinking with her sad, dark eyes each gesture of the lovers' meeting. O Proserpine! What were you thinking then? That you never had, in spite of all your powers, nor ever would again participate in this common goodness of the upper world?*

*The queen of the region nodded, then, her approval and raised her arm to dismiss the lover with his beloved:* You may go. *Orpheus could have wept the second time. He felt so light and strong, empowered by his happiness. Like a silly child he grinned on Eurydice. But before he took the first step to lead her to life again, Proserpine arose from the iron throne and descended to the man and touched his face; and his heart went still.*

*She turned his head to the black mountains of the underworld and to the path that wandered into them: this is the way that they would have to go. Was she instructing him? By the same compulsion, she had turned his head away from Eurydice. His wife was behind him. Now Proserpine touched his eyes one at a time with the ice-cold tips of her fingers, and next his mouth, and she gazed on him severely. Yes, she was instructing him. She was teaching him the condition of her benevolence, and his task: to climb to life again meant always to look forward. Attend to the present, Orpheus; attend to the task at hand. For to climb to life again, even with Eurydice, meant never to look back or to see her following—not until the two were safely in the sunlight and fully alike in that they both were fully alive. In the meantime, Orpheus, let Eurydice attend to you in front of her; let Eurydice attend to the love, while you but trust her attentions, knowing nothing. Going forward meant not looking backward. It meant not seeing at all the very purpose for which he labored. Trust.*

*And what if he should turn around? Then all would be as backward as he, and everything would be reversed, returned—Eurydice lost and dead forever.*

*So it was. There was no help for it.*

*Nevertheless, Orpheus felt flushed with his previous success, and he smiled obediently on the Lady of Avernus. He thought slyly, "I have done something, and more than any mortal has ever done. And what do you ask of me now? Why, not to do something. To do nothing!" He was lighthearted and glad.*

*The queen of the Kingdom of the Dead nodded one*

*more time:* Even so, *and stepped aside. Then Orpheus sprang forward.*

Carpitur adclivis per muta silentia trames,
arduus, obscurus, caligine densus opaca—

*Cheerful and lively was his climbing, not at all like the morbid slowth of his descent. He was strengthened by the assurance that he would have his wife again to love and to hold. He imagined their laughing together in a green valley, and he traveled at a wonderful speed, and this was the more remarkable because the path was steep, and the rock was sharp, and all was thick darkness around him. He went by feeling, his lyre upon his back.*

*Sometimes his foot dislodged a stone, and then that stone would clatter down and down behind him, and at first he measured his progress by the long fall of the stone, and he congratulated himself.*

*But then his hand would disturb a nest of pebbles, and as they rained and rattled away, a new thought troubled him:* What if, *he thought—*

*Or his knee would slip in crawling, and he would gash himself—because the path was arduous, the climb was truly dangerous—and he thought,* What if—

*That sound of falling pebbles: it was the little noises of his own climbing which made him aware that there was not another sound in all these black mountains. Silence. No wind, but for his breathing alone. No creatures, no calling, but his own groaning only. A solid silence surrounded him. He could not hear so much as a foot brush stone behind him, or the tiny gasps of exertion—her exertion. He paused to listen, and the silence was complete. He kept perfectly still and strained his ears, but he heard nothing. The beating of his heart and—nothing.*

*When he began to climb again, he climbed more slowly. He thought,* What if she isn't here?

*Every time he had difficulty scaling a sheer rock, he thought,* What if this is too hard for Eurydice? *He comforted himself in the remembrance that she was still a spirit unencumbered by a body, and that she might merely float where he had to grapple. But then the fact that she* was *a spirit caused him some sharp suspicions:*

*If her state of being was unlike his, couldn't her sort of loving be different from his too? Did Eurydice love him as much as he loved her? He had journeyed to the Kingdom of the Dead on account of his love; that was extraordinary. Would she likewise do the extraordinary, journeying upward to light on account of him? Or was she different, being dead?*

*Orpheus knew himself; he knew his own capacities very well: if it depended on* him, *their reunion would certainly be accomplished. But right at this moment, while struggling for one more handhold in the dark with only the scornful silence behind him, he knew little and nothing about Eurydice; yet everything, everything, her life and his, and the daylight glory of their loving, everything depended on her alone!*

> *Who is Eurydice?*
> *How strong is she?*
> *Where is the soul I cannot see?*
> *Does she love me?*

*Orpheus loved mightily. Was he loved as mightily in return? Could* anyone *match him and love as mightily as he? Orpheus loved deeply, but here was the danger of that: as deeply as his love went, even so deeply did his doubts go now.*

*He broke the silence. He whispered through his teeth, "Eurydice?"*

*There was no answer.*

*The man kept climbing, but slower and slower. He was of two minds. If she was behind him, then he should spur himself and hurry to meet her above and be done with this torment. But if she was not behind him, why, then every step was taking him farther and farther away from her, and his own glad rush at the beginning had only hastened his torment. Then he should have stayed in hell, for this way was a hell more horrible!*

*Which was it? Where was he going?*

*With his hands hooked to crevices above him, and his cheek against the rock, he hissed, "Eurydice? Are you there?"*

*There was no answer. He waited a full quarter-hour, but there was no answer. He heaved his laggard body to another ledge, and by main effort to another—closer? Closer? Or farther away?*

*"Eurydice?"*

*Oh, why couldn't their loving depend on him alone?*

*"Eurydice?"*

*Her name, her name called out, her lonely name unanswered, the name itself became evidence in the growing argument against her. For how could she love him if she did not answer him?—if she would not comfort him? And if she didn't love him, then she would not follow him. And if she had not followed him, than all his labor was in vain!*

*He cried out at the top of his lungs, "Eurydice!"*

*Silence.*

*God, how the climbing hurt him, body and soul!*

*Finally a grey light sifted in the air above. Orpheus saw that he was causing shadows beneath his hands. He was coming to the mouth of the cave. There was daylight outside the promontory of Taenarus.*

*Wretched man! He gained a crest of stone then took to his feet and ran as fast as he could through the final tunnel, gasping. And when he reached the portal, he whirled around. There was no help for it! Shuddering, in a dreadful doubt, he turned around—*

*—to see Eurydice. He saw her. She was there!*

*No, no, no: she had been there.*

*She'd been there all along—but his impatient glance had caught her still in the throat of Avernus, still unready for the violation of his sight; and the looking killed her. Even now before his burning eyes, because of his eyes, the woman was fading, suffering death the second time. This is what Orpheus heard: he heard her say, "Farewell."*

*"Farewell," Eurydice called in a distant echo of her voice, a dream-cry. And when he rushed back into the darkness to embrace and hold her, she was gone.*

◊　　◊　　◊

How long do we go in the gladness and the memory of our sweet experience of Jesus? Well, it can be a long time; but it is always too long. The memory may remain our whole lives long; but the gladness passes away. And why? Because that good experience, once we've left the third passage, is not repeated. Indeed, the fourth passage is the unrepeating of the vision; it is the silence and the darkness of the closure of glory. And it is properly entitled "faith," despite its late beginning in the whole drama of faithing, because, though we still have many things of our relationship with Jesus, what we lack precisely is the evidence that it *is.* We can neither see nor touch nor hear nor thrill in the relationship. Faith is the conviction of things not seen.

Conviction, assurance, these alone—without evidence.

But at the beginning of this passage, so long as gladness lingers, we do not mind (we pay no mind) and therefore do not recognize either the inception or the dolor of the fourth passage. Not yet.

No, we are warm yet in yesterday's retreat, yesterday's worship service, when certain prayers and certain ceremonies melted us to tears and we said in our souls, *The Spirit of Jesus is here.* We are full yet with the rosy gratitude that a prayer was answered, a sickness healed, a hopeless marriage renewed, a burden lifted, an impossible problem resolved, or a human hugged us so tightly, so unexpectedly, that we said in our souls, *This is a miracle: this is none other than the presence of the Lord!* (There are a multitude of ways by which we may recognize the Spirit.) We are warm yet in the palpable success of our determined pieties: that the fasting, the physical deprivations, the disciplines and austerities finally caused our flesh to thaw and fall away, and in an ecstasy our spirit met the Spirit of the Lord; or that our alms-giving, in any of a thousand forms, finally transfigured the face of one impoverished human, and we perceived in her gaunt smile the face of Jesus; or that a persistent study of the Scripture and the devout, repeated praying of the Psalms made the black print of certain words blacker still and bolder before our eyes, so that the verses seemed to rise from the page and enter our minds like living things, and we said in our souls, *This is the handiwork of Jesus—* and privately we bowed our heads, and privately we wept. Warm: we are for some time warm in the memory of the experience . . . of the promise . . . of the Spirit . . . of the dear Lord Jesus.

The experience happens, truly does happen, a thousand ways; may even happen more than once. But always one thing follows: Time.

The days pass. Yesterday flows backward, like the river, into last month, last year. And time itself instructs us.

When the experience (which we thought would continue, thinking that *it* was the new plane of our relationship) does not return, then slowly the warmth cools. Last month becomes a season lost. Then what we do still have feels very cold within us. And what do we have? The memory—whose reality is in the past. And the memory is of a promise—whose reality is in the future. But we are in the present where nothing is because what we do not have is the experience itself or immediate evidence of a persistent Jesus. *With our eyes* we cannot see. Again, what do we have? Mementoes. Promissory notes. Documents which one day long ago or one day yet to come might prove valuable and true, but which today are paper. Scriptures. Doctrines. Books of common prayer, literate, lovely, but lacking, we sadly confess in the silence of our souls, fire. (In the second passage we were, perhaps, angry with these things; we were adolescent then. In the fourth passage we are not angry; we've grown older; we have experienced their value, and so we do not reject them, but continue to honor and use them, yet more and more in wanhope and without a passionate expectation. The faithers of the fourth passage may, in fact, arouse the rage of faithers in the second.)

So what do we have? The darkness in which doubt occurs. And doubt becomes a question. And what do we have? The silence which absolutely refuses to answer that question. So the question recurs again and again to hector us:

*Jesus? Are you there?*

Silence.

*Jesus?*

A silence so deep that it doesn't even whisper: *Trust.* No, it cannot caution. *Only believe,* because it is silence and even these small comforts would break silence, becoming signs, a sort of shadowy seeing, glints of evidence; and the character of the fourth passage is the denial of any evidence. The silence only. Only the darkness.

And what we might not know in such a state, but what we ought to know (though it confuse us even further regarding our God) is that this severe condition placed upon our faithing, this proscription of spiritual sight and sound, is no accident: it is an interdict of God himself. He issues it for our own sakes. Rightly it follows upon the third passage; the third passage prepared for the fourth to come. Rightly it is the perfect inverse of the third passage; the fourth shall cleanse the pride revealed in the third that was, shall purify the faither of pride in the only way possible—painfully, experientially. The fourth refines the third, by cold fire and a caustic loneliness.

For had we, in the third passage, chosen the shape and behavior of the relationshp? Well, in this one it is chosen for us and enforced upon us by command. And had we, in the third, blithely chosen to *do* something, believing our doing worthy and good? Well, in this we are commanded to do nothing at all, but to wait only; to *be* nothing at all in the relationshp, not even testors or provers of the love or the presence of Jesus ("You shall not tempt the Lord your God"), but to allow God *in secret* to be everything of the relationship. We are to be nothing: Nothings can know nothing. Nothings can do nothing. Nothings, accepting their condition, must cease any seeking and should not enact a certain faithlessness by trying to look around to see the signs, but must rest only in the darkness and the silences, waiting on the Lord, waiting on him even for personal being, waiting on the Lord, with the strong, unsatisfied desire, more than they that watch for the morning. That, at this pass, is faith.

Know, dear people—without the tiniest scrap of evidence to confirm it—that this is the will of God.

So we say. All of this we *say;* and all of this the faithing one, about to enter the passage that shall most mature him, may *hear.*

But how does the passage actually unfold?

In the beginning, despite all warnings and the announcement of the interdict, the faithing one thinks, "I can do it." He comes encouraged by his burning love for Jesus and flushed with the success of that love's accomplishments. "What is it after all?" he thinks when time has taken the vision away. "A little waiting. With the promise still inside of me to give me hope. I can do that," he thinks. "I can be still a while. Better to wait in the foxhole than to endanger myself on the battlefield," he thinks, unaware that the foxhole *is* the battlefield of the soul, and infinitely more lonely. In the foxhole one is one's own foe, and thinking is the weapon. And, unaware (because he hasn't yet experienced it) of the completeness of the occlusion, the darkness of this night, he thinks, "How bad can it be?"

*I can do it:* this is the attitude exactly which will be excised. Graver still, this is the declaration which later will cause spasms of an even more horrible pain: guilt. Guilt is the pain of a pride cut away. Darkness is the scalpel.

*How bad can it be?* This is the bravura of ignorance. This is the boast of persons or of peoples in physical prime, willing to hazard a bodily death, reckless of the spiritual (and in need of spiritual refinement). This is the swagger of heroes: the Greek Odysseus before he, and his culture in

general, became King Oedipus; Beowulf swimming fully ar-
mored down to Grendel's dam, before he met the dragon
and his own old age; Lancelot after a thousand battles in
which he gathered worth, but before he faced King Arthur
as his enemy, in which battle there could be no worth at
all. This is not an uncommon attitude, this casual courage
of the good when they are still strong, this pride of nations
or individuals. It is America before its Vietnam. It is the
faithing one, before the doubt that comes in the darkness.

But ask the question without ignorance, and answer it
without illusion, according to those who have gone before
us, Jesus, Abraham, Israel. Then the answer will still our
pride.

How bad can it be?

As bad as temptation—to hurt like the Devil!

Jesus had had his own celestial experience, sweet and
good and signifying. He had heard himself named as "beloved" and "my son," the Son of God: the divine relationship
had been divinely validated, and with it, his identity; and to
make the validation an objective experience and not the
dreams of a fervid mind, he *saw* the invisible Spirit descending visibly like a dove; he *felt* it to alight on him.

But straightway the experience devolved into a memory,
and the dove became his drover; for he had, by the will of
God and the urgency of the Spirit, been led (passive voice)
into the wilderness, whose nature is privation, to experience
which is to experience want. He did not eat for a generation
of days (as Israel was denied, for a generation of years, the
milk and honey of the promised land, living with the promise only, itself repeatedly jeopardized). And now he was hungry. And now the tempter came to him.

What did Jesus have then? He had the memory of the

voice of God, but the voice of God was silent now. Another voice was speaking. He had the memory of a relationship which promised a future glory; but the Father himself was not evident in this wilderness, for hadn't he given the tempter permission to appear instead and to harass his Son? Jesus remembered (and, to give them a present value, had to *believe*) the words, "This is my beloved son—"

Now watch the accuracy of the tempter's attack, the effort to cause doubt in period of deprivation. His first shot targeted those exact words, the truth of that memory, and the very believing of Jesus, whereby he trusted them. The tempter said, "If you are the son of God—" The tempter sought to make a question of the divine declaration, and to make its truth dependent on something else: "Are you really? Are you *really* the son of God? Can you believe that in such a place as this?" It is not denial; it is the first motion of doubt.

And what did the tempter suggest might support the memory, proving true what should be its own proof, being true of itself? Why, evidence! A sign! Something to *see* and to experience here in the wilderness-present. And that sign, so the tempter suggested, ought to be performed by Jesus himself: let him *act* like a son, if he truly is the son of God. Do something! How could it be wrong merely to flesh out the words of the Father, completing them, as it were, and doing it all in love of the Father; for isn't it a compliment to image the beloved in oneself? "Like father, like son" brings father and son closer together, though separated, doesn't it? How could that be wrong?

But the evil in the temptation was revealed by its very form: "Command these stones to become loaves of bread." The purpose of the act would be, at bottom, to satisfy Jesus' *own* hunger, a self-satisfaction both physical and spiritual. Love might have increased, were the act accomplished; but

trust in the words, the memory alone, would have vanished—replaced by trust in Jesus' own divine ability to do
miracles. And Jesus might have *seemed,* but he most certainly would not have *been,* the son who allowed his Father
total responsibility for their relationship; rather, he would
have become the son of himself, born of his own action, so
much like the Father that he would have separated himself
from the Father. He would not have waited for the Lord: it
was a dreadful temptation.

But Jesus said, "It is written—" not even speaking by his
own authority, but referring to collective memory, holding
to memory, trusting the memory. "It is written, 'Man shall
not live by bread alone, but by every word that proceeds
from the mouth of God.' " His faith, then, at that moment in
the dark, silent wilderness, was revealed in no inspiring act,
no martyrdom, no miracle nor wonder of any sort; it was
revealed in that he did none of these things, precisely in
this: that he did nothing! Faith was the life of one founded
totally upon God—nay, upon the words of God issued in
the past against a future promise—nay, upon a quote! Faith
had nothing whatever to do with Jesus' own doing; rather,
it had everything to do with his carefully doing nothing.

But the devil was not yet done. If Jesus himself would
not produce the sign, then surely the loving Father would.
How could he love if he wouldn't protect his son from pain?

So the devil put Jesus in peril. *(How bad can it be?
Well—)* The devil set Jesus at a dizzy height above the city,
saying, "If you are the son of God"—are you, are you
really?—"then let him give evidence of his fatherhood and
of your sonship, that it still is: jump. And do you believe the
words that proceed from his mouth? Then believe these:
'He'll give his angels charge of you—to bear you up, lest

you strike your foot against a stone.' Jump. Surely *that's* a sacrificial act. Surely *that* shows trust. It wants no action out of you; it asks but God's act only. Jump. Or don't even so much as jump. Fall; cease standing; collapse. Can you call that your own doing then?"

But Jesus said, "Again it is written, 'You shall not tempt the Lord your God.' "

No evidence! There shall be no sign. No experience of the hands of angels or the love of God. No voice to break the silence. No seeing in the darkness—no, not even if one's very life depended on it. Even in such extreme circumstances as tragedies, catastrophes, and slaughter; even when any good-hearted mother would repent her decision to force her child's independence, and, seeing him suffer, would run in tears to save him; even then there shall be no evidence of God's love, or of the nearness of God.

Don't ask! It is both presumptuous and criminal to ask. The asking itself would destroy what is—even when you do not *know* what is! For asking is the proof—the treachery—of faithlessness. It is proscribed: thou canst not even turn to see. To believe is to resist the desire to ask.

But there was a third temptation. The devil was still not done with Jesus.

If you cannot yourself produce the sign; and if God *will* not produce the sign; but if you persist in seeking some sign nonetheless, then signs may surround you after all in a vulgar abundance. For there is a third being, besides you and God, who wishes to destroy that relationship. This one stands both willing and able to console you with evidence, if only you will break relation with God altogether; and if you are comforted by this one's evidences, then he has become your god. Here is one thing you *can* independently do: you can cease worshipping the hidden God, the dark and silent one, to worship the bright and voluble devil, loud Lucifer, by loving his visible things, the things of this world.

There was a third temptation. The devil took Jesus to a very high mountain and gave him a universal, nearly supernatural, sight. "Is it seeing you desire? Would you want to *see?* Why, then see everything, the whole world at a glance." Satan showed him all the kingdoms of the world and the glory of them. And he said to him, "All these I will give you, if you will fall down and worship me."

This is the third temptation and the danger of desperately seeking signs: if you seek them, you shall find them. But beware! When you have found them and have begun to rest in them, to depend upon them (any signs whatsoever: the Shroud of Turin, or success in servitude, or the opposite of that, wealth, prosperity, clerical power in political realms, swelling church roles, a nation called godly merely because it is mighty and yours)—when you have found them, you have found the devil as well! These things may be, surely. But they cannot be seen as signs of God, for then they have become signs of a false god.

As for Orpheus, so for us: turning to look for signs of our Beloved banishes the Beloved from our sight and replaces him with the Destroyer.

Therefore Jesus cried with a passion, "Get thee hence, Satan! For it is written, 'Thou shalt worship the Lord thy God, and him only shalt thou serve.' " Even the God beclouded in darkness, whom to serve is to serve unrewarded, for one single word of praise would cancel silence.

How bad can it be? As bad as to battle the devil. That bad. That hazardous. As bad as battling every tendency within yourself—to do, to know, to see. It's a grievous, exhausting war in the foxhole, and devious, because it is war with your very nature, even while it is at the same time (this is what "temptation" means) war with the cunning force of evil. And none appears either to champion or even to commend you. You fight alone. This is the wilderness.

Worse, your fighting is nonfighting. It is to do nothing. You are a nothing in a nowhere.

*Jesus? Are you behind me?*

Here is an anomaly: we took up the cross to follow Jesus; and so we do, when we are nailed to it—we follow Jesus. But following him, repeating in our own experience his, we suffer the question of whether *he* is following *us!*

*Jesus? Are you there?*

For at noon, by the same divine fiat that made light, God makes darkness, and we hang in it. And the cross to which we are affixed, why, it is the hard, unbending command not to turn and see. We hang *on* that command, and the silence torments us. Were we only thieves, one of two criminals, we would hang to the left or to the right of Jesus, clearly in his company and in sight of him. But we are not mere sinners, either mocking him (persisting in sin) or else pleading his forgiveness. We are the faithing ones, called to believe on him; and so we hang precisely where we cannot see him at all.

*Jesus? Jesus?*

Why are you so far from helping me, and from the words of my roaring? O my God, I cry in the daytime. Do you hear me? I cry in the night season and am not silent. Won't you answer me?

Are you as near to me as my shadow—were there light and I able to cast a shadow? Are you both as close and as quiet as a shadow when it is drawn across the rough surface of the earth? How glad I would be to know this! Or else, or else—

*Jesus, have you forsaken me?*

I could suffer the worst humiliations, if only I knew your presence and your approval. But the last humiliation, the true humiliation, the humiliation which would make hollow every gesture of mine and a mockery of all my pain, the humiliation which would shoot out its lip at me, scorning all I did as meaningless, would be your absence. Then I suffer for nothing. I am a worm, whose dying under the mud never did produce a god.

*Eli, Eli, lama sabachthani?*

Worse than physical mortification, worse than any torment my body can experience, is the silence and the not knowing. That *becomes* the hurt to sharpen all my other hurts.

*Jesus?*

Silence.

Is all this for good or for ill? Do I go toward you or away from you?

*Jesus?*

Silence.

*Jesus, won't you speak to me?*

Silence. Believe. Believe. Believe. Yet no one in whom we *can* believe so much as whispers the word "Believe." That is to say, Jesus doesn't say it. All we have for testimony is the memory that once he said it and the written record of his call: Take up your cross and follow me. This, now, is the third level of meaning in that call, and only now, with the experience, do we discover it. God abandoned his son; we suffer that abandonment. As his cross stood in darkness and the cosmic loneliness, so ours *is* sightlessness and silence and the injunction, "Do not turn! Believe. Believe." And the believing itself is served by this, that he does not say, "Believe."

Nevertheless, believe.

But how bad can it be?

(By now that question has grown derisive and vexing—oh, why did we ask it at all—and still it's not completely answered.)

How bad can it be?

As bad as to feel not just forgotten by God, but the object of his casual ridicule, as though he created situations of absurdity, then intensified them past endurance, merely to see how we might react. "As flies to wanton boys, are we to the gods"—or so the suspicion grows when we try in our puny minds to explain the silence, to explain that his promises are followed by silences.

Silence seems to us the proof of not loving.

In solitude we wrestle against such interpretations, born spontaneously or willfully of our human understanding; at bottom, we wrestle against the natural patterns of human understanding, and so against reason itself. We wrestle against our propensity to make sense of senseless circumstances—for who can live in the alien irrationality?

What is reasonable?

God said to Abraham, "I will make of you a great nation." But that man was childless at seventy-five, and his wife was sixty-five. Except that with God nothing is impossible, the promise would be unreasonable. It was made reasonable only in the supernatural power of God, by his own choice to abrogate natural laws and to open a dried-up womb. God's being alone made it reasonable, and Abraham believed.

But then God's being, over the years, seemed to reveal

a certain perversity. For he kept repeating the promise, as though desiring Abraham never to forget it; but he allowed the passing years themselves to belie the promise. The years continued in their natural procession, and the laws of nature did not cease their iron grinding of an old man's body: he grew older. His wife grew older. And though God repeated the promise, he did not keep it.

Why? What was reasonable to think?

Abraham, full reasonably, cried out to God, "O Lord, what wilt thou give me, for I continue childless!" And he said, "Behold, thou hast given me no offspring!" Just how was this promise to be fulfilled? The longer God reneged, the less reasonable it became—because God alone had been its rationality.

Then the Lord made the promise dramatic, by a smoking fire pot establishing a covenant with the old man—but still, he did not keep it. Abraham's believing continued in the continued not-keeping of the promise. So it was. So is faithing. But what is a natural man to make of this?

Finally, the natural man took matters into his own hands, following conventional laws, if not the laws of nature. At eighty-six he conceived a son upon the younger body of his wife's maidservant. He was seeking the reasonable in a promise growing absurd with time. *He* would do something where God had not. But faith consists in the not-doing, even when (precisely when) not to do increases the impossibility of its ever being done. So the son of his doing was rejected as an heir.

And again God re-promised the promise (oh, what is reasonable to think of all this iteration?) again establishing a covenant, this time asking Abraham to sign it irrevocably in his flesh by circumcision; the very fountain of any future family was cut—a reminder that he believed, in spite of every evidence to the contrary, that he would father a son.

But what, finally, finally, was the reasonable thing to do? Why, the sardonic thing.

When Abraham was ninety-nine and Sarah, by calculation, eighty-nine, the Lord appeared again, *again* to say, "I will surely return to you in the spring, and Sarah your wife shall have a son."

Shall a child be born to a man who is a hundred years old?

Then Sarah and Abraham (each in their own privacies) shared in the only reasonable thing left to them: they judged absurdity absurd, and so severed themselves from it; they stepped backward from the seeming nonsense into the sense of a rational, realistic reaction: this is impossible, a promise grown ridiculous and never to be kept, words, words only, albeit words of God. They laughed.

*That* was the reasonable, sane, and securing thing to do. To laugh at the sheer irrationality. To disbelieve.

It is this natural tendency against which we struggle in the fourth passage of faithing: like Abraham, first to remonstrate with God; second to take matters into our own hands; third to laugh, that is, to impose even a bitter explanation upon the secret and hidden actions of the deity—*to make something of the silence after all!*—to suppose, for sanity's sake, that God is toying with us, refusing to signify himself in order to torment us. The silence, we reckon, is proof that he does not love us. And so (oh, see the subtle winding of our minds!) we make of the silence, which is the absence of signs, a sign itself! But an odious one.

And so, if we do indeed laugh in this manner, we have preserved some self-control, not quite quitting ourselves, becoming nothing. And we have ourselves lightened the darkness a little by the lumination of our human reason. And though we may satisfy ourselves that we've not looked around, we have nonetheless *imagined* the scene behind us, painting it in images of human motivation, human (even sinfully human) behavior—and this is perhaps the most savage looking-around of all! "I shall laugh the worst laugh I ever laughed. I'm cursed. God, if I don't believe I'm cursed." We choose of our own recognizance to answer the question of Jesus' presence. We say, "Yes! And bloody hateful it is, too!" Thus we justify a true, rapacious looking—because why shouldn't we disobey one whose orders are so treacherously conceived? He doesn't deserve our humble and hurtful submission if hurt is the only purpose of it! We laugh sarcastic laughter—

And we do look. But we kill Jesus the second time with such spiteful, lying looking. We see to our horror the loving face recede and resolve itself into a shadow, the shade into a nothing. Gone. What had lovingly been there all along: gone. Then we hear a hideous laughter raised through the corridors of our hell, a laughter that terrifies us by its lawless, murderous hilarity, its chaos of sounds—and we are shocked to realize that it issues from our own mouth. It is us—our reason, in the infinities, gone quite irrational, for reason hath no standard now except itself. Apart from God, it is itself a god, and mad. And we! We are responsible this time. We could not *not* act. We could not be nothing. Do you understand how we destroyed the Beloved by looking around? We handled Jesus with our own sullied, human hands, manipulated him, and made of him the nothing. We are the sinners. We have killed him again.

But faithing in the fourth passage had called also for the sacrifice of reason. That is, the sacrifice not only of our independent selves and our willful action, but also of the patterns whereby we live and apprehend the truth. Truth alone was to be truth. Jesus is the Truth. We proposed and then believed in another besides him.

But (again, "But") neither is this grim pass the end of faithing.

It is the issuance of guilt.

And we are getting ahead of ourselves.

How bad can it be? Again, how bad?

How deep the darkness? How dark the silence? How planetary the solitude of the faithing one?

Consider the dreadful irony of the prohibition "Thou shalt not look back, shalt not test whether thy beloved cometh behind thee. Thou shalt not know."

Finally, by grace, Father Abraham had one link to the Lord. He had one single thing to prove that all the promises were true and would be, could be, kept. He had one lone assurance of the love of God, nay, even of the presence and the deity of his God. He had one bare window unto the Almighty, and all the rest was closure: this was his son Isaac, the impossible gift of God, the child of a miracle. And he loved his son more than his own life; and by that love, he knew and he loved his Lord. The gift and the giver were one, each one precious on account of the other.

Now: what sacrifice could bespeak the fullness of Abraham's gratitude and his love? Only, saith the Lord, the sacrifice of everything in one thing.

God said, "Board that window." God said, "Break that link." God said, "Annihilate that single piece of evidence— and know nothing!"

God said, "Abraham."

And he said, "Here I am."

He said, "Take your son, your only son Isaac, the laughter of your life, whom you love, and go to the land of Moriah, and offer him there as a burnt offering upon one of the mountains of which I shall tell you."

More than flesh and bone beloved, Abraham would have to offer up the validating conclusion of twenty-five years of believing the ridiculous, thus making it twice as ridiculous as before. And worse, this time he could not separate himself. This time he was constrained to participate in the preposterous, for *he* was asked to offer the one thing in his life both lovely and divine.

Darkness by his own hand, silence by his knife! Nay, then he couldn't take consolation in blaming or else in innocence. He could not, with the Epicureans or the Existentialists, claim to make the best of a bad situation, which situation was the nature of the universe and not their faults. He could not laugh. This darkness more than surrounded him, he an island of light in it. This darkness penetrated to the soul, and his soul, responsible, went out to it.

How deep the darkness? As deep as anguish.

Perhaps this was the principle behind the second commandment of Sinai, largely ignored today: "Thou shalt make no graven image." Perhaps the danger of imaging God was not merely that people would worship idols and the false gods of their own hands, but rather that they would have created visible signs of the invisible God, compromising a complete faith by a little seeing.

Perhaps the golden calf was never meant by Aaron to be another god besides the true God, but rather the true God mediated to the human senses. It was too terrible an experience to be left alone—seemingly alone—with the mountain and Moses and God *obscurus* each, *caligine den-*

*sus opaca,* completely hidden in a cloud. And as the time progressed, instructing them by offering no signs at all, perhaps they couldn't stand the silence of a muttering, meaningless thunder. Perhaps their rings and brooches, melted into a calf, were no more than the effort to *see,* to turn and see whether God was with them after all, and the calf itself no more than a focus for their love and their thanksgiving.

If these things are the case, it does not exonerate Israel or lighten her sin; it shifts it, rather, from the simple idolatry that we dismiss as primitive to the sign-seeking propensity of all peoples, to the weakness that wants a moderated faith, a mediated relationship, and proofs. ("Are you *really* children of God? Does he *really* love you?") And then it is the sin of our yearning as well.

And then the wrath of God and the outrage of Moses measure the danger of a diluted faith, for it kills covenant after all when it cannot wait upon the Lord, wait absolutely in darkness and silence, allowing the Lord to *be* the Lord of the relationship, while those waiting humbly admit to nothingness. And then both the wrath of God and the outrage of his prophet span the ages, embracing us as well, and we are not exempt from the judgment or the danger.

"Thou shalt not make unto thee any graven image—"

And perhaps this was the transgression of Hophni and Phinehas when they bore the Ark of the Covenant into battle against the Philistines: that they sought the sign of God's presence in their crisis. And the sign alone, appearing, caused gladness to Israel's heart and fear to Philistia; but the sign as *sign* was effectively abolished by God when Israel was routed after all—and God himself must have seemed, in Israel's defeat, defeated.

For not even in our catastrophes is the darkness to be

brightened (though then especially do we beg and plead, beseeching miracles of God) nor the completeness of believing the unseen—the completeness of believing itself—to be modified and therefore diminished.

Believe. Believe. When no one says, "Believe," believe.

And this is the last beatitude, tremendous in its scope, terrible in its implications, yet a beatitude, a blessing of Jesus nonetheless:

"Blessed are they who have not seen and yet believe."

This was not the believing of a Thomas, surely, who required the first stigmata, to touch them. But neither was it the believing of any of the disciples, who stood by gaping. These were not the *beati,* however much they loved him whom they looked on. No, the *beati* were the next generation, who arose after Jesus had ascended. And this quality of believing became that of the apostles only when they faced martyrdom with never a sign to console them. And this quality is ours, who toil farther and farther away, in darkness and in silence, from the glorious moment when we saw the promise—of the Spirit—of our Jesus.

Blessed, those who faith through the fourth passage: they do not see; yet not seeing, they believe; and their believing is in this, that they do not see.

What, in practical terms, does this mean?

That the faithing one is now, in all she does, totally turned unto others and not unto herself.

That by her own will she is self*less,* a Nothing laboring, though she labor never so hard. No, no! She is not inactive during this passage, but very active, exhaustively active, for she is climbing, moving through space and time; but she's in an activity whose motive or whose benefit is nothing of her own, or else she would become a Something again.

That her labor shall have, so far as she is concerned, no success. Others may be blessed by it, but she shall not know that, for success in what she does were a sign that what she does is worthy, that Jesus is in it and pleased. Rather, all her labor will seem, in this world, perpetual defeat. She shall labor *in spite of* defeat—and thus she shall not know whether she is toiling with her Lord or away from him; she shall be given only to believe.

And what does this mean?

That none of her works shall have even the private emotional reward of self-satisfaction; for rest in a job well attempted, if not well completed, is itself a sign and a breaking of the silence. There shall not come, in her nighttime hours, the quiet assurance, "Well done, thou good and faithful servant," either to invigorate her for another day or to signify the value of the day past. She can never be content. *(How bad can it be?)* Rather, all will seem to her, upon the sincerest reflection, meaningless and hollow at the core. This is unreasonable; it is the sacrifice of reason; it can't be reasoned: the harder this servant labors, the hollower will seem her labor and so her life. There shall not be, either intrinsically or else upon her work, any judgment passed to assess it good and right or bad and wrong. There shall be no evidence at all. None. Except that, perhaps, the lack of evidence shall begin to seem, to her desperate soul, a sort of evidence in itself—arguing her abandonment.

What does this saying mean: "Blessed are they who have not seen and yet believe"?

Finally, that she cannot at this pass perform her labors with the purpose of seeking Jesus, as she did in the third passage. He will not now be found this way. But that does not release her from work. Rather, there is *no* way that she can find Jesus since any way is a looking round and a demeaning of faith. No, she is bound to work, and why? Because even so does she herself participate willfully and completely in the absurdity which faithing presently is. Now this is the task of faithing: to continue preaching the dear Lord Jesus; to image him mightily before others in her own being, yet taking nothing of the image nor the solace for herself; to *be* the visible Jesus before others, calling them, in his name, to peace and to security, even while she herself languishes in darkness and the silences, shut up from him. It is a perfect paradox.

But what is the "blessing" upon such blind, unhallowed service? Why, what it always was: progress in the drama of faithing; the continued changing of the relationship between the faithing one and her God, which changing is its life; more specifically, her own maturation—for she shall be made "most poore, most thinne" by it, wretched in the extreme; but only then can she truly disappear into Jesus and imp her wing on Jesus'. God is doing a new thing, however hurtful it may seem. She is moving toward the fall which finally shall further her flight. This blind, unhallowed service is her purifying.

But now we are speaking of the fifth and sixth passages. And though the fourth prepares for these, while she lives in the fourth the faithing one can know nothing of these.

In this time she is commanded to live knowing nothing at all.

◇    ◇    ◇

"Why are you smiling?" said Mrs. Story. "What do you see out my window?"

Outside her window? There was a man urinating in the lot across Mulberry, his back to the street, his legs planted wide apart, a man with a stocking cap on his head.

But Pastor Orpheus hadn't really seen that man till Mrs. Story's question interrupted him. Neither was he aware that he was smiling. He simply had a sense of physical well-being and of hope. He was sitting on her sofa, which was covered with plastic and crickled when he moved.

"It's noticeable, Pastor," said Mrs. Story. "You've been doing it for some time now, no blame on you. We're glad to see it. There was time enough when you wouldn't."

"Doing what?" asked Orpheus. "Wouldn't what?"

"Smile."

Since the spring the pastor had developed the habit of stealing away from conversations or meetings into secret meditation and that smile. His grey eyes would stray and melt. A radiant smile would spread across his face, and then he'd touch his fingers to his cheek as though to feel it or else to keep it there.

"So what are you smiling at?"

"Nothing, nothing," said Orpheus. "Nothing, Allouise. A memory that comes back. I saw Jesus."

"Well, I won't blame that either," she said. "Seems to've made you fit again, and God knows you needed something. You ought to marry. But lacking a woman, Jesus'll do, I suppose."

Orpheus laughed. He had always appreciated Mrs. Story's stern forthrightness. No, it was more than that. They loved each other, that old black woman and her pastor.

He said, "What about you, Allouise? Why do you keep rubbing your hand?"

Allouise sang spirituals like no one else that Orpheus had ever heard, man or woman. It was *her* voice that had accompanied the death of Jesus: "Were you there when they crucified my Lord—" She had been there; so said her singing. She had stood in a dark Good Friday cemetery and seen the stone rolled into place.

And when that woman sang not once nor twice but five times, *Mary had a baby—my Lord,* sang, *Mary had a baby—yes! My Lord!* then it seemed to Orpheus that a black wind blew. The wind, her voice, bore this news high into a bitter night. The wind lamented that such a thing should be, and then it was a cold, furious wind; but then the wind allowed the news to drift to the ground again like snow, and then it was a wind sorrowful and resigned: *yes, My Lord.* It seemed tragical, when Mrs. Story sang of it, that young black Mary should have a baby. But for that baby itself there was no blame; there was only an urgent and piteous love.

When Mrs. Story sang in church, Pastor Orpheus could hardly breathe.

And once she sang in doleful, manly tones that nobody knew the trouble she'd seen. Then a black hole opened in the earth to swallow the souls of the whole black race and every one who heard her. An African man was sitting next to Orpheus at the time, a broad-shouldered theologian come to touch his American generations. But when Mrs. Story sang, *Nobody knows but Jesus,* that African dropped his face into his hands and groaned. "No, no!" he whispered. He was from Zimbabwe. He knew in his flesh the troubles. Yet he murmured, "Oh, no, she should not sing like that!"

Should not sing like that? Nonsense! Mrs. Story said that this was exactly the way it should be sung, that this was the right way and there was no other.

She didn't mean, however, that this way was the truth of human sorrow and the communication of her own experience. Hardly. The woman kept her experiences absolutely to herself. She meant, rather, that she'd been taught how to sing a Negro Spiritual at the Tuskegee Institute, and that she would do no less than to sing according to the rules. She was a woman of implacable rectitudes. If Mrs. Story knew the right, she would do the right. If she didn't, she'd accept the consequences uncomplainingly. In either case, she had no truck with sentimentalities or tender mercies or merciful kindnesses. Allouise Story, retired teacher, was an old black woman, hard as a hickory nut.

Pastor Orpheus said, "Why do you keep rubbing your hand? Is something the matter with it?"

He said *"Rub"* but it was much more than that. Her right hand was laid palm-downward on her left knee; her left hand was a fist, beating the back of the right, ceaselessly. Her lips were pursed in the punishment.

She said, "Why did I phone you? I wouldn't trouble you if it weren't necessary." She said, "And why haven't I been to church a season since?" These were grim questions. "I'd take it kindly, Pastor, if you'd put the bread in my mouth. I can't pick it any more. It's lost," she said, beating the hand, "its strength. And I'm losing the feeling in it."

Orpheus felt a sadness for her which he did not show. That independent woman! When no one else had played the organ at church, she said, though she scorned the quality of her playing. Even now, before him, she sat backward on an organ bench, and in the other room was a piano, neither instrument available to her if her hand was not to be trusted. It cost him some pain to take the wafer from its tiny paten and to touch it to her tongue, to hold the tiny chalice to her lips, since once she would have held it for herself.

Allouise had hammered out a clean life in a filthy city, independent of that city. Hers was a white frame, double-storied house, immaculately maintained on the corner of

Judson and Mulberry, a sort of alien monument, like a boat on dry land. It was surrounded by ghetto and shattered glass. Across the street men lounged against Doc's Liquor Store. Down the street, children with protruding belly buttons squatted and played by the curb. And the lots were soaked with anyone's urine. And cars full of the young would park on these streets blowing forth an acrid smoke, a fume of grass. Greasy curtains hung outside the open windows of the other houses—but in *this* house, with its windows closed, in this living room, was cleanliness and order: a profusion of green plants, an organ, a piano, carpeting to cover the floors and, to cover the carpeting, a clear thick plastic. All the furniture was protected by plastic. There was a silver tea service beside communionware on the coffee table between the woman and her pastor. There were two pictures on the wall: one was of Nat Story, her husband, whose body once had lain in state in this same living room; the other was of Mrs. Jaxson, the mother whom Allouise had nursed through a decade of illness unto death.

It was in this house that Allouise Story herself intended one day to die.

This is the woman to whom Pastor Orpheus administered communion. They prayed the Lord's Prayer—but Allouise fired the words with such a staccato speed that Orpheus could not keep up with her. At each petition she beat her hand.

She made a point of seeing him to the door. As long as she could, she would perform proprieties; for though they did indeed love each other, he was her pastor and a certain formality was required.

But in the months that followed his first visitation, Allouise's affliction grew worse.

It affected her arms so that she couldn't raise them high enough to lift dishes to the cupboard, or to hang clothes up in the closet.

It affected her walking, and she took to using a cane.

She fought back: she had her whole house painted from the eaves to the foundation. She installed new locks.

She stopped locking her bathroom door, for fear she would imprison herself.

And always when Orpheus came (since always he kept coming) he saw her ceaselessly, grimly, beating her right hand.

Throughout that summer and fall, the city began a program of self-respect and beautification. Community development block grant monies were raining down from the federal government into municipal coffers, and municipalities flushed with new energies. But in the neighborhood surrounding Pastor Orpheus's church, "renewal," the city's word, was translated into "demolition."

Orpheus's ministry grew to new dimensions. (What could he *not* do, having done one thing successfully, calling Christ into a dead man? He felt equal to the task.) It was true that most of the housing in this area was substandard, rental property and unmaintained. But here was a reality, that this was the only housing affordable to desperately poor people—and for all its promises, Orpheus saw no evidence that the city would build where it had destroyed. Where were these people to go? The better alternative, he argued before the city council and the Department of City Planning, was to rehabilitate the housing that existed. Pursue these landlords! Force them to bring their buildings up to code. Surely, do not relieve them of their financial burdens by buying the wooden liability and razing it to the ground. Yet, that's what the city was doing: making vacant lots where there had been houses.

"You're eating us up!" Orpheus wrote in the newspapers. With his reputation he'd earned the right to publish a weekly column (his ministry increased—he was running hard again, but with optimism). "You're murdering a living thing. This neighborhood has a long and living history. Old men still can point for me the places of their childhood, and every corner breathes a story. It has a subtle nervous system, does this neighborhood; relatives are relatives of relatives, all still dwelling close to one another. People still walk these streets; they stop and talk to one another; a summer's evening is more busy outside the houses than in them. This isn't the suburbs. Houses do not isolate their several families; rather, houses hold them close together, so that a child can move from door to door, from aunt to uncle to cousin in perfect familiarity—exactly the way a suburban child moves from bedroom to bedroom *inside* his larger house, his smaller space. But you are murdering this neighborhood by cells; you're forcing the people apart—you and your renewal. Demolishing poor houses, are you? Hardly. But exiling poor souls."

Orpheus wrote from a personal knowledge. The evictions touched his parishioners. Lola Jones had no choice but to leave the little house she'd lived in since before Corie was born, and she moved in with her sister—but that was as much as her sister's apartment could handle.

When Corie himself was released from prison on shock-probation, there might have been no home for the young man. For a thousand reasons, though, there had to be a home. Don't talk about shelter against the weather. Don't even talk about a bed instead of a doorway, or that he had no income for renting a place. Talk about the government! If Coral Jones was to be given probation, he had to have an address. That was regulation; that was a condition of the young man's freedom.

"You're coming home with me," Orpheus told him before the release. "My address is going to be yours. Why not, Corie? We're kin."

And Corie Jones lowered his wonderfully soft eyes and said nothing, moved by the gift, and Orpheus loved him.

"You cooked in the Navy, right?" he said.

Corie nodded.

"Then you can cook in a parsonage. Corie, believe it: you're worth something to me." *Come, Lord Jesus, be my guest.* No. Orpheus did not see it as a gift at all, but as natural in the sequence of events. Children should live a while beside their parents; wasn't Orpheus Corie's parent? And Jesus should be near to his disciples; didn't Jesus dwell between the two of them?

Pastor Orpheus put his hand one more time on Corie's neck, once more to stroke his child. "Come home," he said.

So Corie moved into the parsonage and tried hard to wash and be clean, to cook, and to show his gratitude. And he went to church on Sundays. And he strolled the streets on Saturday nights—the signs of a truer renewal than the city's. Coral Jones could smile sometimes, now, on account of: Coral Jones was Somebody.

In this manner did Pastor Orpheus's reputation grow, both throughout the city and in his own community. The congregation didn't mind. In fact, the attention pleased them, and any risk of reprisal for the pastor's loud advocacy was forgotten when Mr. Arthur Williams noted that Sunday's attendance was swelling. He was genuinely glad that the lost—like Corie Jones—were coming back again, that the curious, black and white together, sat shoulder to shoulder in his own small sanctuary: that a new thing was happening.

Mr. Arthur Williams smiled, murmuring, "Yep, we'll have to build a new church before long. Yep."

It was a long period, still, before Orpheus became aware of the congregational favor. He was serving Jesus; that was the truth.

But there came a day of recognition, and then he was uneasy.

Sidewalk crapshooters had begun to nod "Rev" when he walked by, not hiding their game. Straight-up roosters in electric suits grinned at him and meant it. He was never again propositioned by a prostitute—

And then, as he was descending Mrs. Story's front porch steps one day, a huge man shouted at him, "Hey! Hey, man, wait!" This giant peeled himself from the wall of Doc's Liquor Store, ambled over to Pastor Orpheus, and thrust out his hand. "You somethin' else," he said, "and I wanna shake your hand for it. No crap, you unnerstan'? No crap—scuse me; it's the way I talk."

Orpheus put forth his hand and had it crushed.

Blinking, confused, he said, "Thank you."

The big man barked a laugh. "Hey, don'chu member me? Hey, man, don'chu member I showed you my menace? And I figgered to shoot you for a robber? Ha-ha!"

Orpheus smiled. "And it was Arabelle that saved my life."

"Arabelle Lee!" the giant shouted. "Right! You remember me!" He released Orpheus's hand, grinning. "See? I ain't bullheaded. I can change my mind when I meet a good thing."

Orpheus said, "What did I do?"

Immediately the big man hit him on the shoulder, delighted by the question, and turned to roar toward the men at Doc's: "Hey! Listen to this," he cried. "He don't know what he done! Hey! The Rev ain't a hincty one at all! No, he don't preen or put hisself forward!"

This was disconcerting. It felt to Orpheus like a set-up, like the beginning of ridicule, so overstated was the big man's praise, so loud his bellowing. Orpheus grew uncomfortable. There was booze in the man's voice and a strange brightness in his eyes. But the joke never came.

"I'll tell you what," the giant thundered, "this here's a humble preacher!"

Doc's patrons mumbled agreement.

Orpheus said, "What did I do?"

The giant hit him a second time. He shook his head at such humility. "Corie tol' me what you done for him, man, an' Corie's clean, now. *Clean!*" He shook Orpheus like a doll. "Man, you somethin' else," he said. "Mm-hmm. Yes. I think I'm comin' to your church. Ye-es!"

It was a whole new embarrassment that flushed through Orpheus. It was a fumbling distress for the error that suddenly he saw the people to be making.

This sort of praise was wrong. Jesus wasn't in the thing.

Wrong? No, dangerous. It scared him. It scared him because as easily as it came so easily could it change again. This was unstable praise. Worse, it implied the sin of pride in Orpheus and threatened Jesus' absence after all—absence from him, from Orpheus. Then what good was all that he was doing?

"Corie," he said in their kitchen, "who do you think I am? What do you think I've done?"

Corie turned from the stove and considered the question. It had been too earnestly stated to be a joke, and the pastor's eyes were strained.

"You Pastor Orpheus," he said, his voice as velvet as his eyes were soft.

"What are you telling people I've done?"

"Why," said Corie slowly, ducking his head, "the truth, thass all." He looked guilty.

"Corie, what is the truth. Tell me what you tell them."

"Aw, well," said Corie. He turned back to the stove. "That you give me a roof. That you saved, um, my life—"

*"Corie!"* The name came almost violently. Poor Corie froze. "That's *not* the truth. I did not save your life. Corie, only Jesus does that. You've got to understand that what I do I do for Jesus. Do you understand that?"

Coral Jones looked stricken at the stove. "I do, I do," he whispered, full of guilt. "You allus did your work for Jesus—"

"But you! It was Jesus who loved you, Jesus who gave you a home, Jesus who washed you up and made you someone again. Corie? Do you believe that?"

The young man didn't answer. His head was bowed as though about to cry. For Orpheus it was important that Corie believe in Jesus, his own faithfulness was somehow bound up in that man's perception.

But he hurt for Corie, too. He didn't mean to thrash him.

Very gently, then, he changed his tone and the question together. He said, "Corie, look at me." Slowly the head came up and the doe's eyes lay on Orpheus. "Do you love Jesus?" asked Pastor Orpheus.

Then Corie's eyes filled truly with tears. He whispered so softly that he could hardly be heard, "I love *you.*" And he began to cry.

Poor Orpheus! He could not doubt the sincerity of that love; it was whole and human and abundant—but it burned him like an accusation. Jesus wasn't in it. Part of him was glad, so to be loved. But the rest of him felt this gladness like a deadly sin. How much of Corie's misbegotten adoration was his, Orpheus's, own fault? Oh, this was confusing. Was he serving Jesus rightly or wrongly after all?

But there stood Corie in the kitchen, weeping, frightfully vulnerable after such a declaration. There was no help for it; Orpheus could not leave the man in the nakedness of his confession. He went to Corie and put his arms around him and hugged him, whispering, "Love Jesus, love Jesus, love Jesus, O my Corie Jones, not me."

Pastor Orpheus began, in those days, to preach vigorously the presence and the Lordship of Jesus Christ. With extraordinary persuasion (he had the gift!) he pleaded with the people to do all that they did for the sake and in the name of Christ. Over and over again he vowed that his own ministry, though to them, was for Jesus and none other— for the dear Lord Jesus, whom he loved even more than his own life.

And the people believed him. They believed that he believed what he was preaching. They marveled, saying, "How good and humble he is!" And in consequence, they loved him. There is such personal satisfaction in loving a good man.

But Orpheus, in his daily praying, began to pray a new prayer: "Jesus? Are you there?"

He couldn't make sense of this irony: preaching Jesus seemed to be hiding Jesus behind his own face; denying himself seemed to be thrusting himself deeper into the eyes of the people, which shone to look on him.

He prayed, "Can the right be wrong?" He prayed, "And

if it is, won't you make the wrong right again? Can you do that, Jesus? Won't you show me your love, dear Jesus, by doing that?"

*Are you near me, Jesus?*

In time there appeared a certain haunted expression in the pastor's eyes, and behold: the people loved him the more for this mystery. He was so far, so far beyond them in his holiness. . . .

By the autumn of that year, Mrs. Story had deteriorated to the point that she could not climb her stairs; this was a particular trial for her since the bedroom she had shared with Nat was on the second floor. Their bedroom had been shut to her. She had a cot set up for sleeping in the ground floor parlor, and in a low mood she stared through the window at the rental house next door.

Then she could not so much as rise from a sitting position without some aid, and she smoldered at the dependency. Her face grew harder and harder, yet she did not complain. She faced the affliction with her mouth shut, as though it were a storm wind.

She was a light-complexioned woman. Her makeup, when Orpheus visited her, looked a little ghastly, and her lips seemed twisted. She could not control the left hand that applied the lipstick, and she beat the right hand always. She didn't sit to receive him. She leaned back against the organ bench and pretended comfort; she could get to her feet unaided this way and see him to the door.

He laid out the communion elements between them.

"I think," he said softly, "it would be appropriate for you to confess your sins first, Allouise." He meant it mostly as a ritual.

She thought he meant the sins of her life.

She said, "Well," with an air of remembering. "There were transgressions," she said. "Yes, there were some." And she fell silent, staring downward.

Into this silence, finally, the pastor spoke her absolution with true conviction. "I, by virtue of my office as a called and ordained servant of the Word," he said, "forgive you all your sins in the name of the Father and of the Son and of the Holy Spirit."

But Mrs. Story, that old black woman, did not say, "Amen." She said only, "Well—"

Orpheus was bemused by the scruple of her response. He smiled. "You heard what I said?" he asked.

"Yes," she said. No doubt in that.

"And you understand it, Allouise?"

"Yes."

He laid his smile by and seriously asked, "And do you believe it?"

Abruptly the woman folded her arms across her breast and answered vaguely, "Well—"

"Allouise!" Orpheus frowned. "You are not an evasive woman. You never have been. Do you believe that your sins are forgiven?"

The old woman looked down and said, "There's a reason why I'm poorly. Everything has a reason—I believe *that*. What goes around comes around."

Orpheus was growing nervous for the thing he was unearthing. It was monstrous. It was surely not the message he had been preaching in his years with this congregation. "What do you mean by that?" he asked.

Mrs. Story turned a teacher's glare on Pastor Orpheus and reduced him to the size of a boy. " 'He doesn't hold them guiltless that sin,'" she quoted: he knew that she was quoting. "'He will by no means clear the guilty.' He visits their inquity upon them!"

"Then you think that your illness—?" The words flew from his mouth, and understanding took his breath away. What a stern God confronted the woman whom he loved! "Oh, Allouise, no!" he cried, leaning forward. "But God is a merciful God. Why do you think he sent Jesus into the world? It was because he loved the world and didn't want to lay its sin to its own account, but laid those sins on Jesus—*his* account. Allouise, it is not God's way to burden you, but to take your burden away. Do you believe that?"

She sighed and looked away. She said, "Well."

"Jesus is here, Allouise Story. Jesus sits in your parlor with you, all night long. Jesus loves you more than I do—"

For the fraction of a second she softened and seemed to be young. She sent the earnest Pastor a warm glance and said, "I know that *you* do."

But Orpheus received that coquetry like a blow, and he groaned. *Jesus* was mercy, not Orpheus. Orpheus was his servant. It was Jesus whose love counted. "Allouise, don't!" he said too harshly. "Please know the love of Jesus. He is with you always—"

Her face hardened again. "Where?" she said.

"What?"

"Where is Jesus? Show me Jesus."

"Well, if it's signs you're looking for," said Orpheus—

"Signs! Yes!" she said. "I have a sign. I have a thing from God, but it is not merciful." She lifted up her right hand with her left and held it out between them. Then the hardness passed. She lowered the right hand, spread it out on her left knee and began, slowly, to beat it. She said, "Well."

With all his heart Orpheus wished that he had a sign of his own. *Jesus, where are you now?* As deeply as he loved Allouise and suffered with her, so deeply did he desire some sign of mercy for her. Oh, it was more than that: as fiercely as he loved his Lord, even so fiercely did his heart cry for a sign, mercifully, for himself.

But Allouise Story said, "Well," in a tone that dismissed debate, as though to say: We disagree; but you're a kind man by nature, generous and young; you'll grow older, and you will see. "Well."

Almost fearfully, Pastor Orpheus hazarded one more question. He could not leave this most important issue like a boy discredited. "Do you believe in heaven?" he asked.

"That there is one? Yes," she said.

"No. That you will go there," he said.

And she said, "Well."

Orpheus sat back on the sofa; the plastic squeaked beneath him. He gazed at the woman who beat her hand. She had confessed very much after all; and no, her answers were hardly vague. She was a woman of dreadful precision. She lived by an absolute rectitude, under inflexible laws—and he was filled, when he looked at her, with a tragic awe.

*Not heaven? Not salvation? This is the measure of the affliction you face?*

*Nobody knows the trouble I seen. Nobody knows but—*

The earth opened up when Mrs. Story sang that song. The earth gaped black. And the African who heard her bowed his head and said, "Oh, no. She should not sing that way."

*Nobody knows but—*

But Jesus was not in the song, was not there to know her sorrow, nor there because of her sorrow's bidding. Because sorrow wasn't in it either. Sorrow she kept to herself. No, she sang the song that way because she had been taught at the Tuskegee Institute how to sing a spiritual; that's all.

Before he left her that day, Pastor Orpheus prayed two prayers, but they were really one prayer.

"Heal this woman," he prayed, "both in her body and her soul."

And the second was the same: "O dear Lord Jesus, reveal yourself."

Arabelle Lee didn't have the VD after all. She came to the Pastor nearly seven months after their last meeting, when the problem had been raised, to say, "Naw, I ain' got the VD. Well, God's lookin' out for me, I b'lieve. God looks out for his own, is what I b'lieve." So, she hadn't lied to anyone, neither to the department of health, nor to John, nor to God; and she was glad. Life was good. Arabelle Lee was laughing again.

But what she wondered was, did he maybe know of a place where she could stay.

Was Arabelle moving?

Yes. She had to.

Pastor Orpheus grew concerned. Because John was beating her again? But he saw no marks. Arabelle, high-boned, was strikingly beautiful. Perhaps the man was forcing her to go?

Well, yes and yes to both. Or, at least—yes, in a little while. Not yet, but soon.

Did she mean that he would start to beat her soon?

Yes. In four months, maybe.

And then he was going to kick her out?

Yes. Yes! Arabelle was so relieved that the pastor understood.

But Pastor Orpheus understood nothing. How could she time the beating to come?

By when, she said, she'd begin to show.

Show what?

Show a pooch in her belly.

Ah. Ah. The pastor leaned back in his chair and said, "Ah!" He covered his face and repeated the sound. "Ah. Arabelle, Arabelle, you are pregnant."

She nodded vigorously at his insight. "An' you know me," she said. "I ain't the kind can jus' go get an abortion. It's my baby, Pastor. It's my flesh an' blood, and I'm going to have it. But," she said more slowly, "it ain't John's, y'know, 'cause he's in no mood for babies, an' he uses a rubber, see, an'—"

And four months from now—

Right! Four months. Did the pastor know of someone that would take in her and Tulip, and maybe care for Tulip while she—

This is what was happening in the ministry of Pastor Orpheus, in his congregation and in the neighborhood: nothing was happening. No one seemed to be changing for the better.

The distress grew sharper in him, and the darkness intolerable.

For all his arguing in behalf of housing for the poor, the city came like an iron maw, munching homes and seeding grass; and people were displaced. His reputation put him before the city Council, the Optimists, the chamber of commerce; his reputation, together with his rhetoric and his obvious commitment to the "Good," bought him smiles and plaques; but his reputation was utterly meaningless in the municipal assizes.

Nothing happened.

Arabelle Lee sought him out, but never thought to change her way of life, just her habitation. She perceived no evil in her habits, and Orpheus's own severe morality was "his thing" and no model for her at all.

No, nothing happened.

The silence of God was killing.

Nevertheless, so long as Orpheus continued to preach and to be where the people needed him, they felt blandly embraced by their God. This congregation grew.

Some fell sick, and the pastor prayed with them. In their extremity they swore renewed commitment unto Christ; but once their health was restored, they couldn't remember precisely what that meant—this, though they had chewed on the body and had drunk the blood as perfect and powerful signs of their new communion. The sign itself seemed not to signify. It was lost in the fogs of persistent habits. Orpheus found himself, even during the distribution of the Holy Sacrament, while laying his hand on the people's heads, pleading, *Are you in this? Are you near me, Jesus? Is this right or is it wrong? Do they receive these elements, if they do not change, to their forgiveness or to their damnation? Am I too careless with your body, and am I to blame? Or do I feed them rightly, giving them your opportunity to cleanse them after all? But I don't see the evidence! O Jesus, which is it? And where are you?*

Silence. Treasurers talked about money. The council began discussions about erecting a new building for the growing congregation. Jesus seemed a pretext. Everyone loved Orpheus for his extraordinary presence—and for the suffering in him that was mystic and incomprehensible. He was holy. He was a blessed asset. He grieved. But he loved these people. They seemed to be children, after all, sheep in need of a shepherd. But whose sheep? His or God's?

*Tell me!*
Silence.
*Jesus? Jesus??*
Silence. No sign whatsoever. The darkness only.

"I have another sign," said Mrs. Story. The expression in her face was hard to read. Orpheus thought he saw a sly triumph; but her tongue kept darting out to lick her lips, and that looked like fear. "Want to see it?" she said.

They were in her kitchen, the breakfast table between them. Mrs. Story had been reduced to a wheelchair and couldn't roll it well across the carpeting; so Orpheus came to the back door, where she could wheel on linoleum and receive him.

"It's what I'm praying for," he said.

"I don't think so," she said.

With her left hand she slid a piece of paper across the table. He picked it up and read it.

An official letter. The city, its Department of City Planning, announced that it was purchasing all properties in the block bounded by Judson, Mulberry, and Bellemeade; that it planned to demolish the buildings in order to clear land for a projected shopping center.

"This is your house," said Pastor Orpheus. "What are they doing now? Your house isn't substandard. Oh, Allouise."

"My house," she said, "and my rental." Mrs. Story owned the house next door as well, a small income. She pushed a second letter toward him, a duplicate of the first: they dealt with her as though she were two separate people, which indicated that they didn't know her after all, and to them she was no one. "They can have my rental," she said, and then she did not say: *But I want to die in my own home.*

Pastor Orpheus looked out the kitchen window and saw a bald-headed man urinating against her fence. He fell silent and thought. Then, very quietly, very carefully, fully aware that the woman was likely to turn him down because she loathed to be dependent, he said, "I have some influence. I write a column in the newspaper. You are my parishioner, and this is a callous outrage. Allouise, it would be right, it would not be wrong, if you let me fight this thing."

Now she looked the old lady that she was, somewhat hunch-backed in her wheelchair, her head bowed down, tired. But she didn't answer him yet.

Softly, he pursued her: "Do you suppose they have the financing for this shopping center?"

She smiled bleakly. "Do they ever?" she said.

"No," he said. "They never do." It was the DCP's practice to ballyhoo a plan at its beginning and so to garner an upbeat publicity, to spend for demolition, and then to let the land idle while hoping that the first publicity lured money. That kind of recklessness made their demand for Mrs. Story's clean and well-kept home all the more noxious. "Please," said Orpheus, "can I fight this thing for you?"

Allouise Story gazed at him a long time, beating her right hand. Then she said, "Whatever"—and his heart leaped up inside of him.

"You don't mind," he said, "if I threaten to expose them in my column?"

She bowed her head.

"I'd have to use your name and tell your story."

He wanted this established right at the beginning. She was a private woman; nobody saw her sorrows!

She touched the letter with her useless hand and murmured again, "Whatever."

Pastor Orpheus nearly burst in his excitement. His whole

body trembled to be up and gone. It was with an almighty restraint, then, that he reached his own hand to hers, that he held her soft right hand a while, then rose and kissed it. Oh, how he loved the old woman!

And how grateful he was, finally, for the chance to act— *to act!* To act on her behalf, because he loved her. But mostly to act on Jesus' behalf, because if Orpheus could stall the city on this one, then he would have brought proofs to his ten-commandment woman, clear evidence that Jesus was here, that Jesus loved and guarded her—signs of the mercy of God! Signs, sweet Allouise!

But he was not being foolish. He had enough experience with the city to know that his success was not assured. Yet, this time it was possible. And look: if success were achieved in spite of the odds, why, the odds themselves would increase the glory of the thing, making it a marvel after all, a miracle. See it and believe, sweet Allouise!

It was all good. It could not be bad. She had a right to her own home, to die in it.

*Oh, for the lady's sake,* Orpheus prayed, Orpheus pleaded with the God he could not see, *let me prevail. She needs to know your love.* This was the blameless side of his prayer, the selfless side, born of his care for Mrs. Story.

But the same prayer had a perilous side, blameworthy after all, because it came of faithlessness. Orpheus could not abide in the silence, believing. This side of his prayer referred to the whole of his ministry and begged one thing for himself alone: a sign.

Deep, deep beneath the righteous rationale, *For the lady's sake,* was a worried Orpheus, wailing, *For my sake, Lord!*

*I need to see you, dear Lord Jesus! Are you near me?*

• • •

This is what Mrs. Story did: wheelchair-bound, she went a-traveling.

The woman was made in the image of her God, as stern and determined as he. Her character was carved out of stone tablets. She did not intend to suffer her affliction passively. And since the doctors of her city had by now displeased her (they patronized her; they gently poo-pooed the woman's analysis of her own sickness), she packed up and traveled to Mayo Clinic in Minnesota.

That old black lady went in her wheelchair. She set her jaw and crossed a nation. On the way up she fought the airport crowds without a weapon. For ten days she matched both will and wit with the white doctors, judging, in the end, the entire clinic and all its operations "White!"

In the airport, for her flight back home, Mrs. Allouise Story bought an umbrella.

And then she was found to be sitting in her parlor again, gazing through the window at the rental house next door, frowning.

"They do not know," she said about her renters, "how to clean up after themselves. I'm going to paint that house. I'll give them a sign that I'm watching, and then they won't forget me."

And she did. She had the whole house painted black.

This is what Pastor Orpheus did: he invited the Superintendant of the Department of City Planning to a private conference in his office. And because this pastor had earned admiration for his austere labors in the inner city, and because this Superintendant had publicly declared himself to be "a people-person," he came.

They sat facing each other in the tiny study, Pastor Orpheus masking a tremendous mixture of anxiety and excitement. He commanded his face to seem commonplace, and his manner to be casual.

The Superintendant sighed. It was, he said, the end of a very hard day. Orpheus asked after his health.

"Tired, tired," admitted the Superintendant, and then he went on chatting a while, complaining about the pressures of his office.

Pastor Orpheus nodded, sympathetic. This is how people talk to pastors, and how pastors are supposed to respond.

The Superintendant chatted about his sailing boat and his vacation and his mortal need of both.

The pastor nodded.

"But," said the Superintendant in a joke, "you didn't ask me here to get another counselee, ha-ha. What's on your mind?"

Orpheus said, "Allouise Story. She's on my mind."

The Superintendant smiled. "Who is this?"

"She's a parishioner of mine," said Orpheus, his heart racing, now that they had come to the moment when he meant to issue a perfectly secular threat, but his face mild. "She lives in the clean, well-kept house on Judson and Mulberry, directly across from Doc's Liquor Store."

The Superintendant's face, too, resolved into blandness: knowledge was gathering behind it. He said, "You've heard, of course, that we've evicted Doc. We're cleaning up the neighborhood."

Orpheus said, "This is what I've heard, that your office has given Mrs. Story notice as well. Are these actions to be taken as the same action? You want to buy her house."

"Well, yes. Yes." The Superintendant's eyes went hooded and still. "It will benefit the whole neighborhood. There is a coalition of businessmen prepared to build a shopping center in the block bounded by Judson and Mulberry—"

Pastor Orpheus said, "Do they right now have the financing to build?"

"What?"

"Are they solvent? Is the money *now* in place, so that as soon as this woman's house is demolished they will construct their shopping center?"

"Of course not," said the Superintendant in the chill terms of realistic business practices. "They mean to sell—"

"In other words, Orpheus repeated his question, "is there sense to your sequence?"

The Superintendant ignored this and repeated himself: "They mean to sell shares, Reverend Orpheus, to gain the financing. First they have to create faith in the project and enthusiasm for it—"

"But before that," said Pastor Orpheus, "they do *not* need to buy and bulldoze Mrs. Story's house! Do they?"

"Well, there are procedures."

"Let me tell you about Mrs. Story. Mrs. Story is not Doc," said Orpheus. "Neither is she someone's image of the welfare poor. She is old, sir, and sick, and there isn't a stain on her. And her life would move the people to sympathy, if they heard of it. She has managed to keep order and cleanliness in the middle of the inner city—which you announce you are cleaning up. In other words, she's managed a miracle; and her perseverence would move the people to sympathy, if they heard of it. She nursed her mother in that house for years. She lived for years there with her husband until he died. And now she does not want to leave the place. I'm not exaggerating or sentimentalizing her life. This is all true. Plainly, she is a good woman, and her goodness, if the people heard of it, would move them to sympathy."

"Why do you tell me this?" said the Superintendant.

"Because I can't think of anyone less deserving of the

injuries which your practices and policies commit. Because she could become a perfectly unimpeachable symbol for the many whom you wound. Because the sympathy of the people could be turned against your department like a weapon—and you will hurt yourself this time if you proceed with taking her house from her."

The Superintendant sat quietly. He didn't protest the pastor's language. Merely, he watched Orpheus through lidded eyes.

"I write a column," said Orpheus as calmly as he could. Here was his munition.

The Superintendant said, "A widely read column."

Orpheus nodded and said, "I'm not asking anything unreasonable. I do not intend a campaign against the department. I ask only one single thing: that you do not force her to sell until this coalition of businessmen has its financing in place. In fact, I am asking you to *be* reasonable. Let her stay until there is good, substantial reason for her to move. Don't make it a meaningless move. Do you understand this? Because if you move her too soon, sir, I will write her story in my column; I will gather sympathy on her behalf; and by that sympathy, I will charge the DCP with cruelty." Orpheus swallowed.

The Superintendant nodded.

But that was not enough. Orpheus said, "Do you promise this?"

The Superintendant said, "I'll see what I can do."

More harshly than he wished—but the tension was hissing at his teeth—Orpheus repeated, "Do you promise that?"

After a single silent moment, the Superintendant suddenly allowed a smile to bloom on this face, and with hearty assurance he said, "Of course. Of course. Why not? Our policies can make space for the Mrs. Story's of the city—"

He was already rising from his seat, taking the lead. Orpheus popped up himself, not desiring to be led, seeing that he'd set himself to be the aggressor in this contest. The conversation ended. Orpheus was glad. He'd begun to tremble, finally, and he didn't want the Superintendant to see him trembling.

When he was alone, he stood at the window, whispering aloud, "Jesus, Jesus, Jesus, please—"

*Be here!*

"Oh, Pastor! What's the matter?"

In fact, he was not standing at the window, but leaning heavily on its sill and trembling as though he had a fever. He turned around and saw Dolores Johnson in the doorway. He wasn't surprised; she regularly came to the church to drive her mother home. Stella Johnson was her mother, the cleanliness of the congregation.

When Dolores could see his face, her hand went to her mouth in a little gasp. "Are you sick?" she said. She stepped toward him. "You're so white."

He smiled. "And you're so black," he said. It was a joke, a way to turn attention from himself, caught suddenly in a private moment. But it was also true: he had always taken pleasure in the simple looking at her skin, rich, deep, and reddish black, shining at the cheekbones.

She flushed a ruddier color and focused the more intensely on him.

"Are you feeling poorly?" she asked.

"I'm just tired, Dolores," he said. He was. Her appearing and her kindness made weariness to soften all his bones. "Just tired." He smiled again. "Did you see a man in a three-piece suit leaving when you came? He's the City. The City makes me tired."

All at once Dolores took two steps forward, closed the distance between them in the tiny study, put her cheek to his chest, and wrapped her arms around him. "I want to cry for you," she said.

She was so small, this near. Her frame was so delicate. Her hair, pure black, smelled of coconut. He raised his two hands spontaneously and touched her back, feeling ribs. Almost he patted it, a gesture of affection.

Instead, he dropped one hand and with the other patted her shoulder.

"No, I'm fine," he said. "I'm fine. Did you want to sit and talk? Dolores, I'll get you some coffee." He moved, and she let go, but he didn't get coffee, and she didn't sit.

They stood, not looking at each other; only now did the discomfort twist inside of him. Confusion made him blush. He said, "I have to go now," but immediately felt the silliness and the transparency of the words. "Dolores," he said, "don't cry for me. Cry for the people, if you want. They have the need of it; and they have my love. Cry for Jesus. I mean, cry *for* him, pleading that he come—"

"He's here," she whispered.

"What do you mean by that?" Orpheus asked, truly looking at her. He wanted to know.

The woman of sympathies said, "Ever since you came, he has been here. When you cried Good Friday—remember?—I felt that he was here. On Easter you said, 'Why do you seek the living among the dead'—see how I remember?—and I knew that he was here to stay. Oh, Pastor!"

Orpheus was caught between two things. Either she spoke the word that he absolutely needed to hear, or else she was mistaking Jesus. He didn't know how to ask that question.

"Pastor," she said, "you're wearing yourself out on account of us. So says my mother, so say I. I've never seen anyone give so much, be so kind, love so much. I—" she said, and stopped. "I—" she faltered again. And then she said, "That's Jesus, isn't it? In you?"

Orpheus said, "I know that Corie Jones has supper ready and your mother is waiting."

It was dark outside. They were deep in autumn, close to winter, and the world was cold as well as dark.

But here was a wonder. Here was a joy uncomplicated and good:

The old eyes of Mrs. Allouise Story were dancing when Orpheus came to visit her. She was sitting in the parlor beside her cot, not in the wheelchair but on a wooden stool. Her makeup still was misshapen, but the woman was smiling.

"Look," she said, but then immediately changed her mind. "No, let me tell you first." She bent her head and engaged in a dark chuckle of gladness.

Pastor Orpheus smiled, not knowing why.

Mrs. Story said, "It was anger, don't you know—pure, cussed anger that did it for me. I never thought it would be anger."

She pointed through the window to the black rental house next door. "I was sitting here, looking," she said, "when that woman stepped out on the back porch, and the first thing I thought was, 'She's three weeks overdue with her rent,' and I began to calculate what she owed me. But then the second thing was this: she was carrying a plate of gnawed bones and garbage. Right before my eyes she slung those bones back-hand into the yard, all over new white snow. She turned to go in again, and I was so angry at the mess, so angry at that woman—that I stood up! Ha-ha-ha! Pastor, these old legs forgot to be crippled. I stood up. I took two steps to the window and then noticed that I was walking. What do you think of that?"

The black lady leaned backward and laughed.

Orpheus joined her, laughing.

Mrs. Story said, "Look, look." And she did it. She stood. She trembled on her legs; she was holding her arms out for the balance; but she was standing.

And from the height of that stance she seemed to be shouting at Orpheus: "Do you know why I bought an umbrella in the Minnesota airport? Why," she cried, "to poke people out of my way. Ha-ha-ha! I'm a mean, mad old woman. I jabbed calves and kneecaps and made a path for myself. No, I never thought it would be my madness that made me walk again. Ha-ha-ha!"

Orpheus called in his mind, *Jesus, is that you?*

She had begun. She was not done. From that day forward Mrs. Story determined to climb her stairs to the top and to make her house her own again.

And she did not mind if Orpheus stood by, praying.

Day after day she approached the low steps of the staircase and gripped her leg at the joint. She bent it, lifted it, and placed a foot one step up. Then she dragged hard on the bannister, hoisting herself body and soul upward. It was an exhausting trial: she leaned, breathing, on the bannister before she attempted the next.

It was exhausting, and it put her into awkward, unflattering positions; therefore, Orpheus took it as a pure kindness that she allowed him to witness her weakness. But she wanted his prayers, now, and he prayed them.

With the stony, horned forehead of a Moses, in Deuteronomic language, he prayed, "Jesus, strengthen this woman!" He prayed with the excitement of an outrageous hope. Oh, they labored together, that old black lady and her pastor, one grunting and the other shouting prayers. They made noises in the silences. They streaked the darkness with their laughter.

"Allouise," said Orpheus, "he's a merciful God after all, isn't he?"

And Mrs. Story, struggling one step upward, muttered, "Well," said, "let's say that he's keeping the bannister from breaking, but it's me that's doing the pulling."

"But you will get to the top," said Orpheus. "That counts for something."

"I will. *I* will," she grunted. "And I will sleep there, where Nat used to sleep. It's my house again." She meant she had the run of it; but Orpheus saw another meaning, and another sign.

He said, "Yes, Allouise, and thank God for that. You may be climbing, but God is keeping your house for you. I talked to the Superintendant. I don't think the DCP will risk demanding the place."

She said, "Well."

He said, "He *is* a merciful God."

She said, again, "Well," and attended to the task at hand.

In the middle of December, Allouise Story finally stood on the landing at the top of her stairs. Like a celebrant, she raised her hands still higher than her head, and then she slapped them together in triumph. "Thank the Lord," the old black woman whispered. "Oh, praise the Lord in his tabernacle. Praise him!"

Behind her, below her, small in an honest humility, Orpheus looked up and grinned. *This is you, Lord. This is you then, Jesus, isn't it?*

·   ·   ·

Twice that month Mrs. Story succeeded in coming to worship at the church. Twice.

Once she merely sat among the people.

But the second time was Christmas Eve, and Pastor Orpheus persuaded her to sing. He shaped the service to her song. Night shaped itself to her singing. The stained-glass windows were black, but candles burned in each, and the church lights were low, so it was a firelight that trembled throughout the room.

She sang sitting in the front pew, facing from the people. Orpheus watched her shadow.

She sang, *Mary had a baby, my Lord,* and it seemed as though a black wind blew. *Mary had a baby, my Lord!* Louder and louder the song insisted this birth, like a lamentation which would not be comforted. It grieved upward to the ceiling beams: *Mary had a baby, Mary had a baby, Mary had a ba-aby—yes! My Lord.* Down and down the black wind came, till it sank to the floor in sorrow—because it seemed a tragical thing for Mary to have her baby, a costly, disastrous thing; yet for that baby, Oh! have a care!

Orpheus closed his eyes into a more personal darkness, and his heart said, though he knew better, *No! She should not sing that way!*

He thought, *Allouise, does it mean nothing to you that he's given you your legs again, and your house? He is a merciful God.*

Twice she came to church. Twice. And then no more.

Four days later, before the New Year, Orpheus came back to the parsonage unexpectedly, midmorning. He was so tired that he sat a moment on a folding chair in the dining room without removing his coat. The walls seemed to hang wry around him, and he thought this strange. He considered a moment, foolishly, how that walls are not to be trusted.

It was snowing outside. He pulled his coat tighter around him.

And then he heard a sort of sobbing in the extra bedroom. The sound was barely audible, but it repeated itself several times over until he was sure that he heard it—and his heart was moved. His Corie Jones, he thought, was crying.

Orpheus got up and went into the kitchen. He drew a glass of water and carried it to Corie's room.

He knocked once, opened the door, and entered.

But one step was as far as he got. He froze with the glass in his hand.

They were not even under the blankets. Corie still wore his undershirt and stockings. The woman—the woman was Arabelle Lee—had a half-slip rolled up to her waist, and her bra hung from her shoulder by one strap. They lay on their sides, their legs entangled—and for a flash stared back at Orpheus, confused.

In the instant that Corie leaped up, Orpheus withdrew and closed the door.

"Pastor!" Corie called.

Orpheus returned to the folding chair and sat down, the glass of water still in his hand.

"Pastor?" Corie thrashed about in the bedroom, making a fearful noise.

Orpheus covered his face with one hand. This was the child? This was the son whom he called back to life? This was the man in whom he had seen Jesus? Jesus was in this man? Had he? Had he? Had Jesus been in him after all? And if he truly had seized Corie Jones, then why had he dropped

the child again? What, O my God, endured? Where was the
divinity that lasted? What holiness was not a fraud?

*Jesus Christ, where have you gone?* Orpheus felt physically sick for all the casual immorality that persisted around
him unchanged, that now had trespassed into his own home,
into one whose righteousness he needed—

"Pastor?" Corie stood before him. Orpheus did not un-
cover his face. He felt the young man shift from foot to foot.
Corie had shoes on now. "Well, I didn't mean for you to
come—" The sentence died, killed by its own self-conscious
idiocy.

A silence enveloped the two of them.

Orpheus heard a floorboard creak, and smelled Arabelle.
There was a mute exchange. The front door opened and
closed. Orpheus thought: *It's snowing outside.*

Corie said, "Arabelle, she said John beats her, and gon'
beat her near to death, soon. Said she lookin' for a man, a
protector. Said she needed me—" Suddenly his voice skid-
ded upward to the high whine of misery: "Ain' you gon' talk
to me again? Pastor?"

Orpheus hadn't moved. He didn't move, and he didn't
answer.

Gently the glass of water was removed from his hand.

"This for me?" Corie asked pitifully. "You got thish'ere
water for me? Well, thank ya."

Orpheus heard swallowing. He said, "Get out."

"Pastor," whispered Corie. "What did you say?"

Orpheus breathed it very quietly: "Get out."

"You want to be alone some? I unnerstan'; I'll jus'—"

"Get out. Find a new address. That will be your address.
We'll tell the parole officer together. Get out." Orpheus was
shivering in a strange way, as though he ran a fever, as
though the snow were inside the room.

"Mean, leave," whispered Corie. "You mean, like, leave."

"Arabelle is pregnant. She's using you, that's all. She wants a man to pay for her baby—"

"Pastor," said Corie gently, "I know that."

*"Ahh!"* It was a groan, torn from his chest. "Corie. Corie. I'd rather you were ignorant." Orpheus drew a deep breath, shivering. Was his own virtue no example for the son whom he'd received into his home. Had he no effect? Orpheus lived according to a fierce, ascetic restraint, putting to death the flesh inside himself. Was that nothing to Corie Jones? Jesus Christ, nothing. "Get out," he sighed. "Just get—out."

Corie didn't say another thing. The floorboards complained of his passage, though he seemed to be walking as softly as he could. He went back and forth several times between the kitchen and his bedroom, sniffing. There was a rustle of grocery sacks. There were moments when Corie stood near enough that Orpheus could feel the heat of his body. But he never uncovered his eyes to look.

In the end, the front door opened and shut, and Corie was gone.

Orpheus said aloud, "It's snowing outside," and continued to sit in the same position, shivering, shivering, wanting to cry.

Dolores Johnson saw Pastor Orpheus step out onto the porch of the parsonage. She waved her hand and began to walk toward him, but he didn't see her. He was swaying, and his eyes seemed closed, which was strange.

"Pastor!" she called. Puffs of white breath floated from his mouth, as though he were talking. "Pastor Orpheus!"

Now he turned his face in her direction. No—his eyes were not closed; yet they had a wallowing sightlessness about them.

"Corie?" he said.

She smiled. "It's me, Dolores."

Pastor Orpheus took a step down to the sidewalk, then suddenly slumped to his knees in the snow. His head dropped to his chest.

Dolores ran to him, kneeled beside him, and gathered his shoulders against herself. "Are you all right? Oh, Pastor, you are so pale."

"It's snowing," he said.

"Yes, yes—"

"Corie, it's snowing. I can't send you into the snow. Come home—" Then he swooned altogether, and she let him slide down into the snow. He was much too heavy for her. He stood six foot one in good health and better days.

"Neurasthenia"—nervous collapse.

Orpheus had, so he was told, a nervous breakdown. The doctor spoke in broad terms of overwork and kept him in the hospital four days, then prescribed bed rest for another week and two more weeks thereafter of a relaxed life. No work. Preaching? No, no preaching, either. Stay out of the church. Watch TV, read novels, walk. Too bad his mother was dead; he could have gone to visit her. But ministry was too disturbing for the time being. Let it be. His people could do without him for a while.

Well, and they did.

Mr. Arthur Williams visited him in the parsonage because he was the head elder and represented all the people. But his eyes looked suspiciously at Orpheus in slippers.

Dolores came because she had been the one to call the ambulance and felt a personal responsibility. She brought the bulletins to him on Sunday afternoons. She brought flowers and sat an hour or so.

It was in one of Dolores's bulletins that Orpheus read, on Monday morning, of Mrs. Story's admission to the hospital. No one had told him. Everyone was protecting him from churchly troubles, and he grew angry at the news— angry and bitter, both: the irony was that she had been in the hospital at the same time he was, one floor above him. Mrs. Story had been so triumphant at Christmas. What was the matter with people? Why hadn't they told him of her relapse? Who gave them the right to make decisions about things so critical to his life?

Rest, Dr. Kraddock? Damn your "rest" when Mrs. Story pines. He loved her. He was responsible for her. And now especially, when everything else was failing around him— everything!—it was in her life alone that he was finding the precious presence of God.

No, Dr. Kraddock: he could not be healthy apart fom his hard old woman. He needed her more than he needed rest.

On that same Monday Orpheus found Allouise Story sitting on the edge of her bed, surrounded by a blizzard of papers and leaning toward a hospital tray. She was trying to eat soup. The sight wounded him. She held the spoon in her fist, like a child, tipping it always too soon, so that the liquid ran down her chin and soaked the towel at her breast. Old black lady, spilling soup.

She saw him.

He slumped heavily into a chair facing her, dizzy from the effort of coming. They looked at one another for a while, neither smiling, each of them infirm.

She spoke first. "What goes around comes around," she said. Her eyes and her mouth were as sharp as a ferret's. It was the rest of her that had gone dull again. Her legs and arms had swelled since last he saw her. Her face hung slack to one side. Without makeup, her skin was mealy. She said, "The only way to beat old age—die young." But she was not smiling.

Orpheus kept gazing into her eyes. "It's snowing again," he said.

She said, "I tell them how to lay me down. I tell them how to turn me, how to sit me up. They think I'm a meddlin' old woman; but they do not know the pain of their twisting me. And," she lifted her chin a slight degree, "I choose not to let my knees show. I choose!" She, too, kept her eyes on Orpheus, and their little talk passed into silence.

Finally, it was Mrs. Story who lowered her voice to kindness and spoke the more personal word. "Well, Pastor," she said, "how are you?"

He smiled thinly. "Passable," he said: her own expression.

"The pastor needed a nap," she said.

He bowed his head.

"I prayed for you," she said, and Orpheus was moved. It hadn't occurred to him that someone else would do the praying.

"You knew I was in the hospital?"

"I knew," she said.

He was a little uncomfortable, suddenly, with the open attention. He deflected it. "So I rested," he said lightly. "So why can't Allouise do the same? Why aren't you resting?"

"Rest!" she snorted. "What else does an old woman do but rest?"

"Yes, *what* else?" He indicated the papers strewn over her bed. "What's this official-looking stuff doing in a hospital room? What are you busy about, Allouise?"

She closed her mouth and pierced him with a narrow eye, as though considering how to answer. Then she murmured, "Oh, well. Buying a house."

Orpheus came half-way from his chair, tingling.

"What?" he hissed.

"Buying a house," she said. "I have two weeks to buy a house, and two to move."

*Jesus!* The lights were going out, not slowly—suddenly. Darkness cloaked his soul and the face of Mrs. Story; darkness filled this room; darkness covered the whole Godforsaken planet. *Jesus! Where are you?*

"Allouise," he whispered as though strangling, "why?"

"Why, you say. Oh," she muttered wearily, defeated, "why, he says. Because they told me the time was up and my choices were down to one, is why. Who am I to fight them any more?"

Orpheus made a vulgar gesture of disgust. He meant it for the City, but he said to Mrs. Story, "So you gave in to them."

Suddenly her eyes were blazing. "Don't you question an old woman," she snapped. "No, *don't* you! If I can't walk, I can't fight. If I can't eat, I can't argue. If I can't climb my own stairs no more, nor turn my body—" She subsided before the futility and took a cold control of herself. She said, "I'm buying a house."

But Orpheus was past control. He burned with spite for the Superintendant of the DCP. This was evil! This was malicious betrayal and clear provocation. Orpheus had one weapon in place and was not about to admit hopelessness, however defeated Allouise felt.

He gazed at her. "Let me write about it," he said.

But Mrs. Story looked down and began to shuffle through the papers on her bed. She said, "I haven't seen the new house. Found it in a catalogue. I'll show you the picture—"

He said intently, "Let me expose this treachery in my column. Everyone—"

She said, "Can't find that catalogue. This is a laugh: all the bankers will have to come to this old woman's bedside to sign for two houses—"

Orpheus fairly croaked, "Everyone will know what they've done to you, Allouise. Public opinion, Allouise. It can be a mighty thing to force the DCP—"

She said, "A girl writes my letters for me." Still shuffling helplessly among the papers, she said, "I can only make my mark, now. I'll make my mark on the contracts—"

"Allouise!" he cried. "Do you hear me? We've got one weapon—"

*BANG!*

The woman hit her tray so hard that the soup bowl spun away. She glared at Orpheus, the bridge of her nose gone white.

In a voice so low it shamed him, she said, "I heard you. I'll hear no more. Do you think I want my private troubles thrown at every front door in the city? No more, no more, I'm dying, no more. And do you truly think you would do one bit of good?" Her nostrils flared. "Write merciful Jesus in your column. Don't write me."

So Orpheus was taught by a voice that could teach. The last light went out. He sank backward on his chair and raised his hands before his face, as though inspecting the palms of them. It struck him as a piteous thing, how empty his two hands were. There was a cry deep in the hollow of his soul. There was a shout down there. He felt it swelling. Therefore he kept his mouth shut and stared at his two hands, because if he said anything at all, it was likely to be that shout.

He was not a pastor.

He was not a servant of the dear Lord Jesus.

He was not Orpheus.

He was nothing.

Then Mrs. Story nearly killed him another way. That old black lady leaned forward. She pushed his two hands down and slowly placed her swollen hands on either side of his face, and looked at him without winking. "But I love you, Pastor," she said.

Immediately he took her hands and clung to them.

And immediately again he put them aside and rushed from the hospital room. Her word had meant no more than "Farewell." And his own terrible shout had exploded inside. It threatened to erupt—

This was the shout, in anguish and in bitterness. This was the accusation and, at once, the pleading question that dearly wants an answer. This is what Orpheus roared into the darkness: *My God, my God, why have you forsaken me?*

And this, pitifully, is how he made his shout:

He wrote a letter.

Did he know the futility of his outrage, the puling uselessness of his complaint? Yes. Yes. That exactly is the anguish in it, that Nothings can hurt so horribly, can roar so mightily, knowing that no one at all need pay attention.

To the Superintendant of the Department of City Planning, he wrote a letter. Perhaps he might rouse an apology or the squeak of a moment's remorse. That was in his mind, too: that any sound is sound in the silences.

He wrote, "Justify, sir, the early initiation of the purchase of Mrs. Allouise Story's property, which action has forced her into a move sadly premature."

He wrote, "Your people approached her before she had begun to look for other property, before she had any desire to look. *They* forced her to search out housing. She didn't ask. Why was she approached at this time? Is the money— as you promised me it would be—in place for financing and building the shopping center? Say so, and I will be satisfied; but I am gravely doubting it now. Doubting, sir, the humanity of your department. Doubting our own communication with one another. Doubting any promises."

Why had they approached her at this time? Orpheus suspected it was because he was himself incapacitated and disarmed.

Shouting his shout, he wrote "And it may seem sentimentality to the offices of government, but it grieves me that Mrs. Story had to direct this final (and likely unnecessary) move from a hospital bed! She has not so much as seen the house in which she must live out the last part of her life. Oh, sir, show me that it was necessary. Do you think she is satisfied with your terms? No. She is making the best of a circumstance which is out of her hands. Show me that it *had* to be done! Or, as long as it stands empty, I will burn to see an empty field where Allouise Story's house once stood."

February was miserable. The snow persisted throughout that winter; and in February two blizzards in a row shut people into their houses for six days, cut off from one another. One of those days was a Sunday. Orpheus held worship for six people. They didn't sing. They spoke the hymns.

Then, when people were moving about again, it was told him that Mrs. Story had trouble sleeping in her new house. A friend sat through the nights with her, dozing in a nearby chair. Orpheus wished it had been him, but it wasn't. There was nothing, now, that Allouise could do for herself. She was totally dependent on others—for eating, for eliminating, for bathing, for lying down in bed.

Orpheus contemplated her descent.

One night she began to thrash violently beneath her covers and to moan. "What do you want?" said her friend, but she only threw her head from left to right. "What do you want?"

All at once Mrs. Story leaned up in bed with a sudden, astonishing strength, and she cried out clearly, "The horses! The chariots! O God, O God, the horses!"

Then she tried to make a telephone call; but she could only beat the bedside table with her swollen, impotent hand—and the friend was forced to restrain her so that she wouldn't fall to the floor.

The next night she died.

On the day of her funeral, as was the custom, men from the mortuary brought her casket into the little sanctuary two hours early and set it immediately in front of the chancel. They went back and forth, placing flowers all round the coffin, stamping snow from their boots, chatting. Finally, they opened the coffin lid and left. Orpheus sat down in the first pew and gazed at Allouise. It was snowing again. Few people would venture early into this weather. He expected to be alone awhile before the funeral.

But he wasn't alone long.

The church door opened behind him, then bumped shut. Cold from the outside air, Dolores Johnson sat down beside him.

"Have you come for your mother?" Orpheus said. He did not look at her.

Neither did she look at him. "For her," she said. "For Mrs. Story. For you."

"Ah."

They gazed at the old black woman. It was so quiet in the sanctuary that they could hear the feathery brushing of snow on the stained-glass windows.

Dolores said, "Are you mourning Mrs. Story? Is that why you are crying?"

Orpheus didn't answer her right away. He put his hand to his eyes. "I didn't know I was crying," he said.

"I'm sorry she died," said Dolores. "I'm sorry she died."

"Oh, well—died," said Orpheus. He rubbed his face hard with the flats of his hands. "Can I talk to you?"

Immediately Dolores turned to him and said, "Yes."

"No, no, don't answer. Just let me talk. Just—" He drew a breath and sighed. He made fists and put them in his lap. "It should be said. I'm sorry. Someone should hear it. Here you are."

"I am," she whispered.

Orpheus said, "I am guilty of this woman."

"Pastor—"

"Hush. No. Please, Dolores, let me say it. I am the serpent that swallows the living. I—" He touched her shoulder a moment, then stood up and began to pace in front of the coffin. "The City wanted Mrs. Story's house. I wanted her soul, and I was the worse thief. I was using her to prove— to me, to *me*, don't you see—that Jesus was here."

Suddenly he leveled his gaze at Dolores and said, "This is a confession. I am confessing my sin to you."

She kept her eyes on his. "That's all right," she whispered.

"You needn't forgive me. There is no forgiveness for this."

"That's all right," Dolores repeated. She tried to smile and failed.

Orpheus continued to pace. "You can't buy a gift," he said. "You can't command it or seek it or think that praying would cause it to come. It wouldn't be a gift, then. You can only wait on it, whether it comes or not. The waiting," he said, "the waiting without yearning or complaint or blame or self-pity or suffering or pride or expectation or any feeling for yourself at all—the waiting, Dolores, *that* is faithfulness." He touched the coffin with his right hand. "I couldn't wait. I just couldn't. That is my sin."

"Well," whispered Dolores, "that doesn't seem so—"

"I demanded the gift of the presence of Jesus, that he should talk to me and love me, that he should cry out of Mrs. Story, *Here I am! Here I am, alive, approving you.*"

"Pastor—"

"Dolores—everything that I did for Mrs. Story was wrong. My reasons were wrong: I was serving me, not her, not Jesus. Listen to me. If I had done the same things exactly, but emptied of myself—just done them for their own sakes alone, not asking if they were right or wrong, not seeking some good from it—then everything I did could have been right. Listen to me: if they succeeded, I wouldn't swell. If they failed, I wouldn't suffer. I would have been free. And that old lady would have had something worthy after all, a son to love her. That would have been enough. Oh, God help me!"

Orpheus leaned on the coffin. He almost, but not quite, touched the woman's passive face, the white and waxy nails on her hands. She was not smiling. Severe old woman!

"Dear Allouise Story," he whispered, "I killed Jesus between us every day. Why did I do that? I didn't rejoice in the thing we had, as though it were enough. It was enough. You knew that. The day alone was enough. Pain was part of the day. Pain was sufficient. Jesus was—Allouise, Jesus was in the sufficiency, wasn't he? And I might have witnessed that for you. I might have *been* that. But I wasn't, with all my damnable, faithless yearning. What did I do? I killed Jesus."

Dolores began a protest. Orpheus whirled and pointed a finger toward her. "No!" he said. "I made a torment of the very gifts God gave to me. This old lady was his gift. And Corie Jones was a pure gift of God to me. But they weren't what *I* wanted; they weren't exactly what I was demanding from God—so I smashed them to make them fit. Do you know what I did to Corie Jones? Smashed him. Smashed him, just like Mrs. Story—to hell. Dolores, do you understand this?"

He was leaning forward, glaring at her. She shook her head. She said, "I understand that you are hurting. I think you want to cry—"

"No. No," he said. "No, I don't have the right to cry. No." Suddenly he raised his voice so that he could be heard in the basement of the church: "Stella? Stella Johnson! Here is your daughter, come to take you home."

Orpheus received a response to his DCP letter. It was, in fact, no response at all.

*Eli, Eli, lama sabachthani!* he had cried, and lo: it did not so much as thunder. It simply swallowed up his cry without a blink, without an echo. It was as though someone should hear one cricket in ten thousand: his cry had been a cricket's chirp.

This, on the third page of a very long letter, is what in fact the Superintendent of the Department of City Planning wrote:

"Your third question concerned Mrs. Storey [*sic*]. Her home is needed for the shopping center. Mrs. Storey was treated fairly under the Uniform Relocation Act, as are all persons affected by relocation."

Neither before that paragraph nor after it was the Superintendant's Storey or the pastor's Story mentioned again.

Nothing. A life—the life of an old black woman, hard in her rectitudes—a whole life simply disappeared in cold, official prose.

Her houses were torn down, one white and one coal black. To this day there is no shopping center there, but a snowfield in the winter and a green lawn in the summer; and Doc's old building stands across the street, hollow-eyed, staring at an emptiness. No one indicated regret. No one so much as giggled at the joke. There weren't even enemies to hate.

How complete was the failure of Pastor Orpheus.

◊    ◊    ◊

So, the fourth passage began in gladness. And then the fourth passage demanded a faith without seeing, a ministry absolutely unrewarded, a trust without immediate and evident assurance, a loving that continued peacefully through utter failure and defeat—precisely as Jesus' love not only seemed to be but was in fact his unqualified defeat in his execution. (This is the third level of meaning in his call, *Come, follow me.*)

Some of the faithing ones stay here, within this passage, and go no further. There are two kinds of those whose drama is accomplished at this pass.

1. Some truly had no pride inside. Some (but not Simon Peter) truly denied themselves even unto a spiritual death with the third passage, so that for them the fourth was the natural consequence. They gave up control because they truly did not desire any. They had died. They resigned reason, because the fact that they were both living and dead at once was already an absurdity; the whole world could continue unreasonable and not offend them. These are the sweetly faithful, who ask nothing for themselves. Abraham

on Mount Moriah; Jephtha's daughter; Jael; Rahab; Mary, the mother of Jesus at his crucifixion; and she who dried his feet with her hair, whose name is to be remembered forever because she saw the death before it was and did not dispute it but prepared him for it: Mary. (Remarkable! How many women are named within this company!)

For these, anything at all is a gift, because nothing at all is expected. They live even wretched lives in glad contentment, for that they live at all. And they will rise again to eternal life with the shock of astonishment, because they had not counted on that either. The Lord was their Lord, not their own continuance. And if the Lord chose silence, well, that was his prerogative because he *was* their Lord. No, I don't think Jephtha's daughter accepted death because she thought she'd rise again; that is too reasonable an exchange. Rather, she accepted it because she was obedient—even when the command was senseless at its core.

These I take to be the *Lamed Vavnik*, the Righteous Ones, on account of whose righteousnes the Lord does not destroy the world. They have no knowledge whatsoever of their righteousness nor of its effect. There are no signs for them to see. But we, the poorer ones, receive the benefit—and though we do not see the signs either, we live because of them.

Unto you, O Lord, be everlasting praise for this handful of the faithful, who live in the darkness without looking back, who do not utter questions in the silences. They are your glory, surely.

2. Others, unable to stand the darkness or to conceive of a God willfully silent, quickly content themselves with signs as proofs of God and revelations of his character. Signs shall light the darkness for them from this time forward. Signs shall console them—signs, the hands of God. Signs:

the Church, its doctrines, its creeds, its practices, its Scriptures and tradition.

Creeds? These people rest upon the speaking of a creed, both on the speaking and on the creed, these two. They believe *because of* a particular Credo and not solely in the object of the assertion, *credo,* "I believe," himself. They pause in the anteroom, as it were, where there is light, fearful of the darkness in the hall beyond, where the Lord is fully Other to them. The utterance becomes the proof that he, who is thereby uttered, is true. Much is invested in the precise language of that utterance, and they will fight for it—fighting, in fact, for their God. These soldiers are debaters, fighting not on his behalf so much as for his existence. It is not that, by the creed, they reach blindly for their God, nor that, in the creed, they patiently await their God's *selbsttätig* reaching unto them. Rather, it is that God himself is *in* the creed, possessed and proven thereby. The creed is the sign.

Emotions? If music moves these people, they are persuaded that the Spirit is abroad. Art and architecture, rhetorical magnificence, the vaulting tones of a massive organ, or a vaulted ceiling—these lift them up, and they are elevated. And since it is evident that they were passive in the experience, acted upon by outside forces bearing the name of the Lord, they are satisfied that the forces are divine, proofs of the power of Jesus and the presence of his Spirit. Signs.

These are good, religious people. They are Moses at the bush; Gideon; the whole order of Israel's priests; Zechariah before Gabriel (but not yet Peter). God is mediated unto them. All their surprises were sought or prayed for or explained in advance. For them the seraphim will not fly up, suddenly, on six wings; the seraphim are fixed and beautiful.

For them the temple will never fill with smoke, except there be a reason. They will speak in tongues; but the Bible will reason the speech, and their own reason will make a sign of it, establishing both degrees of blessing and security thereby. Or else they will shun glossolalia as unreasonable, fanatical, strange, and subversive to God's good order therefore. And those who do and those who don't accept the speaking in tongues will not be much different one from the other, since each shall have founded God—their relationship with him and their knowledge of him—upon some comprehensible sign, some something else.

But these all may love God by loving the signs of God. Their flesh has its touch, their eye its vision, their ear its sound, their tongue its taste: God is mediated unto them *like* them, and they are comforted, loving one not different from themselves. Well, this was the mercy of the incarnation: flesh that flesh could comprehend. It is a gift of God and should not be blamed.

Only, these people halt *at* the incarnation. In experience they do not follow all the way to the abandonment of the cross—or, if they should discover themselves on the other side of the cross after all, they are Thomas, demanding the incarnation again: "Unless I touch—" It is the flesh of Jesus printed with his death, and not the death of Jesus swallowing his flesh to nothing, which characterizes their faith and their pause in faithing. Signs. They stop at the signs, in an ordered, familiar world.

But that is no evil thing—so long as they do not impose powerfully (they will always be the more powerful) their own defining explanations, their lesser consolations, *their* world and its orders upon the third group of faithers, those who move through the fourth passage into the fifth.

This group is not as peaceful as the *Lamed Vavnik.* Neither are they as battlemented as the Sign-Satisfied. They are highly vulnerable and could be killed.

The fourth passage began in gladness. But its end— which is at once the beginning of the fifth—is so bitter that one feels *all* to be at an end.

The end of the fourth passage is a sin, but more than a sin: it is the sin revealed and no longer to be denied. Thrice did Peter, for his own life's sake, deny his Lord. And then the cock crew. And then he knew.

It is the sin revealed, but that revelation is greater than a merely personal awareness: Jesus, against whom it is, sees it too; and we see him seeing it. After the crowing of the cock, so says Luke, "The Lord turned and looked at Peter. And Peter remembered the word of the Lord." Not only did he know his sin: he knew that his Lord had seen it. But that glance of the Lord was "Farewell," for immediately he was snatched from Peter's experience and delivered unto death—for which death Peter himself now became responsible! No, *he* was not dying, as he swore he would. No, he had not denied himself, as Christ had asked him to. He had denied the Christ, and Christ was dying. What, then, was left for Peter but to live with his sin? The Lord, who might have released him, was gone and gone for good. Therefore his own future was shut up against him. It was a wall of hopelessness against which he could only weep, bitterly.

It is a sin at the end of this passage, and sin ends it. It is a sin that destroys all goodness in the future, but worse: it destroys, too, all goodness in the past, for we say, "Now I know my motives." And we say, "Selfish motives turn all good works bad." And we say, "No! I had no right to content myself in deeds done for my own contentment." When Peter saw the Lord seeing him, then all that strong man's promises of faithfulness, of sticking by the Lord even unto death, were not good nor even neutral; they were evil. Guilt goes backward. Guilt is retroactive. Guilt poisons every word and every work that can be remembered.

And we are Peter.

At the end of the fourth passage of faithing, at the beginning of the fifth, we see the face of Jesus one more time; but it was our sin that caused him to look at us. It was not our love but our sin that called him up. And this is the judgment we perceive: his face is not appearing, but vanishing. We, who demanded signs and the success of our own holy labors, who made these things greater than our Lord (whose Lordship is his freedom from any created thing) because we needed to believe in them in order to believe in Jesus, we denied his very nature! We commanded *him* to be dependent on visible signs. We killed, in our lives, his transcendent autonomy. By our faithlessness, our doubt, our mistrust, we had all along been seeking to exchange the hidden glory of the immortal God for images resembling mortal humanity.

And when the signs go cold and futile, lacking life, now, not because the Lord denied them but because we denied the Lord *by* them (that dreadful confession is necessary), then we are Peter. With him we go out to the narrow street between two walls, the wall of the culpable past, the wall of the hopeless future, and weep bitterly.

# The Fifth Passage: Guilt and the Final Refinement, Dying

*Orpheus stood looking backward on the promontory of Taenarus. To all the world he seemed a man distracted, trying to remember something. Or else it seemed as if he'd heard a sound and was listening for it the second time to learn what it was.*

*In fact, for Orpheus there were two stones growing.*

*Can stones grow? No. And then, Yes. If the stone is in the world, it seems, to short, mortal life, always to have been there but only just discovered. That stone merely is. Orpheus was looking at the door to Eurydice in the underworld, and lo: it had become a stone. There was no tunnel, no descending any more, and no door, but sheer stone only, with neither fault nor seam nor feeling. He said, "I did that. The serpent first, but I killed her the second time." He said this without moving, still looking backward. He said it without emotion because he was guilty; he alone was guilty; he did not deserve the sweet release or the self-expression, the seeming strength, the seeming consolation which emotion allowed—or the greatness of heart it implied. Orpheus was no hero; he didn't roar his sorrow. He was guilty only.*

*And so, the second stone.*

*If the stone is in a human breast, it can grow indeed. It can bulk so hard against the ribs that it flattens human feeling to nothing. And the man that carries such a stone in him can feel the weight of it, but that is all he feels.*

*Orpheus's heart was not great. It was a stone. Guilt kills everything else, even tears.*

*So Orpheus left the promontory of Taenarus. He hung his lyre on his back and wandered away, thinking,* There is no Eurydice. *No Eurydice, and so no love within him nor faith in loving any more. He could neither love nor receive the love of others. That made him an exile wherever he went.*

*Where did he go? It didn't matter. To the Rhodope Mountains. To Haemus, swept bare by the cruel northern winds. For three years Orpheus wandered aimlessly, unsurprised by the brutalities and the desolations of the world; and when anyone tried to love him in that time, he responded with a cold, stony heart—as hard as the door to hell.*

*He didn't know what he was doing. There were women in Thrace who were drawn to him as much for his indifference as for his music. Their hearts hurt when he walked by, but he passed them unseeing; so their love and their torment increased together.*

*And what did he do? That didn't matter much either— not, at least, to him, though it affected the world profoundly. He sang. It was his nature to sing. But he sang a passionless, despairing song of the vanity of things, the senselessness of living—and the skill of the music said,* This is the truth. *Orpheus hardly knew what he was doing; he had resigned all sense of responsibility when he quit caring; nevertheless, he was* poiētēs *and a "maker" still, and the beauty of his music persuaded those that heard it, and they wept grievously to see the utter hopelessness of their lives. Orpheus didn't weep. He felt nothing. But softer hearts did, and he caused a universal lamentation by his song.*

*In fact, he sang the earth to autumn; he closed the world in winter.*

*And this is how, in the end, he brought about his own death:*

*One day, in Thrace, he sat singing on a naked hill. His music was so sad that the sky began to cry; a cold, dreary rain came down. Farmers looked up at the grey clouds and felt wretched, but they worked the harder at their harvest, fearing that it would turn soon to snow.*

*His music caused the nightingale to stop singing, stunned by a beauty greater than her own and a sadness deeper than she had ever known.*

*And his music caused a marvel among the trees: they moved. Unrooted by the song, they moved one by one in slow procession toward the singer. They came and forested his hill. The oak tree spread branches over him. Poplars, lindens, beech and laurel and hazel surrounded him—so, too, the silver-fir, the ilex, the sycamore and maple. Willows removed themselves from the water and came, together with the lotus. Boxwood, tamarisks, myrtle, viburnum with her dark blue berries, and ivy and vines all darkened a forest where he sang. And like the sky, they wept: the trees began to drop their leaves. Autumn is the weeping of the trees.*

*But this miraculous motion of the trees drew the attention, too, of the Thracian women together with the Maenades, the priestesses of Bacchus. These were no longer sympathetic. In three years they had lost sympathy for the man who acted so superior in the face of their love. Too often his cold behavior had made fools of them. When they followed the trees, then, and saw who sat in the midst of*

*so remarkable a worship, they were torn immediately by
a fury:*

"It's the man who despises us!" they hissed.

The Maenades were unrestrained. Their hair whipped
wild around their heads, and Bacchus burned in their
blood.

"Arrogant Orpheus!" shrieked one. She seized a spear
and threw it at him.

"Orpheus!" screamed another, "who laughs at our love!"
She hurled a stone.

Then all the Thracian women began to fling whatever
they could pick up, and those that had crossbows shot arrows. They didn't think. They wanted him to suffer. They
turned into a mob.

But everything they threw fell down at his feet! So long
as he kept singing, the music softened stones and turned
the spears aside. Natural things didn't want to hurt this
man.

Oh, how that enraged the Thracian women! They
wanted more than his suffering now. They wanted his
blood. They wanted him dead. They filled the air with their
shrieking. Worse than the beasts, louder and louder they
howled, until their vengeful noise drowned out the sound
of his lyre—and the charm was lost.

A stone hit Orpheus in the throat. It broke the skin and
took his voice away. He touched his lips and found blood,
then leaped up running; but the women streamed down
the hillside after him, maddened, excited by the weakness
they had seen. They rained clots and pebbles and rocks on
him, and brooches and pieces of their clothing.

Orpheus ran to the farmers harvesting their fields—but
when these saw the savage women following him, they
dropped their tools and escaped with their lives.

*And the women shrieked delight. Some fell on the oxen left behind and slaughtered them. Others seized the fallen forks and hoes and mattocks and bore down on Orpheus with the speed of insanity. He could not outrun them. At a riverbank he turned and stretched his arms out to them. He moved his lips, but there was no sound, no voice, and no one heard the word he tried to speak. Into his stomach went the hayfork, and then the women of Thrace were beating him down. He went to his knees; he sank backward with his face to heaven and his mouth wide open, and he died.*

*In the end, his body lay in pieces on the ground.*

*In the end, his head was severed at the neck; his lyre lay silently by. Even in the running Orpheus had not lost his instrument—*

◊    ◊    ◊

When a sin finally surfaces, then it can be taken away. When his sinful condition is no longer hidden from the sinner himself, but he sees it with the righteous eyes of God and therefore knows it clearly *as* sin (which knowing will always be a feeling as well and experiential), then it is where it can be confessed and then, by God, abolished. This, as painful as it is, is the process of guilt; and it is good.

But for the faithing one in the fifth passage of the drama, the goodness is hidden behind two tremendous ironies:

First, it is not a single, isolated sin that has arisen; it isn't what he has *done.* Rather, it's his whole character which is sinful; it's his pride of personhood and the cause of all his doing: it is what he *is.* If God should abolish such sinfulness completely, then God would abolish the person, too. What then? How does one pray for the cleansing that will blot him out of the book of life? Does he pray for mere oblivion, and can that be counted as forgiveness?

Second, when this sort of sinfulness surfaces, it does so with the *anagnōrisis*, the sudden and incontrovertible recognition, that the sinner has all along been cutting God off; that that precisely *is* the sin; and that he discovers this sin only in God's final leavetaking, for then the symbols all go hollow, rousing him to the truth: it is Jesus' *vanishing* face which wakens Peter. (Or else, like King Saul this sinner does not realize that his "worship" is cutting God off until God cuts him off.) And what then? If the very effect of the sin is separation, the destruction of his relationship to God, to whom shall this sinner pray for forgiveness? To the degree that he grieves his sin, to that same degree he is convinced of God's departure. What good is prayer? Well, he is sadly persuaded that it can be no good, and he despairs.

No, he sees no goodness now. The door, once opened and shut—it cannot be opened again.

The faithing one is now most desolate. And now his desolation is obvious to the world because he does not persist in a mask of Christianity: he sees no good in that any more—not because he thinks that God is not good, but rather because he knows that *he* is not good, that he is wretched wholly and has failed his God. Oh, the faithing one (finally, finally) knows his transgression, and now his sin is ever before him, never forgotten: it is his very nature. Therefore he does not argue his condemnation, the spiritual solitude which he suffers, because he is convinced that he deserves it. (That is the hardest confession of all; it is made to the void, so there is no goodness nor hope in making it; it concerns the only being left in his world, that is, himself; and it declares the utter worthlessness of that being—one worthy only *of* the void. It is the hardest confession because the sinner now sees with the righteousness of God, and so despises this single being in his world, that is, himself: *You deserve it. I deserve it!* Yet, as hard as that confession is, he finds himself making it, compulsively, all the time.) No, he does not argue against his sentence. He finds the judgment of God to be blameless. The lack of any argument, in fact, this resigned acceptance, this spiritual indolence, is the desolation that the world sees.

He sees no goodness in the world. He sees no point to the consolations others offer him: their very love for him discredits them in his eyes. What truth could they tell him if they cannot see him, the greatest of sinners, truly? No, he sees no goodness in any relationship any more. And, soon, therefore, the world will see no goodness in him nor any faithing in his persistent melancholy. First he will make them sad; then he will make them offended; and then they too will cut him off. And what will he say to that? Why, something to frustrate them all the more: he will bow his head and say, "I deserve it."

Well. Is there any holiness in this passage, then? Can there be goodness to such wintry despair?

Yes.

But what is the faithing one doing after all when he seems so intent on doing nothing? He is dying. Or, to speak it more precisely, he who could not die before, by denying himself according to the Lord's command (because his nature was unable to chose not to be)—he is being killed all the day long.

And what is the goodness of that? This, that he, willy-nilly, is following Jesus to the cross. Finally he is enacting the fourth and deepest meaning of the holy *vocatio: Follow me.*

. . .

1. *Follow me* meant "Come from the world. Find hiding underneath my wings." It was a sort of death, but an easeful one. We died to a very demanding world.

2. *Follow me* meant "Deny yourselves." Make little of your own desires; mortify your flesh. That was a death more difficult, to suffer both Christward and Christlike; but it nonetheless had the promise of possibility (we *could* do it), the promise of reward (we could do it *for Jesus*), and the flattery of our own powers (*we* could do it, not the Lord). So, this dying wasn't total. Also, it glowed with hopefulness.

3. *Follow me* meant "Suffer the abandonment of God. Suffer to know him as he is, unmediated—which is not to know him at all. Suffer *his* complete control of the relationship: trust absolutely." This, too, was a death—not to the world, nor to ourselves, but *into* a fullness of relationship with God. Ironically, we felt that this death we could most easily die, since it consisted in our doing nothing. And some of us did—and these, then; were done. But for Peter and for the most of us, this was the death we could not die. Instead, our inability to die it has finally raised into our consciousness the very truth of our natures, and it has prepared us for the death we *shall* die—

One more time the dear Lord Jesus whispers (but we do not hear him, and we would not believe him if we could; he does this thing, not we) *Follow me.*

Jesus Chirst drank the cup which the Father would not remove from him. He drank it in his dying on the cross. Be clear, dear people: what was that cup? What did it contain?

There is no doubt in anyone's mind that it contained his physical pain. In fact, this is what we, sympathetically, most focus on—perhaps because it is the easiest pain to contemplate or else to understand. He was whipped, mocked, spiked, and left to die of exhaustion and exposure.

Yet, sadly, that is not unique unto him. Others have suffered greater bodily torment at the hands of a cruel humanity.

So, what did the cup contain?

Well, the wrath of God, the judgment of a just God against this cruel humanity. And that means a number of things in deadening succession—to understand which is to marvel both at the suffering which Jesus took upon himself and at the depth of his love for us.

"The cup of wrath" means that Jesus' was a spiritual suffering far beyond the physical spilling of his blood. He was suffering the divine punishment of his Father, stored up throughout the ages and equal to the sin committed throughout the ages—judicially equal. No Roman cross could match the rage of an angry God. Whole worlds shall one day be cindered by that rage. But this God was Jesus' Father. It was upon a Son that God accomplished the sentence. Not only did Jesus take unto himself the wrath reserved for all, but it came from One with whom he'd had communion from eternity, One who now turned a furious face upon him. No amount of imagining can comprehend how the loss of that love multiplied the pain of punishment.

But it is even more than that. "The cup of wrath" means that Jesus drank down the sin that deserved this punishment. He drank it; it became him; he became it. St. Paul says, "He made him to be sin who knew no sin." *Jesus was sin,* the thing itself. There could be no comfort, no solace, no psychological nor spiritual escape from the fullness of the punishment. Look: Jesus did not "bear" the sin of the world, as though a certain filth clung to him or covered him or even crushed him, but was not cosubstantial with him. If that had been the case, he might have earned some honor (and so some consolation) by the sacrificial love wherewith he loved humanity; he might have endured the pain by reminding himself that it was not *his* pain to bear, but ours—and so he would have separated himself somewhat from that pain, preserving a piece of himself as worthy (how he loved!) to survive after all. We, in retrospect, do that for him; he did not do that for himself. For him, nothing was worthy, and nothing survived. Behold: while he hung upon the cross, Jesus did not represent but *was* the cruel humanity whom God despised!

He was the loathsome thing itself.

And therefore, he bowed his head (can we understand the horror of this thing?) and said, "It is right. This is righteous." Not "it is right that someone suffer for such sin." Rather "it is right that *I* suffer; I *am* the sin. No one deserves it as much as I do, since everyone else is one only, and a few sins each, while I am all and all the sins together! I deserve what God, in wrath, is doing unto me."

Now the old saw, that "God hates the sin but loves the sinner," is a false comfort. This sinner was the sin. God the Father hated the thing that his Son had become.

But so, too, did the Son: Jesus' instinct and character and love was ever for righteousness. He did not lose his vision of righteousness on the cross, as though he might think his sinful condition were all right, a justifiable thing to be. Then he might have raged back at the raging God and so preserved some stature and some worth (as Satan does) by warring against the Supreme. No, he still knew sin as foul and hateful. Therefore (can we understand this sorrow?) with the Father, Jesus despised himself! When God the Father turned away, leaving him alone, Jesus loathed intensely the single being left within his world, that is, himself.

He understood, and he approved the abandonment of the Deity. It was right that the Father disown him. It was right that he should suffer so. It was right that he should die. There could be no qualification of that simple rightness, no appeal nor amnesty nor mercy—none. Any of these things would have been wrong.

Then what did the cup contain? The fullness of human sin, the righteousnes of wrath. And to drink it was not only to die, and so to be released (how the suffering soul longs for death; but death was no release for Jesus). To drink it was to be fixed in the full knowledge of personal sin forever; fully to experience the spiritual, judicial, and eternal causes of Death Itself (that which brought it into being), discovering oneself to *be* the cause; and fully to experience the divinely fashioned retribution which Death is.

What is the cup?

It is the *Dies Irae,* the Last Day, the abolition of ignorance.

It is Hell.

That is where Jesus went. But first he said, *Follow me.*

4. *Follow me* means—to hell?

No, of course not. But at the same time, Yes.

Emphatically, Jesus went through *that* death, eternal death, for us and in our stead. He drank the cup on our behalf in order to save us from that cup. And Paul, who called him sin, said that his being sin was "for our sake . . . so that in him we might become the righteousness of God." This is the Gospel.

But there is throughout Paul the persistent "in him," the constant occlusion of our lives into the death of Jesus—into the totality of that death, which fullness is much Paul's point.

And Jesus said to his disciples of that cup, "You will drink it," and of the caustic baptism with which he was to be baptised, "you will be baptized."

What did he mean? That his drinking canceled our need to drink? No, he didn't say that. Then what did he mean? That his drinking would be of no effect for us? Of course not. His coming at all would be nothing then.

But what did he mean? This: that his drinking first would give grace to our drinking second; that our drinking, which otherwise could have no consequence but that we end in Hell, might have good consequence after all. Without him, our drinking (which would certainly be decreed by God on the Last Day) would damn us. With him, our drinking can be cleansing: the lifting of our sin before our eyes; our suffering both the knowledge of the sin and the righteousness of punishment; and then the killing of that sin, which is— since the sin is us—the crucifixion of ourselves, forever. We die. In him the wrath was drained and done; and then he rose again from the dead. In us—although the drinking may *feel* as acid as heavenly wrath—it is not wrath at all, but a savage love to purge us; and then we too will rise again from our lesser deaths. ("Do you not know that all of us who have been baptized into Christ Jesus were baptized into his death? We were buried therefore with him by baptism into death, so that as Christ was raised from the dead by the glory of the Father, we too might walk in newness of life." Newness, now!)

Ours is the same cup as his. But it is different because he drank it first.

His cup was the thing eternal. Ours is an exercise.

His cup cast a long, long shadow. Ours is the shadow.

His was made of the iron *Is,* but ours of the clay *Would Have Been.*

He suffered the drinking because he knew beforehand

the horrible truth entire; we drink and suffer in order to know.

He saw himself therein, reflected on the fluid.

So do we—see ourselves, in order to see him. For he who drank the cup to the lees then took up his place within the cup. He is the wine inside it now.

Therefore, it is the same cup, but different.

*Follow me.*

◊     ◊     ◊

"I remember Reverend Peters," said Mr. Arthur Williams, who was sitting almost knee to knee with Orpheus in the parsonage dining room. "Took good care of this house, him and his wife. She was a painter, y'know. Very pretty pictures on the wall. Now, they didn't have anything very new, understand, but it was all good and matching. I think a pastor of ours should have good furniture." Mr. Williams nodded several times to underscore his point. "Think you'll ever fix the place up, Pastor? Folding chairs, y'know. Looks kind of like you're passing through."

"I don't need much," said Orpheus.

"No. No, that's true," said Mr. Williams, unconvinced.

But then, Arthur Williams hadn't been able to persuade Orpheus to buy a car in all these years, nor to marry, though either acquisition would have improved appearances for the pastor, for the parish and, by association, for Arthur himself, who was pleased to be the head elder.

"Well," he said, "can't argue with success. Ha, ha."

Orpheus didn't ask him what that meant. Williams was changing the subject, preparing to reveal the reason why he'd come. He was a man of parts, the owner of a Buick, a bald head, and an ample stomach. He observed what he took to be the amenities: amiability, addressing people according to their titles, shaking hands, and pleasant small talk always before arriving at the point. He avoided conflict and fancied himself something of a peacemaker therefore: if nasty words weren't spoken, why, then nastiness didn't exist, and everyone was happy. Mr. Williams made himself deaf to nasty words. He certainly never used them himself. It was marvelous to him, however, how often he had to overlook the nastiness in others.

He was also a man of foresight. He said so. He crossed his legs as best he could on the folding chair, locked his fingers across his belly, and said, "I'm the kind of person who plans for the future, Pastor. Always have been—is why I could take a early retirement. Now I'm thinking of the future of our church. You noticed that we have to put up extra chairs almost every Sunday? I have. We line the aisle with chairs and we stick two new rows in the back. That's good. That's good. A credit to you, yes. Well, I can't see it being any different, except to get better." He beamed, patting his stomach. "And I have given it thought. We got to build a new church, yes, yes. Yes, a new church building—first new building in the inner city in generations, yes." His eyes misted at the prospect. He was genuinely moved.

Orpheus had, to this point, endured Williams's talk and his presence passively, watching the man with small interest, but watching him.

At the word about a new building, however, his stomach tightened.

"Why?" he said.

Williams blinked. "I just told you why," he said. "We need room."

"That's a reason. That's not *the* reason," said Orpheus.

Mr. Williams was confused, "It ain't?"

"I suppose you'll want to dedicate it when it's finished."

Williams smiled again, to be talking of the future again. "Yes. Sure," he said with some enthusiasm. "We'll have a big altar area, so we could stick seven, eight preachers in there for a dedication—you in the middle of them."

"To what god will you dedicate it?" asked Orpheus.

"What?"

"To whom do you plan to dedicate your new church building?"

"Well, sure. To God—sure. Everything for God. I don't—"

"Or to human pride, Arthur? A monument to our success? As though that's something praiseworthy? Arthur, I'm sick of human pride."

Arthur Williams was frowning, trying to follow. "Pastor," he said. "I don't know what you're saying, but I'm saying you're a good pastor. I'm saying you fill the church like I never seen in all my years here, and that's Sunday after Sunday. You preach good sermons, there's a fact. So we got to have more space. Now, I talked to others and they agree with me, so it was time I talked with you. Here I am, talking with you."

Orpheus subsided. He felt mortally tired, impotent before the Arthur Williams's of the world, isolated in sorrows he could not explain, and finally too indifferent to try to explain anything. He didn't know this Arthur Williams of contentments; neither would Arthur ever know him, though he would always think he did—a prejudice too thick to breach. Besides, it was nearly nine o'clock at night, and it was raining. Orpheus said simply, "Don't do this thing." But he said it meekly, and Williams smelled capitulation.

The older man became avuncular.

"Ha, ha!" he said, "Ha, ha! I see the problem. You're so modest, Pastor. Such a humble man. Yes, that's it. You don't want to take credit—but credit's due you."

Orpheus felt a furious rash of guilt break out on the back of his neck. He bowed his head, angry at Williams, angrier with himself.

Arthur Williams took that bow as further humility, confirmation of his words; so his next words sounded positively pastoral. He could be infinitely gracious to those who thought him right.

But the words he spoke burned in Orpheus; guilt swept through him like nausea.

Williams said, "You're a good man, Pastor. The best we ever had. Mrs. Story wrote it in her will that she wanted it anonymous—but I think I can tell you: she gave all her money to the church, is why we can talk about building now." The man leaned forward and put his hand on Orpheus's knee. He lowered his voice to imitate intimacy. "She was a hard old woman," Williams said. "It's not wrong to say, she had tight fingers. But you, Pastor—you did such good things for her in her final days, you stood by her and comforted her, that look what she did. She gave her money to the church—all on account of you."

Abruptly, Orpheus struck the man's hand from his knee and stood up so violently that the folding chair clattered backward.

Now, that might have been taken as a nastiness, even by Arthur Williams, except that someone began almost in the same instant to beat at the front door of the parsonage. The sequence was backward, but Williams was practiced at reversals: he accounted for the pastor's behavior and his own bruised hand by the knock at the door.

It was no knock. It was brute pounding. And a man's voice outside was roaring, "Reverent! Reverent! Reverent!"

Orpheus went to the door. It was an enormous face, pressed to the window and shining with rain, and it was wrathful.

Orpheus opened the door. The rain and the man burst in.

"Where is she?" he demanded.

Williams sat up, sensing nastiness.

Orpheus said, "Who? And who are you?"

The man stood five inches taller than Orpheus, broad-shouldered, soaking wet and smelling of industrial coolant.

"Arabelle! Arabelle!" the man roared down on Orpheus. "Where is Arabelle!"

"You're John," said Orpheus.

"No shit," he said. "And you're the reverent she been runnin' to, fillin' her head with notions. Now she's gone, an' I wanna know where."

"John, I haven't seen—"

"Took ever' damn thing she owned and some a mine, too, my stereo. Took the damn kid, an' clean gone, man."

"John, look—"

"I don't take that shit off nobody, here? An' that woman been wrong-headed from day one, an' you, man—you messed wit' her, makin' her snotty, so that she th'ew you up to my face whenever I said somethin'. Jesus, man. Jesus! Where'd she go?"

Orpheus raised his voice to a pulpit tone. John kept ramming a finger into his face. Boldly he pushed that hand down and at the same time said loudly, "I don't know! Listen to me. I haven't seen her in three months, not three months. I truly don't know where she is. I'd help you if I could."

John fell quiet a moment. As big and angry as he was, there was something pitiful in his eyes. Orpheus pursued the quiet with questions. "When did she leave? This morning?"

Low, like muttering thunder, John said, "Two weeks."

"Two weeks?" said Orpheus. "And *now* you go looking for her?"

"I been thinking on it," growled John. "I been meditating on it." Rage inside of him curled like a cat flicking its tail. He had great black nostrils that swelled each time he inhaled, and beer soured his breath. "I been thinkin' backward on ever' damn little thing that woman done me. An' now I'm ready, an' now I want to find her."

"Two weeks, John. She could be anywhere. She could be in Atlanta—"

The big man's head lowered before such a thought and such a distance. His spirit was already turning to leave—perhaps to check out Atlanta. But Arthur Williams perceived an opportunity to make peace of nastiness. He spoke up, surprising both that he was still there.

"No, no, it isn't as bad as all that," he said cheerily. "I thought you knew, Pastor, or else I would have told you, ha, ha. Word is, Arabelle Lee has moved into the projects. She's sharing a room with Coral Jones, because he was eligible—Hey!" cried Williams. "*Hey!*"

John's eyes had ignited like fuses. His black face had twisted into storm. He drew back his right fist and drove it like a sledge with all his body weight into Orpheus's throat, sending him backward into the card table.

"*Hey!*" cried Arthur Williams.

John glared down at Orpheus a moment, trembling.

Orpheus was writhing, trying to breathe. Just now it wasn't the pain that bothered him, but the fact he couldn't breathe.

John turned and went out into the rain.

Williams leaped up, hurried to the front door, and stood there, crying, "Hey! Hey!" into the night. "You can't do that!" Like a little dog barking. "Hey!" When he was satisfied that the assailant was gone, he closed the door and returned to lean over Orpheus. "You all right?" he said.

Orpheus just couldn't draw breath through a locked

throat. He forced some out, and it sounded like gagging; but he couldn't suck it in again. The tears started running from his eyes, but he wasn't crying. Curiously, he was aware of everything. He knew precisely the nature of the pain in his neck. He remembered the sense of something collapsing when John's fist slammed against it. He tasted salty blood in his mouth. He felt his eyeballs popping a little right now, going bloodshot, he was sure. He just couldn't breathe, that's all. His gut convulsed for the breath that wouldn't come. He thought that he would probably panic in a moment; but there was no panic in him now—rather, a sort of resignation: *Oh, let it be. Lie still and let it come.*

"You should bring charges, you know that?" said Arthur Williams. "You can't just let a thing like this pass." He was leaning close to Orpheus's face. "I mean, this is criminal. You going to press charges?"

No, Orpheus realized that he wasn't going to panic after all. He ceased writhing, stretched out on his back, and let his eyeballs roll upward. He was thinking, *And why not? Let it be.*

But then Arthur Williams brought his own face monstrously close to Orpheus's and for an instant it seemed the man was going to kiss him. He had very soft, very spongy lips—and warm. He had stubby fingers, which he forced into Orpheus's cheeks, separating the jaws. He blew a pipe-tobaccoed breath into Orpheus's mouth, drove it painfully past his throat and into his lungs; and that was how Orpheus came to breathe again.

He was not grateful.

So they said that Pastor Orpheus shouldn't preach a while after that incident. They voted him five, six weeks vacation. Well, the man could hardly whisper, let alone talk, let alone preach. But their pastor had grown strange and stubborn during the winter and the spring, and he preached despite their kindnesses.

Neither did he press charges again John Sutpen. He didn't even report him to the police.

It wasn't as if his sermons were all that great, either. They were bookish things, preached from the pulpit and with notes. He'd never used notes before; and he'd only used the pulpit early in his ministry, when he was still green. So what? So he seemed green all over again, a seminary graduate uncertain of himself. And no one wanted to complain, but, "Could you hear what he said? I couldn't, and I was sitting in the third pew. The man don't talk no more. He squeaks."

But this was the situation: Orpheus was not preaching for the people, neither for their sakes nor really to them. He was preaching for himself. Not that he found comfort in, or even took meaning from, the words. No, he was preaching because it hurt to talk. Sound came from his throat as though it were a steel file scraping the tissue of his tender larynx. Then, after preaching, his Sunday afternoons and Wednesday nights (it was the season of Lent) were spent in a lacerated agony when he couldn't so much as drink water. And as long as his throat was aggravated from healing, he continued a forced fast. He grew thinner; his eyes grew larger, and his cheeks sallow. He was doing all this on his own account. It hurt to talk—and he *wanted* to hurt.

Not that it made any difference. Not that he had even thought it through. Simply: he deserved no better. The state of his life and the state of his conscience were the same this way.

No, it made no difference. This was no sacrifice to God, no Lenten deprivation; God wouldn't acknowledge it since God would not acknowledge Orpheus anyway; he had turned away from Orpheus in disgust, as well he should. And Lenten fasts lost meaning when Lent itself did. What was the meaning of the death of Jesus, the Son of God? Only that Orpheus was a bastard. Because it didn't matter what the world thought, or the Church, or the people of his congregation (it didn't even matter that they were perfectly right where they were themselves concerned): Orpheus knew certainly that in the little world which he and Jesus once had occupied, he had killed Jesus. That's what Lent led up to, the dreary reminder that he himself was constitutionally the nullifier of the Christ.

The pain in his throat and his forced fast merely expressed this truth aloud. He wasn't about to lie any more nor to play the hypocrite—at least not with himself. He'd sinned enough.

The killer of Jesus? The nullifier of Christ? Oh, yes, yes—in more than metaphoric senses. Orpheus was inclined to agree with John: he was responsible for Arabelle's departure. He had not raised Jesus up within that woman's sepulcher of a life. Mostly, he had wanted to be free of her; he wearied of her amoral sexuality and her parochial religion, her streety self-centeredness. He deserved the punch in the neck. John had come to the right place. Worse, Orpheus had killed the Christ in Coral Jones, wherein he had most clearly seen the Christ. It wasn't Jesus whom Corie betrayed by permitting Arabelle's power over him. Their sex in the parsonage had in no way betrayed Jesus. Jesus wasn't exiled by their sinfulness, or else Jesus would never have chosen to enter a sinful world at all. No, Jesus, outrageously, forgave. Rather, it was *Orpheus* who had been betrayed! It was Orpheus who could not handle the offense. It was Orpheus who did not forgive, but exiled poor Corie from the house and from his life—Corie, so quick to believe that he was a

Nothing and who looked to the pastor in order to see his Lord. If Arabelle, even in her slattern, lascivious way, made Corie Jones Something again, why shouldn't he go and live with her? Orpheus, the arrogant, the heartless, so cruel to Corie Jones—Orpheus killed Jesus for Corie, nullified the Christ by taking up Christ's place in Corie, and then vacated the place altogether. John was right to strike him. The pastor deserved to have his breath and his voice destroyed. How perfect, that a pastor who lied should be condemned to whispering only.

Of Mrs. Story he couldn't think at all.

He didn't write his sermons any more. He read those that others had published, in order not to distort the truth for the people of his parish. And God was not here for him. Should he let that terrible word creep into his preaching? No.

But for him, for Orpheus, God was not. Not because God was not powerful. Not because God was not good. God was good. *God* was good. Orpheus was not good. This man's nature—his habitual action, the things he didn't even think about, the very ministry he once thought holy—was devious, antithetical to God, God's opposite. For Orpheus, God was not. He despaired. Why shouldn't he eat food? Did he have a right to food?

But did Orpheus love Jesus in these days? Oh, my dear! Orpheus loved Jesus with his whole heart, his whole being—more than he had when he smelled his Jesus on the breath of his mother and learned his name. His love was the sickness in him; he fought terribly to put that love away, because it was his damnably distorted *loving* that had screamed for Jesus when he couldn't see him, his selfish *loving* that had banished Jesus to death again. Did he love Jesus? Orpheus loved nothing but Jesus. But he'd killed the one he loved—what blame on him! And since his beloved was gone, there was no love left for him in all this world. *Let it be. Let it be.*

Orpheus despaired. He didn't complain of that. He simply sat in a bare room on folding chairs not even his, and despaired.

On Good Friday he squeaked a sermon written by someone who meant to be consoling, someone too timid to speak accurately of Death, Christ's Death or the Death upon humanity. It was nonsense to Orpheus, but he presumed the writer knew better than he how to be kind to people, so he chose it. And on this Good Friday he did not cry.

Nevertheless, when the church cleared of its cheerless people, he felt a touch on his shoulder and turned around.

It was Dolores of the rich black skin.

"How are you, Pastor?" she said.

He nodded. He whispered, "Fine."

She gazed at him a moment. She said, "It always rains Good Friday. But on Easter the sun always shines." She smiled meaningfully on him.

But he did not smile in return. His face sat blank before her. So she lost her smile too, and in a moment, without another word, she hurried from the church.

Easter Sunday the sun did, in fact, shine; and Dolores twice sought him out to tell him so, once before the service, poking her head around his study door, and once after it. "I told you so," she said brightly in the study. But the second time she met him it was with a forced brightness.

A whispered Resurrection Service has a deadening effect. People had muted their singing, as though they were in a hospital ward. A blank-faced celebrant does not encourage unbounded praise. If people came with true gladness of soul, they felt a little guilty about it. And Dolores had been dabbing at her eyes periodically throughout the worship. So it was with false brightness and a teary glitter in her eyes that she repeated outside the church: "I told you so, didn't I? The sun always shines on Easter."

His answer did not come immediately. There were people lined up behind her, waiting to shake his hand. And though he was not immediate, her feelings were. Suddenly she covered her face and rushed down the steps to her car.

Orpheus was not oblivious. He saw that and he suffered for her. But his thought, as he shook the next hand, was *This is who I am, now. This is what I do: I hurt people.* He despised himself.

He despaired.

Mr. Arthur Williams said that he didn't like to talk about other people behind their backs; but he said that he was the head elder and had been for ten years now, and that he'd been a member of this congregation for many more years than that, and that he bore a certain responsibility, therefore, for the health of this congregation—and did anyone know what was happening with Reverend Orpheus?

Arthur Williams conceded that the blow to the pastor's throat—when was that, two months ago?—deserved sympathy and would take any man backward some. But he had to admit at the same time that it was that blow which opened up his, Arthur Williams's eyes, and he saw—we have to be frank about these things—a certain dereliction of duty in the pastor. And he wasn't the only one. For example: Reverend Orpheus never reported the incident. Now, either he was careless or weak or else too coddling of the low-life in the neighborhood; he did, in fact, seem to give them much more attention than he did to respectable members of the congregation—and he had since the beginning, come to think of it. Why did young Corie Jones deserve all the attention *he* got? There's another perfect example. Mr. Arthur Williams didn't want to say for sure; he just wondered whether the Reverend's values weren't upside down. He knew for a fact, in fact, that Reverend Orpheus had slacked on visiting the shut-in and the sick—even before he took the punch from John Sutpen.

Well, he was the first one to acknowledge that the reverend was overburdened. But whose fault was that? The elders didn't ask him to take on the city, to fool with housing. No, he did that on his own. And what good was it to the congregation if the man worked himself to death? Look: he'd knocked himself into the hospital. A lot of people pitied him for that; and Mr. Williams knew that those people might not like to hear it, but let's be frank: one, Reverend Orpheus wasn't taking good care of himself, so the church suffered; two, he was up and out of his bed *weeks* before the doctor released him; and three, he'd been morbid ever since. Morbid before that, to be sure, but snappish and gloomy and downright grim since. Does that help the church?

Mr. Williams mentioned these things aloud in meetings or in the churchyard after services or when he met members in the course of his day.

Whenever someone brought up the subject of the pastor's poor preaching, Arthur Williams brought up the subject of the reverend's poor health, and they both shook heads together, and Williams allowed as how it could have been avoided. Then he would say, "It's something else. Something's got into him. I just wonder what that something is. Hum."

Whenever someone observed that the reverend was looking sicker these days, Arthur Williams made observa-

tions on the man's lifestyle: bad eating habits, solitary behavior, and a bare house, nothing in it but folding chairs and
a card table. They shook heads over the strangeness of the
man and wondered why they hadn't really noticed it before,
since he'd always been that way. "Yep, something's got a-holt
on him."

Whenever someone made the mild complaint that the
church's parsonage, of which they were proud since not too
many churches were able to give their pastors a house, was
being neglected and looked like the house of poor folks,
what with folding chairs and card tables only, then Arthur
Williams wondered out loud whether Reverend Orpheus
had ever meant to stay among them any way. Folding chairs
didn't look like roots to him. They looked to him like the
furniture of someone passin' through.

He was, he said, merely considering what was best for
his church.

And in elders' meetings he several times brought up the
topic of building a new church building, saying, "I have a
dream—" This, finally, was the core of Arthur Williams's
complaints against the Reverend, that he had scorned a very
dear dream.

On the Tuesday after Easter, Dolores Johnson brought
Orpheus a lily. At ten in the morning she rapped cheerfully
at his front door. He opened it to her with some discomfort
at the contrast between them, and she stepped quickly into
the living room, glancing from corner to corner.

He'd been awake since five; he wore jeans and a T-shirt.
But he had the punk disshevelment of sleep about him still,
unwashed, uncombed, thick in his motions, throbbing in his
throat. His house must have smelled sour because of his
presence.

But Dolores smelled of a light, springtime perfume. Her hair had a fine knot at the back, and she wore a bright dress to contrast the deep Caribbean black of her arms and face. Before her nodded the tall, white lily.

"I had it on the altar in memory of my Papa," she said. "But now I bring flowers to the living. I want to give this to you." She smiled. The furnaces beneath her cheeks glowed darkly red. "I didn't think anyone else would give you one." She glanced around. "Where should I put your lily, Pastor?"

Orpheus shrugged. He'd never furnished his house for lilies. "There?" he said, pointing to the floor below a dining room window.

"Oh, Pastor!" She wrinkled her nose at his lack of taste and began to test the lily in various places. She took a long time moving it here and there, bowing low to set it down, stepping back to see.

He stood watching and knew that there were other reasons for her coming. She might have just handed the lily to him and left.

Finally, as she was kneeling with her back to him, he squeaked, "Dolores," and she froze. She didn't turn around, but she spoke quickly as if to forestall any word of his:

"Pastor, how are you?" she said. "I mean, how *are* you?" She held her hand cupped beneath the petals of the lily.

To her back he whispered, "Fine."

"I know, I know, you told me that already, but I can see, and I know it isn't true." She was gazing at the lily. "Don't you think I can see things? You should talk to someone. How are you?"

She gave him a silence in which to answer, holding her body very still. But he, too, held still and said nothing at all.

Very low, as soft as her dark skin, she said, "I am Dolores Johnson."

He said nothing. She dropped her hand from the lily and put it to her knee, leaned lightly on her arms and lowered her head. "You are Orpheus," she said, nearly whispering. "You are suffering. I know that. I see it every day in your face. I have always seen it—sad eyes, sad eyes, your sad eyes hurt me; and I think, *The eyes of Jesus.* I'm not no one, Pastor. I can be hurt by the sadness—"

Orpheus struggled to keep his face calm. His breast constricted at her words. It irritated him that she should be talking about his face, his eyes: a kind of invasion. He wished he had his whole voice. He wished that he was clean and not musty from sleep. All this put him at a disadvantage.

And she shouldn't be saying these things. No. He was distressed by the direction she was taking. He whispered harshly, "Dolores—"

But she stood up immediately, saying, "The lily needs water," and breezed into his bathroom. She shut the door, and there was a moment of stillness in the house, her lily lonely in a corner.

Orpheus thought, "That bathroom is not clean"—but she was clean, and he felt a certain entrapment.

When she came out again, she had no water. "No glass," she muttered, glancing through a doorway into his bedroom.

Suddenly she disappeared into the bedroom.

"Dolores!" he squeaked.

She didn't answer. The sound of snapping blankets came out.

He sighed and followed her until he stood in the doorway.

Busily, busily, she was making his bed. No, no, this was too intimate a gesture. No, she didn't have the right.

Orpheus said, "Stop that."

But she didn't stop. "Someone's got to take some care of you," she muttered. She tucked blankets and yanked them tight, as if driven or angry. The room had the shade drawn. He could hardly distinguish her face, but her perfume brushed the air.

"Stop it, stop it!" he hissed.

Suddenly she hit the bed with the flats of her hands, her fingers spread wide, her body bowed at the waist. "I am Dolores Johnson," she whispered, and Orpheus heard that she was crying. His flesh tingled. "I am not nobody. Am I nobody to you?" She raised her face; great white eyes appealed to him. "Pastor, you held me in your study. You put your arms around me. I held you, too. That wasn't nothing. I have carried it in me ever since, but you never said anything about it."

Orpheus remembered that. He bowed his head. What did it matter that she had initiated it? But that *was* nothing— or it should have been nothing, or—

His bowed head softened her voice. Tears moistened it. She said, "Who found you when you fainted on the sidewalk? Who came and held your head for you? Who suffered for all the suffering you were going through? Please. Please," she whispered in a tiny voice, a baby's voice, beseeching: "That was me. That was Dolores Johnson. Don't you think my heart grew big and hurt for you? Pastor, is that nothing to you?"

Orpheus folded his arms across his stomach, which was twisting painfully. This was so wrong. There was no way in which this could be right. He felt such a burning fear rise up in him, because the trap was tightening and he didn't know how to be free himself except to cut it, except to wound Dolores, the child, the woman, so defenseless before him—so beautiful. No, she was not nothing! She was someone! But he, Orpheus, he was a bastard. *He* was nothing—

Dolores said a horrible thing. She stood up straight, her white eyes gazing at him across his bed, and she grew bold, and the tears seemed gone. She said, "Do you love me?"

A groan escaped him, as though he had been kicked.

She said it again, in simple, perfect clarity: "Do you love me?"

"I love," he said, and paused. "I love you—all. I loved Mrs. Story. I love Corie Jones. I preach, and I see the faces, and I love—"

"No!" She raised her hands. She held them in front of her and fairly cried: "I am Dolores Johnson, Dolores Johnson! *Do you love me?*"

Orpheus threw himself from the room. Deep in a whisper he said, "Jesus Christ, where are you?" He went into the dining room, into the light again, and sat on a folding chair, and bowed forward with his fingers locked behind his head.

But Dolores was swift, came instantly to his side and kneeled, and he felt her like a fire there. She was crying. She said, "Don't you know how much I love you?"

He knew. He knew. And, by the arousal in his own body he knew how he could respond. But, with everything else, his burning sexuality accused him, and he whispered, "You can't! You can be a friend. I can be your pastor. But you cannot love me like this!"

So tiny, like one pebble in a stream bed, Dolores made the declaration: "But I do." Then she put her dark face soft upon his leg and sobbed.

How wrong the whole damnable world was! How evil was the soul of Orpheus. This is what he did now, whether he wanted to or not, because this was his nature, this was the vile truth of his condition: He hurt people.

Dolores, weeping against him—Dolores was righteous and gentle and kind and beautiful and undeserving of the pain he caused her. *You are not nobody*, he thought, but he didn't say it; he couldn't say it; he could not encourage her misbegotten love. *You are somebody, child. Oh, child, you are somebody. But I belong in hell!*

Out loud he whispered, "You ask what you can't have. You don't even know what you're asking for. You call me Pastor. I am no pastor. I am no pastor. I am not worthy. *Kindness hurts me.* Ah, Dolores, get up. Don't touch me any more. Go away. Go away."

He felt her forehead on his knee, the gentle motion of her sobbing, and the tears all down to his flesh. Her weight was upon him. The knot of her black hair was under his eyes. He did not know if she'd heard him. She did not move. She wept. And he did not do the things he yearned to do: to touch her black hair with a hand of peace, to hold her very tightly, and to love her—

One more time he forced the words through his wretched throat: "Dolores, you are killing me. Go away."

When she didn't, he stood up himself. Her face slid down to the metal chair. He went into the bedroom for his keys, then walked through the dining room to the front door.

She was glaring at him, then, furiously.

"You can't do this!" she said, but he kept walking. He didn't turn to look at her. "After what I told you," she cried behind him, "you can't just walk away from me. Pastor!" she cried. He went outside, but didn't close the door on her. "Pastor Orpheus!" He walked on the sidewalk to the church. From the parsonage he heard her wail, "I am somebody! I am somebody! I am somebody!"

Should a lily be left to die? Should it die the slow death of inattention, drought in a little pot? A lily has no fault. It is white, silent, and innocent, caught up in forces it neither caused nor understands. A lily does not deserve to starve unto its death.

But Orpheus could not abide Dolores's lily in his house, accusing him from the corner of his dining room.

He thought of planting it outside, but it would accuse him there as well.

He buried it.

With a shovel and a hole in the earth, he put her lily out of sight. It seemed right. He was dying, too. He preached sermons stillborn, and he fasted.

He began to look very old.

Orpheus neglected his ministry sorely, despite warnings from the leaders of the congregation. He exchanged his duties for a folding chair, and it began to be noticed by people who once had praised him—that he stank.

One notable event preceded his death, and then there was the death.

The phone rang at one-thirty in the morning. He was not asleep and answered it on the second ring.

"You coulda had the decency to tell me," said the voice, "but you led me on instead." A voice so bitter it sounded metallic.

Orpheus said, "Who is this?"

"Nobody, Pastor. Jus' nobody."

"Dolores?"

"Go to hell."

Her words were slurred and unrepentant. She was either very tired or loosened by liquor. Orpheus closed his eyes. Behind him was a trail of the slaughtered; she was one of them. This is what he did to people, now—

"Tell you what?" he whispered.

"That you are gay."

A wild rush of surprise swept through him. *Gay?* "Gay?" he said. He was prepared, these days, to accept any accusation, but this one bewildered him. What did it mean? Where did that word come from?

"Oh, yes," said Dolores. It came through the receiver like *Oooo, yes!* "I talked with Arabelle at the Come-Back Inn. She told me Corie's feelings for you. She told me the feelings she saw you had for Corie Jones. She told me how broken up he was to be kicked out of your house—and she's been patching him together ever since, and she knows it's you in bed between them still—she knows. You ruined Corie Jones—but everybody loved the high and mighty Reverend Orpheus, Minister of God, the Goodness of the Inner City, takes boys in and gives them beds. Oooo, yes! You could have had the decency to tell me—"

"Dolores, Dolores, what could I tell you? It isn't true!" This bubbled up like a bile in him, sour in his mouth. He didn't think, or else he would have said nothing. "I love Corie, but—"

"Said so! Said so you loved him, and didn't I hear you say so,—when you wouldn't love me?"

"—but not in *that* way. I've never, I have never been to bed with any—"

"I was so stupid!" she whined in the receiver. " 'Corie!' you said when you fainted on the sidewalk, but did I think anything of that? No. 'Corie,' you said, 'Come home, come home,' you said, like a lover, but I didn't see it—"

"But I *did* love him—"

"I've got no problems with homosexuals," she kept driving her anger into him. "I've got terrible problems with liars, hiding behind your Jesus, looking down on us so proud, so scornful, sneering—"

"I do not look down on you! You are more good and more beautiful than I could—"

"Shit!" she said, horrifying him. *This* is what he'd done

to her? Immediately he clapped his hand over his mouth, to silence himself, to argue no more. She was right. She was perfectly righteous in her judgment, because his sin was his whole being: he could not look at himself except he saw a human thoroughly iniquitous. Then shut up! She could accuse him of nothing so sinful as he truly was; therefore, all her accusations were accurate. He embraced all sin. He writhed physically while he held the telephone: he *was* sin, and despised himself for it.

"Shit!" she said, "and now you're going to tell me that you didn't dig a ditch and throw my flower into it—the same as throwing me into it; did you think I'm *that* stupid, not to understand? Shit!"

He didn't answer. She was right because she was righteous. Righteousness is greater than rightness. He bowed his head before the judgment and said nothing.

Her words began to slide to street-speech. "So what you got to say for yourself, Reverent?"

Nothing. He said nothing.

"Tell it to me," she said, "Tell me straight. Say you ain' gay, an' maybe I'll b'lieve you—Reverent."

He kept the phone to his ear, but he said nothing. He did not deny it.

Her voice changed once more, for the first time sounding like the deep-fleshed Dolores whom he knew. It took a tone of pleading: "Pastor, *are* you gay? Won't you answer me?" *Just tell me. Tell me. I will believe you. I will love you again.*

He didn't. To argue this judgment seemed to imply arguing any judgment brought against himself, and he didn't have that right. Not any more. Not any more. He despised liars no less than she did. He would lie no more.

He said quietly, in a true voice and not a whisper, as

though some miracle had loosened his tongue and given him speech again: "I love you, Dolores. I love you."

She fairly shrieked, "Go to hell!" and rang off.

And this is what his soul said. His soul said, *I am.*

In a formal meeting of the elders and the entire church council, scheduled for the Saturday before the Pentecost and held before all interested members of the congregation, Reverend Orpheus was given the opportunity to defend himself against the allegations which certain members of his parish had brought publicly against him. They met in the basement of the church, the "fellowship room." There was a strange man among the company, an Authority of the Greater Church, who had come to arbitrate the difficult and heated exchange which everyone expected. He came to arbitrate; he stayed to validate—for it was remarkable to the whole community how quietly Reverend Orpheus sat before his accusers. He denied nothing. They had not realized, until now, when he denied nothing, how base the man had been. They were astonished that he could have carried a hypocrisy on so long, fooling so many people, until the truth was laid before him and he hadn't a word to say, denying nothing.

The meeting consisted chiefly of three parts: the formal placement of the charges; the confession of the accused; the immediate suspension of the guilty man's powers, his rights, and his ministry. This is what the Authority of the Greater Church validated.

And this was the death of Reverend Orpheus, who, except he were a minister of Jesus, was nothing.

Orpheus came to the meeting wearing polished shoes and a vested suit which he'd had dry-cleaned for the occasion. It hung loosely on his hungry frame. He sat in silence.

Mr. Arthur Williams presided, his stomach bulking with authority. He had learned the word "malfeasance" and used it often. He struggled *not* to use the word "gay" nor the word "homo" but the word "homo-sex-yule" completely and with dignity. He'd been unable to persuade Coral Jones to attend, but he could understand that a young lad (who had, in the end, proven his masculinity upon as pretty a woman as Arabelle Lee) would not want his reputation smeared, and he excused him. Yet he referred often to the danger Coral Jones had been in while he lived with Reverend Orpheus: the boy could have been ruined for the rest of his life—and he a member of this Christian congregation.

One thing of Coral's which Mr. Arthur Williams had been able to bring, however, and which turned out to hold a great significance for the Authority of the Greater Church, was a memory of something that Reverend Orpheus once had said. The Reverend once said that after Jesus Christ was crucified he had not risen again, but stayed dead. Mr. Arthur Williams mentioned this but casually, unaware of the fire-power it contained. But when the Authority of the Greater Church suddenly stiffened with keen attention, Mr. Arthur Williams repeated it several times over. He learned a new word, then, one that sounded as vicious and effective as a rapier: "Heresy!"—and he complimented himself privately on having done his homework.

So the accusations against Reverend Orpheus multiplied.

Arthur Williams said, "A Miss Dolores Johnson, who was baptized in this Christian congregation and raised here and who was taught her Sunday school lessons here—I taught her myself, as best I could, you understand—says that Reverend Orpheus said that Mrs. Allouise Story is in hell." He sighed a little for such a long sentence, then looked at the Authority of the Greater Church. He said, "No minister should ever say such a thing about a good member—should he?"

The Authority looked to Orpheus for a response. When it did not come, as none had come to this point, he said, "Well, Orpheus, what do you have to say for yourself?"

Orpheus, his face sagging and blank, said, "Yes, I said that."

The Authority could only shake his head.

Many of the people could only just shake their heads. They felt very embarrassed to have been deceived so very long—embarrassed actually to have *loved* this man so deeply. Mr. Arthur Williams felt that he was leading the meeting very well. He'd had a little stage fright at first, but now he knew that that was silly. With God's help he was doing a fine job. His hands locked comfortably on his stomach.

Let it be known that many people were crying in their souls. And that some of their tears appeared in their eyes. The love of these was no imposture; they had not been hurt by Orpheus, nor had they taken any personal pride in the good days of his ministry, but had merely been blessed by him. These gazed at their Pastor, pleading him to say something, to argue something on his behalf—for their own sakes, or else their hearts would break. If he had only said, *I'm innocent,* these would have stood up in a body, aligned themselves with him—upon his word alone—and split the church in two: so great was their commitment to a man who, they believed dearly, had made so great a sacrifice for them. They yearned, they trembled to hear the words. But they were beaten silent when they heard, finally, what he did say.

Orpheus was given a chance to speak. Sitting still, his head slightly inclined to the left, looking at no one at all, he spoke. Partway through his speaking several people began to sob, two women and a man, and no one came to comfort them; everyone was too personally involved in the moment. The Authority of the Greater Church was rendered uncomfortable in the extreme.

"When I was still a boy," said Orpheus in a soft, smooth voice; he didn't whisper any more. His throat had healed. "When I was still very young, and when I cried, I knew what to do with my tears. I did it, and God blessed me for it; Jesus looked on me and loved me for it. This is what I did: I gave my tears to Jesus. And this is what he did: he took them. That was my sacrifice, when I was just a child.

"Well, I'm grown old, now. And I will not cry. Not today, not any more, because Jesus will not take my tears any more and they would only run like acid down my cheek. I will not cry.

"Jesus cannot take my tears.

"Jesus would not even know that I was crying.

"Because," he said so softly that they leaned forward to hear, "I am so much worse than what you say I am—"

There arose a universal gasp. The sobbing began now and did not cease.

"I am more sinful than you know," said Orpheus. He took a breath. "Arthur—" Mr. Arthur Williams snapped his head up, shocked to be named. He didn't want to be named now; he shot glances toward the congregation. But Orpheus, with a sort of shivering restraint, continued. "Arthur, you were wrong to save my life. It wasn't worth the saving. I've suffered too long what you did for me, too long, too long. Oh, but I don't blame you, Arthur. You didn't know. You're a kind man, and now you're making up for the mistake. This is right. What you are doing now is right."

Arthur Williams murmured, "No one's saying you didn't build the church up—"

A man covered his face to cry. Two women let their tears run openly. Those who loved the most were the most betrayed, and Orpheus shuddered to hear them. *This is what I do, now. This is who I am—*

Aloud he said, "I hurt people."

Then he said *Yes* five times over: "Yes, yes. Yes, yes, yes, I hurt Corie terribly, and Allouise and Arabelle and John Sutpen and Arthur Williams—and Dolores Johnson. Who shouldn't I name? Everyone." He sighed deeply, wretchedly. He seemed small in the oversized suit. "I've imperiled this people and their faith. I have," he lowered his voice nearly to nothing, to a ghostly breathing: "I have denied the Christ before them and in them. I am not worthy to be called by his name. I am not worthy of one of you. I am not worthy to be loved or to love. I am not worthy—to live." His voice was dying away: "I am not worthy to be called a child of God. I am not worthy. . . ."

He stopped. He simply stopped. Dead silence filled the room, except that three people wept softly. Who knew what should follow this confession?

Finally, Orpheus raised his hands as though in a blessing and exclaimed from the fullness of his heart, "Thank you, people; thank you for hearing me. Good people, kind people—thank you." He dropped his hands to his knees and bowed his head. He was done.

So then: the third part of the meeting came with merciful speed for the defeated man. In five minutes the process was begun for stripping him of his office and ministry. Mr. Arthur Williams called for a motion and received it. The parish approved it with a vote voiced in misery. The Authority of the Greater Church validated it. And so. And so. Orpheus would not appeal. And so.

People arose, then, in various attitudes, some rushing

out, some shuffling solemnly away in narrow file, some standing uncertainly at first as though something should still be
said, some sitting rather longer than others—but none of
the people, none of them, spoke. None.

Orpheus kept his head bowed in order to relieve them
of the pain of looking on him and wondering what to say.
He was the corpse in the coffin, and the wake was over.

Then there was only one presence in the room, one
watcher left. Orpheus lifted his eyes: Dolores Johnson. She
had been one of the inconsolable, one of the women weeping throughout his confession, and he hadn't known it till
this moment. She was gazing at him, weeping still—and he
loved her. He loved this poor, sad woman with all his heart.

She began to shake her head back and forth, back and
forth. "It was only a gift for you," she whispered. "It was the
best thing I could think of to give. I had nothing else to
bring. But it was harmless, it was harmless. Why did you
have to bury it?"

Coal-black hair, a rich and burning flesh, a heart as innocent as her lily, though she did not know that: Dolores.
Orpheus looked at her and saw that she was utterly beautiful. She didn't deserve to bear his guilt, the guilt of him;
but he knew no way to take it away from her again. How
could she understand it if he should say, *All this is right,
and I despise myself?*

He said nothing. She turned and left.

Reverend Orpheus, severed from that which was life for
him, was dead.

He did not cry.

◇     ◇     ◇

I truly honor the little monk St. John of the Cross, even
as I do that more bemisted figure whom I cannot see but

who teaches me, the author of *The Cloud of Unknowing*. These are mentors to me, together with others of the long mystic tradition. It moves me, how peacefully they name and recount the most relentless torments, assuring me that the darknesses are of the Light and that the anxieties are of God. They dwell in paradox with a dancer's ease and lightly. They make the moves of faith which Kierkegaard described as a balletic leap so perfect that, on landing, the dancer seems never to have leapt at all, but perpetually to be standing still.

John of the Cross says,

And this is the characteristic of the spirit that is purged and annihilated with respect to all particular affections and objects of the understanding, that in this state wherein it has pleasure in nothing in particular, but dwells in its emptiness, darkness and obscurity, it is fully prepared to embrace everything to the end that those words of Saint Paul may be fulfilled in it: *Nihil habentes, et omnia possidentes.* For such poverty of spirit as this would deserve such happiness.*

And in the next chapter:

This darkness should continue for as long as is needful in order to expel and annihilate the habit which the soul has long since formed in its manner of understanding, and the Divine light and illumination will then take its place. And thus, inasmuch as that power of understanding which it had aforetime is natural, it follows that the darkness which it here suffers is profound and horrible and most painful, for this darkness, being felt in the deepest substance of the spirit, seems to be substantial darkness.

It is one's very nature being purged, says John of the Cross. When the nature, the habitual and characteristic core of

---

*Dark Night of the Soul*, Book 2, Chapters 13, 14 (New York: Doubleday Image Books, 1959).

one's being, is taken away, this can feel no less than a death. This is no surgery nor amputation, the cutting of a piece from the whole, leaving behind something of the whole to suffer the loss. No, this is the annihilation of the center, so that *all* the pieces fly away, nameless, mute, and senseless: scattered. Nothing is left *but* the emptiness. This is death.

Nevertheless, it is a dying at the hand of God, whose hand even now remains a *creating* hand. It is not without its merciful purpose (though the dying is precisely the blindness both to God and to his purposes: in darkness). Therefore, St. John says of the soul:

> In this way, being empty, it is able indeed to be poor in spirit and freed from the old man, in order to live that new and blessed life which is attained by means of this night, and which is the state of union with God.

The old man dead: the new man born. This "old man" is not a homunculus within one, but is oneself. Thus, death. But the new man's springing forth is not merely prepared for by the dying of the old; rather, its birthing *is* the dying of the old; they are one thing, one event, one horrible and merciful occurrence. Thus: union with God.

In the fourth passage, the faither's true nature was brought to surface, even into the awareness of the faither himself, so that in the fifth passage it could be killed—so that in the sixth passage another might be made alive again— But we get ahead of ourselves.

I say, I honor the mystic who made me to understand the holiness and the goodness of this most fundamentally personal suffering, the infinite gain in the absolute loss of self. By him I accept (I do not say I understand; it is beyond reasonable understanding; I stand in awe of, I see as true and trust, I accept) this divine irony: that only when finally

I have nothing do I possess anything, may I possess all things; that "having nothing" means, in its extreme, not even having the self to act as owner or possessor, and makes *impossible*, then, the possession of anything, for I am not there to say, "It's mine"; but that Jesus *may*, then, dwell in me, in *my* name saying, "All is mine, all is thine," and I say, without saying it, "Then all is mine as well." That irony. I accept that irony. I accept completely that this is the single foil to the Devil, who showed me all the kingdoms of the world and the glory thereof, promising to give it all to me if I would only bow down and worship him. He promised to make much of my "self." But the foil is that my "self" dies, has nothing, deserves just nothing, wants and asks for nothing—in order that the King of Creation, the Beautiful Savior, may abide in the empty tent of my being, bringing all creation with him.

I say, I honor him who presented to me such a wonder.

And yet—I maintain a gentle, loving quarrel with him as well.

For John of the Cross would abstract this dear, deadly process from the stuff and tumble of physical human existence. His sense of experience is spiritual purely, as though it took place in a monk's cell only, apart from the marketplace—nay, in a monk's skull, in his spirit, apart from his daily, bodily routine; and the reduction of that routine, and the persistent diminution of attention to the physical world and the physical body both, *releases* the spirit for a freer experience of the fires of the love of God. John of the Cross does not say these things directly; but he, by virtue of his context and the tone of his discourse, seems to take them for granted.

I would argue, rather, that the spirit and the body are divisible only because they are two methods for beholding one singular substance. There is but one person. Yet obsevors of that one person may see as many people as they have eyes for the seeing: a physician sees a broken arm, while a mother sees a broken heart; they recognize two sources for the child's tears, and if they work in concert, they shall together dry those tears, healing arm and heart together—yet it was but one child all along. Likewise, the life of the spirit *is* the life of the body. Or, to say all this another way: God leads the faither unto himself not in a manner divorced from daily and worldly experiences—in the secret regions of his soul only—but *by means of* the stuff and tumble of physical human existence. It is not a secret piercing of the heart that kills the faithing one, invisible to the eyes of other people. No, it is by the actions of those people themselves; it is in the very intercourse of community and words and feelings, bruisings, touchings, the casual greetings and the catastrophic attackings; it is in the downsitting and the uprising that God shapes the drama which kills the sinner. The spiritual drama of faith is enacted on the stage of this world, bodily and under sunlight. Faithing occurs in the experience of the whole human—the human whole; and though we may outline a general pattern to the drama, naming for it six passages, it is always performed in particularity, with loving attention to each individual actor.

For these two reasons (that no element of the faithing one is incidental to the holy process, but all elements combine to make his being, all elements being material in the hands of God; and that each one's experience, though collectively named, is peculiar unto each)—for this reason, that faithing is "real" in every sense of that word—I have traced the drama of one person; I have persistently set before you a Reverend Orpheus in flesh and blood, that you might touch the thing and know that it *is* touchable. In him, perhaps, you may see that spirit and body are of a piece, that the worldly battering of the body *is* the Holy Spirit's handlement of the soul, that the one merely wants the interpretation of the other.

Death shall come, dear God! The righteous execution of the sinner shall, by the gracious will of God, occur—and it shall most certainly have spiritual consequence; indeed, it is the spiritual interpretation of the event which names it a "death" at all. But it happens in the world and evidently. It takes place visibly before the eyes (and by the actions) of those who truly see but do not understand what they are seeing. That they do not understand does not mean that they do not see. No, it is not hidden from them. It is an error to think that the process of faithing transcends the stuff of the world, and therefore to seek God only in the heavenly places. What is hidden is the meaning, not the sign itself. In Jesus's day, many people saw the signs, but misinterpreted. And those who picked St. Paul from the road, in order to lead him to Damascus, knew that something happened, though they couldn't explain it. And when the Father spoke to Jesus, the dull-eared *did* hear; they said, "It thundered."

Well, the dear John of the Cross so occupies himself with interpretations that he ignores the signs, the physical instruments of God, the mental, emotional, social, economic, and bodily *causes* of spiritual consequences; and as a result, many suppose that the process of faith is divorced from the stomach's growling and fleshly experience, that it is itself the divorcement.

Death shall come. In what arena shall it occur? In the world's arena. By whose hand shall you be put to death? By the world's hand—though God shall turn that evil thing to good. And why will the world kill you? Because you loved

Jesus more than you loved it: it hated you. You severed yourself from its values. By not loving it, you became a curse upon all it loved—that is, upon itself, since it loved itself. And you loved Jesus in a way it could not tolerate: you loved him despairingly.

Had you loved him happily, the world might at least have been glad of your happiness, calling you silly, perhaps, but recognizing value in happiness for its own sake. But your persistent, undecipherable, isolating, and cursed despair is intolerable to its own merry romp to happiness, and it will preserve itself by killing you.

What, exactly, shall that killing be? It shall be the stripping from you of any worthy identity *in* the world. It will annul you in its own sight. It will punish you by ostracism. It simply will not recognize your rights of existence within its sphere any longer, so that it need not be unsettled by your presence. It will hate you out loud or silently—but you will feel the hatred. You will be made to know your *self* by the isolation and by the pain inflicted; and then that *self,* in the world's eyes, simply will not be. This may be perfidious. This surely shall be crucifixion. But (and here is how you shall be assured that it *is* a death) you shall bow your head and say, "It is right. I deserve no more than this." For in the knowledge of that *self* you saw nothing good. This is how you shall be assured that it is a death: you shall no longer defend yourself nor fight to be. Self-defense—even taking offense—still clings to self and to being. But you won't even hate the world that hates you. Oh, this is the loneliest, most abasing word, this word of your own annihilation: you will say to the world's execution, "Yes." And then there shall be no more of you, for you shall have lain down and died:

By the world (that which does not know the Spirit of God).

In the world (that which is the experience of this daily life, all that is the creation of God).

From the world (and you shall not expect so much as another rising of the sun or a tomorrow).

And yet, even now, do we love Jesus?

O dear people, made holy in these unspeakable trials, how can I tell you this remarkable thing? Yes! We still love Jesus. But now that phrase is a pale and spectral representation of the truth. We do nothing *but* love Jesus; it is all we can do. Moreover, the love has become substantive in us: it isn't so much what we do as what we *are*. Finally, when all else has been burned away and when the very self has fallen into dust and nothingness, doing and being have become the same. If any should touch us now, they touch the love of Jesus. And should we put forward, now, our hands—which are not our hands but Jesus' hands—and touch another, why, it is the love of Jesus that touches that other. There is no identity left unto us but this: that we love Jesus. There is no life in those who are individually dead but this: that they love Jesus.

It is at this point that the words of St. Paul tremble on the very edge of expression, though we cannot yet express them. It is now that the experience which he declares has become our experience, though we cannot yet declare it— but it is *experience* and no longer the inscrutable catachetic of our youth, *experience* and no longer the scriptural foundations of doctrine, *experience*, our own Way, our vital Truth, and, since we are otherwise dead, our very Life, no longer the metaphoric expostulations of a holy man. This, though we cannot yet speak it, speaks for us; this, in the first person singular:

I have been crucified with Christ; it is no longer I who live, but Christ who lives in me; and the life I now live in the flesh I live by faith in the Son of God, who loved me and gave himself for me.

This is not parabolic language. It is not a symbolic utterance. Nor is it an effort to reproduce in the visible world invisible things. It is the plain report of a historical experience. It happened. Paul shared in the sufferings of Jesus, "followed him." Paul became like him in his death. And so, at the end of the fifth passage, we.

But there yet remains this difference between Paul and us: he is able to express the experience; previous to the sixth passage, we are not. And this is because it is not yet objectified for us, nor a memory. It is the single fact of our beings; we are still submerged, still drowned in the experience. We are still slumped on the cross. We cannot *know* it, but can merely *be* it. It is a terrible, terribly sweet time: we are dead. Blissful death! "With the baptism with which I am to be baptized, you will be baptized—"

Do we still love Jesus?

Oh, we love him so much right now that there is not another shred to our existences besides that love, nothing in us separated from that love, no, not so much as the wit or a nerve to *know* that we love him. *We love him without knowing it!*

But that hardly matters any more. Truth need not be known to be the truth. (How arrogant, ever to think we make truth true by knowing it!) And we who participate in the truth need not know our own participation, truly to participate. Indeed, the highest form of love is not compromised by the personal reward of knowing that it loves. The highest form is ignorant of itself.

No, it hardly matters whether we realize our love or who we are. In other words; it hardly matters whether we rise again. The passages might rightly end with the fifth, consummated in our deaths and in the purified love of Jesus: "It is finished!" Indeed. It is enough and more than enough.

But see the great love wherewith the Father has loved us!—that now he showers upon us blessings not only beyond our deserving, but also beyond our imagining. For as Paul came to know and so to express the wonder of the working of the Lord, so we too are raised again, *both* to experience *and* to understand the complete unqualified loving of Jesus. And since these two—to be the subject of an experience which is at the same time the object of our knowing, at once to be the actor within and the viewer without—are contraries incapable of occurring in the same singular being, but since they nevertheless *do* occur within and for us, this is a miracle. Resurrection is a miracle of God. The sixth passage doesn't have to be. That it is, is an astonishing grace.

#  The Sixth Passage: "I Have Called You by Name"—Resurrection

*This is what the ancients say:*

*At the death of Orpheus, the whole world mourned, and mourning was all that it could know. The birds rose up wailing, calling, crying, lamenting for Orpheus; and when they perched they puffed their feathers in a miserable effort to be warm, because the world went cold without Orpheus. The trees—all of the trees, and not one forest only—the trees, like widows that tear their hair, sheared the leaves from their branches and flung them to the winds, and the north wind whirled them high into a leaden sky. The world was bitterly cold. The rocks lay down in a dreadful, eternal vigil, mourning. And the rivers swelled with their own tears; the rivers wept such floods that they broke their banks to run unstable across the land—like mothers who stumble, in their grief, around the fields, looking for their children. Then one river—her name was Hebrus—found Orpheus's head and lyre lying side by side. She caught these up in loving waters and carried them away, two sad mementoes of the man.*

*And this is what the ancients say:*

*As that lyre floated down the Hebrus, it made a melting, mournful music. More marvelous still: as the head went nodding in the waters, its waxen tongue moved too and murmured mournfully, "Eurydice."*

*And the banks of the river replied:* Eurydice.

To sea: then out to the mothering sea the head and the lyre of Orpheus were carried. They rode her rolling bosom till there was no land, no green nor stable thing around them any more, only the father sky to see them and the mother sea's embrace. And then, in that region of the round infinities, gently, tenderly, she opened up her womb and received them down inside herself, the lyre and the silent head of Orpheus, like seeds.

No, the world knew nothing but mourning then. And the world was cold.

But this, too, is what the ancients say:

The shade of Orpheus himself was sucked below the earth, as all the mortals at their ends are sucked, into the Kingdom of the Dead.

But behold: he was no longer an alien in this place, but a citizen. It was his place, shapen for him because he came this time unburdened by breath or body—dead! He had come home. Moreover, he came with this graceful advantage, that he had been here before: he had no fear of the familiar.

No, it was a breathless joy that filled him. No, he was himself the thing called Joy. In joy per arva piorum—excited, Orpheus rushed through the blessed fields in search of his Eurydice.

And he found her. She found him.

Eurydice came to Orpheus limping still from the bite of the serpent; and Orpheus ran as a mass of wounds; but they laughed. They laughed at the vision they must have made, scarred by the sorrows of the upper world, limping, hobbling, coming together. They laughed, and they fell on one another's shoulders, and they embraced each other in their arms, and only the embrace, then, silenced the joy of their laughter. They bowed their heads and loved each other.

*Finally, this is what the ancients say:*

*Together, like with like in a realm like them, Orpheus and his Eurydice go walking now. Sometimes he follows her while she precedes.* Mirum! *His eyes on her, he sees her lead. He knows she knows the way. He is content to follow. But sometimes, now, he goes before her—and this is the gift whose sweetness he could not know except that once it was denied him: he may look back. Whenever the yearning takes him, he may look back on her in safety, look back and see, and see forever, the face of his beloved, smiling, seeing, and loving him in return. They make a circle, these two. The circle is eternal.*

*Or so the ancients say.*

◊ ◊ ◊

We are Peter. Here, where the fifth and the sixth passages meet in a single event (it is one event, but it ends one thing and begins another; therefore it *looks* different in the approach than in the departure) we are still Peter, meeting Jesus on a beach.

These were the preliminaries: that Jesus had answered Peter's bold oath "I'll die for you" by saying, "No, but you will deny me three times." And then Peter had, in fact, manifested the essential iniquity of his being by denying him three times; and Jesus had nailed Peter with the consequences of that denial by a look, by the glance at Peter in which poor Peter recognized his sin.

Then Jesus rose from his death (his resurrection, of course, must precede ours—but *we do not fully know nor enjoy his resurrection except in ours!*) and met Peter on the beach. There, it was the love of the Lord that killed him (as it kills us). And it was the love of the Lord that raised him up again (as it raises us). And both consequences he accomplished with a single touch, a single, twice-potent dialogue.

At breakfast Jesus recalled the threeness of Peter's denial by wringing a threeness of protested love for himself. Three and three: thrice cancel the Lord, thrice commit thy ways to him. In the Gospel of John, three does not appear so commonly as to make this repetition insignificant; and though the words that Peter then declared seem good and binding ("Yes, Lord, you know that I love you"), they remembered, in the very speaking, words that had been murderous and divorcing. It was *two* confessions that Peter was making at once, though he didn't realize that when he began to answer—a confession of sin and a confession of faith. But take the first one first:

Jesus was forcing Peter to perform a crucial discipline: a confession; a painful *metanoia* or turning away from the sin that had been himself; a denial, now, of the Peter that was, a denial fully as effective as the denial that had abolished Jesus from his life; an abolition of Peter; a death. He died. And therefore the Scriptures say of Peter that he *elypēthē, "was grieved* because he said to him a third time, 'Do you love me?'" *Lypē* marks a terrible suffering of the soul. It is both more intense and more salutary than the *lypē tou kosmou,* the sorrow of this world. In Peter it was *kata theon lypē,* a grieving on account of God. God did it. Jesus questioned Peter, and old Peter was made to feel the sorrow, and by the sorrow to know his utter lostness, his own particular hell, and by that knowledge finally to appeal to Jesus for redemption—which appeal was, finally, the anguish and the reality of his third (no longer proud) protesting, "Lord, you know everything; you know that I love you." Thus did he cry out his love. But he also whined it, seeking, pleading. That is, he could be nothing but his love; but at the same

time he believed his love to be dependent upon the knowledge of Jesus; the proof of the love in Peter was the knowing
in Jesus: "You know everything." Peter was nothing on his
own: it was a confession marvelous in its humility. The man
alone was sweetly, dearly dead. He could not be, except that
Jesus was.

But though he was dead, he was also coming to life again!
This, in the same singular event and by the same dialogue
with the same Lord.

Mark the words above, "made to feel . . . to know . . .
to appeal." They are the passive turning active. One who
may feel, and know that he is feeling, and act upon his
knowledge, also *is*. And note: the grief that was his killing
was likewise the stimulous of his waking.

Love is a cruel fire to consume the unlovely that the
lovely might step forth. God is this love. And what is the
burning but *kata theon lypē?*

Those are St. Paul's words, "a godly grief." He used them
when he wrote to the Corinthians, exalting in their sorrow,
accepting cheerfully the paradox that the same thing may
both kill and quicken:

For even if I made you sorry with my letter, I do not regret it
(though I did regret it), for I see that that letter grieved you,
though only for a while. As it is, I rejoice, not because you were
grieved, but because you were grieved into repenting; for you felt
a godly grief *[kata theon lypē],* so that you suffered no loss
through us. For godly grief produces repentance that leads to salvation and brings no regret, but worldly grief *[lypē tou kosmou]*
produces death.

"Peter, do you, do you, do you love me?" What a gentle
execution! It looks backward to the sin only in allusion
(though Peter's memory, his conscience, makes it real
enough to grieve him). On the other hand, it looks forward

in concrete detail, in commands, and in the trust that these commands shall be carried out—it looks forward in specific realities to new life in discipleship: "Then feed my lambs," "Oh, tend my sheep," "and feed my sheep." It more than gives Peter something to do again, it gives him a position significant in the kingdom of God and in the coming of that kingdom. More than that—yea, even more—it gives Peter an *identity,* a reason to be, a thing to be, a double-bounden relationship between the shepherd and his sheep, the king and his citizens: it gives him himself. *Peter is, again!* This is more than rehabilitation. This is resurrection.

Is it any wonder (oh, yes, it is a wonder!) that Jesus should, as a pure, unboughten, undeserved, and unexpected gift, repeat the invitation with which he initiated the long relationship between himself and Peter, should repeat it now with a fullness of meaning (meaning bled from hard and desolating, sanctifying experience) "Follow me"? It is what Jesus says. He says, "We do continue: it is not lost." At the same time, he says, "We begin anew, perfectly new, as though none of this had happened." Yet he says, "We begin aright and perfectly righteous *because* all this has happened." What does he say at the end of the Gospel, which he said at the beginning?

He says, "Follow me."

*Mirum!* There was a fifth level of meaning to the invitation all along: to life!

Who can conceive of the love of Jesus, that it is not the mildy good whom finally he calls, but the abject and the dead? But resurrection never could be for the living. It is nothing for the living. It is only for the dead. Yet for the dead, it is everything.

And we are Peter: dead, so dead that we haven't even

the existence wherefrom to repudiate our sinful natures: the whole of us died in the dying. "You will look for me tomorrow, and I shall not be."

Even so. But God created out of nothing. And into the lifeless dust he blew his breath, and into the mindless disciples he blew his spirit. It was precisely death and the dustiness that freed us to be the handiwork of God again.

As creator, the Spirit of Jesus descends to us. Perhaps as *re*creator. "When thou hidest thy face, all things are dismayed; when thou takest away their breath, they die and return to their dust. When thou sendest forth thy Spirit, they are created; and thou renewest the face of the ground." And the inbreathing is this, that the only question asked is "Do you love me?" And the only word that can answer—since it is the only word given into our empty beings by the Spirit—is "Love." Or, in a verb: "I love." Or, in a verb that lodges in its object, finding reality there, and so existence: "I love you." *Oh, dear Jesus, how I love you!* It is a spontaneous, unaffected reaction. It is no lie, for there was no alternative thing to say, no other choice. It is all that we had. Nay, it is all that we *were.* We are responding to the question with our very beings. Our beings found expression at the urging of the question. When we answered, by the grace of God, we came to be, for this is us: that we love Jesus.

Do you love me?

Our hearts pump blood with a high and pounding rhythm. But that blood *is* the love of Jesus. It bears no other life than that. He is the life.

Do you love me?

Our minds think thoughts in a delighted, whirling rush, as though the thoughts were flocks of birds circling in the air. But all of the thoughts are one thought, a yearning Jesusward, the infinite ways in which the mind can say, "I love you." Jesus is the way and all ways of the mind.

Do you love me?

Oh, Lord, you know all things. Truth *is* your knowing. You know that I love you!

Our beings consist in this, that we love him. But our loving depends upon his knowledge of it; and the expression of our love / beings depends upon his kindly asking the question of us, whether we do. He gives us to say so. Hear, then, the specific gift which is our resurrection: it is that we are given *to know* that we love Jesus. He asks. But then he allows *us* to answer. When we answer, we hear the truth in our own mouths. It is the Spirit in our mouths, for we could not have done this thing; yet it is our own mouths. We hear ourselves to speak. We hear ourselves: We are, and we know that we are. The truth dwells in us. But the truth expressed reveals its dwelling-place as well.

Do you see? Jesus doesn't ask us in order that he might know—but in order that we might discover that *we* know. Jesus never tested our faith for his own sake, but for ours, to show us what *we* are.

Thus, our resurrection is by a dialogue, a questioning and an answering. And that is right, for faithing ever was relationship: in relationship we do rise again. And language has returned to its holiest and primal function—in the mouth of God to create. Or perhaps to *re*create.

The truth is in us; there we hear it. But this is because we have always been within the Truth, like the chrysalis being shaped unto our birth. There is no tighter relationship, than that each entwines within the other, causing one another being. Jesus is the Truth. "In that day you will know that I am in my Father, and you in me, and I in you." Such a statement is the interpenetrating conundrum of being. Holy being. The sinner's existence was a solitude. But the existence of the resurrected being is symbiotic, one life in two. This infant is not lifted into being until it has touched another being, realizing at once the face it touched and the fingers with which it touched. For us, that face is Jesus, smiling, permitting our baby pats on his most lovely eyes. For us, the fingers are our love, tingling with life *only* in the touching. But did anyone notice, first, his hand upon our wrist? That he it was who drew our fingers to his face and taught us how to touch?

Do you love me? Child, do you love me? Baby, baby, do you love me?

Ah!

Come. Follow me.

Ah.

Now we know it well enough to say it: we know it by the experience.

There was no other way for Orpheus to come to Eurydice, to love her wholly and wholly to be possessed by the love of her, than that he die and be like her. All things between her death and his were necessary, truly. He did not mistake. Merely, all these things conspired to kill him rightly.

Likewise, our coming unto Jesus is not the escape of death nor a saving, either of him or of ourselves, from death. Not the coming; not the process, the drama. It is dying itself. And though, between our sense of his crucifixion and our experience of our own, there seemed to be a pitiful number of false steps and folly, yet it was all embraced by faithing, and in that sense it was right. No, not that we were righteous, but rather that righteousness was served by all of it, even by our pride and the manifestation of our sinfulness.

In this broken world, given the characters we bring unto the drama, it had to be. We go through death to meet our Jesus, wholly to love him, wholly to be possessed by the love of him.

But here the myth that instructed us so well, and the reality that we well discover in the Lord, part company.

For in the end the death-states of Orpheus and Eurydice linger. They remain shades in a shadow land. They remain projections of the human imagination. Within their story, they end dead. Within the world they persist as symbols only.

We, on the other hand, though we are a story, a wondrous history, are no one's imagination, but the creatures of a Creator. He is the teller of this tale, telling it not in the spheres of imagination, but in this world, in space and time, in fact. We do experience his telling it. We end alive, beginning.

The love at the end of the myth is the expression of human yearning, desiring dearly that it should be, but despairing of its being.

The love of the sixth passage of faithing, however, *is*. What the Greeks but dreamed of, God doth give. Not as shades, but flesh and blood we experience the resurrection (*both* here and again hereafter). They were wise in their empty utterances, the Greeks. And we may be fools beside them, hardly able to utter a word well made. But God fills the utterance with his reality. God validates all chattered words with his own Word, which from the beginning was the substance of all creation. He makes it historically to be. No, we do not follow cleverly devised myths when we make known to you the power and coming of our Lord Jesus Christ, but we are eyewitnesses of his majesty and love. We, the dying, die into life. We shall live. We shall most certainly live—which is love. These are the same. For then the Resurrection and the Life, the Lord himself, is all in all for us.

We rise again, dear people, with identities of angels, whose contemplation and whose service is ever upon the lamb.

The mouth of the Lord hath spoken it.

Now these two wonders fall together: that we discover the rising of the Lord in our own; but that our rising consists in this, that he calls us by name, making us by making us his. Finally, this is the third function of language, by God accomplished.

Sweet, sorrowful and laughing Mary Magdalene, talk to me. Tell me: what was it like to rise again, and to be?

All in a single word he called you from the occlusions and the pit. By one word only he called you into life and light and clapped you with identity. Tell me, tell me: what is such a borning like?

Lady, I know the sorrow that precedes it. I, too, have been bereaved of my beloved, and I have seen his pale form harden to a corpse. And when I sought on a Sunday morning the little consolation of serving him still, I found I could not find so much as that. I, too, was denied the ministrations and was left hopeless, helpless, useless at an empty tomb, nothing to do, nothing to give any more. For you this impotence came because the body was gone and you knew not where it lay. For me the impotence came because the signs were gone and all the world was a hollow tomb, signifying nothing. First his death, then death itself surrounded us, and then we died.

I know the sorrow that preceded it, how that it made mute fools of us. You and I, we cried so hard that our tears blinded us to the abiding truth. We went wailing questions—

"Where is he? Where is he?"—morbid questions, since they asked not where he lived, but where was the place of his death: "Where is he?" neither hearing nor seeing answers, yea, though the angels surrounded us, because grief was the only thing that we could know then, and tears filled the whole round world like an ocean, though the tears were only in our seeing. O Mary, I know the slender bend of your sorrow and the whiteness of your knuckles and the writhing of your forehead—

—and the irony, too, that the absence of his body, our deeper death, was his springing into life again, one thing and the same thing.

Woman, I know the sorrow. Oh, tell me of the joy.

When that vision of a man came toward you through the garden, had you no notion what was about to be? Did nothing shiver in you? No, I suppose not. Poor Mary! You thought him the likely and worldly figure, a gardener. Or when that man asked you two questions (always, always asking questions, wasn't he, which demanded the personal answer and so relationship! To another Mary: "Do you believe this?" To Peter: "Do you love me?") did no alarm go off in your system, a twitch of the nerve, a recognition? Didn't you hear that the first of his questions was the same as the angels': "Why are you crying?" Ah, but you didn't know that they were angels and messengers of heaven, because you *were* crying. Nor, poor Mary, could you know that the second of his questions was nearly the same as the first he ever asked the disciples, the initiating question by which relationship began: "What are you seeking? Whom are you seeking?" In this way he had inaugurated his whole work of salvation among the people, Mary, opening doors to discipleship. In this way too he prepared time and space and you for your own resurrection. Didn't you know? Didn't you catch your breath at the holy familiar? Didn't you feel the enormity of the next event about to break for you? Oh, Mary, it makes me giddy to think how close in your darkness you stood to the precipice of life, *not knowing*. I want to laugh aloud at the tragic look on your face. I can hardly stand the waiting—and your misery isn't miserable any more, but the plain wrapping of an unspeakable treasure, the wrapping about to be snatched away. To me it is a wild hilarity that your dreary interpretation could be so wrong and so right at once. You said, "Sir, if you have carried him away—" He did! This man did! This gardner indeed had carried himself away, on the legs of his own most glorious life!

Sad Mary, lost Mary, ignorant Mary, Mary in mourning—tell me!

What was that next instant like? How is it, to be found and suddenly to burn, in every member of your being, with life?

How is it, suddenly to be?

As God spoke all creation in the first place, so it was *his* word that woke you. He spoke it, no one else. He conceived it, and he gave it breath, and he sent it forth into the world. *But his word was you!* You were formed in it. By that single word you came to understand all things in a trice. It clothed you, and you took up being in that word.

And how he said that word revealed unto you who he was: not only that he was and was alive, but that he loved you, too, and that his promises were true, and that in the same instant, by the same word, he was keeping his promises for you: peace, as the world cannot give peace; a joy complete—and life.

One word! He chose no other word by which to raise you from the dead, by which to work one wonder and a thousand, than your own name.

He said, "Mary!"

The shepherd called his sheep by name, and the sheep *became* a sheep, knowing his voice and knowing that she was known by him. How did it feel, little ewe lamb?

He said, "Mary!"

The Word, by which the world itself was created, created yet again, anew, from above, by love instilling love that she might love him in return. How did it feel, little baby, born not of blood nor of the will of the flesh nor of any human process, but of God? He the speaker, you the spoken; his the voice, but yours the name! The Lord God said "Light!" and there was light; the Lord Jesus said "Mary!" and there was a Mary. The Lord God said, "I have named you"; and the Lord Jesus said, "You are mine." Oh, Mary, Mary, Mary, sister mine: how did it feel?

There are certain little fishes that, when they hatch, are taken into the mouths of their mothers. How is it, to be born in the mouth of the Lord?

He said, "Mary!"—and you, *strapheisa,* turned. What a turning that must have been! Surely, this was more than the turning King Saul experienced when the Spirit of the Lord came mightily upon him that he might prophesy—when he was "turned into another man"—for you could see the subject and the object of your turning. You outstrip Saul! Is it the wondrous turning which the Lord performed in times past: who can turn the rock into a pool of water, flint into a spring of water?—who turned the psalmist's mourning into dancing?—who takes a curse and makes it a blessing? Are these the ghosts of meaning, the constellation of images that attend upon your turning? Is this what he did for you, and how it felt?

Or if not, sweet, laughing Mary, you tell me: how did it feel to name him with the old name not as remembering but knowing that he heard it and gave it goodness in *your* mouth? Oh, didn't you feel singularly powerful, saying "Rabboni" again, boldly asserting the relationship, declaring to him that he was "my own"? He named you that you might entitle him! You were alive. You were *so* alive.

Or how did it feel to name him with the new name, knowing the absolute truth of the title, although you spoke it into the dull ears of the disciples, because you had seen that Truth? Didn't you feel a wild vitality, crying, "I have seen"—and then you said it, the first to say it upon his resurrection, the first in whose mouth it could take its plenitude of meaning, embracing the universe with authority— *"the Lord"?*

He named you. He raised you, that you might announce his resurrection to the world. It is all one. In his rising was yours; in your rising is his made known. And so you *more* than came to be when he named you, precisely because *he* named you (this is what creating has been from the beginning and what language in the mouth of God has done): you came to be related unto him, which is love. And more than a merely static relationship, a fixed identity for you, it became an active relationship because he who made you also gave you something to do. Behold this woman: a being with a reason to be. And if she has a reason, then she also has a future toward which she moves with purpose and in hope. She has a ministry again, serving him, the source of her life, by crying his life, his title, and his love into the world.

O dear Mary, my sister, how I love you. I watch you lift your skirt the better to run, to run from the tomb into the city, to run without weariness but in the joy of an endless energy and with supernal purpose. I watch you burst into the disciples' hiding place, and I love you. I see the very radiance of your face as you touch the poor men, one by one, with your eyes. I see the eagerness with which you gaze at them, yearning for them to believe the thing you are about to say, so that they, too, might come to life and be blood brothers to you. I hear you draw breath to speak— and I love you, dear, because it is my Jesus bright in you, and because you are now hidden perfectly in him, and I cannot understand the mystery of that new relationship, but shan't I love you deeply, deeply, completely and innocently on *his* account? I shall. I do. It is the sole response that I can have to the wonder before me, the thing you are and are about to do: that I love you.

No! No, Mary. No, there is one other response in me when I hear the laughing music of your language, the Truth particular and universal in your speech to the disciples, the Word in your words, the Confession, now, of Faith. It is to beg you, my sister, my saint so far ahead of me:

Won't you tell me of the raw thing itself, of the thing made primal and eternal, of Life? Won't you tell me how it felt to say,

*I have seen the Lord!*

◊   ◊   ◊

When Orpheus was a little child, he had the odd habit always to forget the hiding place of one Easter egg. Year after year his mother hid one egg in the same place. You'd think he'd remember. But year after year he forgot about that place, and so he always came up one egg short.

In fact, she hid six eggs for her son; and the custom was that all day long, from the dawning till the dark, he could look for them. So he would wake in high excitement even before his mother was up and run through the house dribbling giggles wherever he went, crawling under furniture, peering into cupboards, scanning mopboards, checking corners.

Six eggs exactly, one for each of the letters of his name, each one dyed a different color: Orange, Red, Purple, White (his mother's idea, since she couldn't think of a color beginning with the letter *H* and she pronounced the word *Hwite* anyway), Azure, and Yellow—ORPHAY!

By the afternoon he would always have found five, but the sixth eluded him. Poor Orphay's spirits would droop. He would look over and over again in the same places. Sometimes a little voice in his head would whisper, *There it is!* But the voice lied. It was only his own desire whispering to him, causing an instant of false gladness. *There it is!* But nothing was there.

Now, his mother would watch his searching with delight. All day long she maintained her delight—and especially when the hiding place was the same this year as last, no different. That intensified the joke and the joy when he should finally see it, remembering not only the place, but also his forgetfulness and himself. What Orphay forgot was to look any place else but on the first floor of the house. He never remembered that his mother could creep so close to him while he slept and he not know it.

So then, what revealed the sixth egg to him was her laughter. It was always her laughter. And then he went to her, laughing too.

Suddenly he would hear his mother's bubbling laughter from above him. She couldn't contain it any more. She was in his bedroom. And then he would remember. *Oh!* Up the stairs the child would race, giggling silly, ready to explode. Into his own bedroom—and there, beside his bed, was his mother, sitting on the floor and laughing helplessly, shaking her head, the tears running from her eyes, holding up an egg for him to see: ORPHAY! Her laughter was her love for the dumb boy. Oh, how she loved her son in his stupidities!

Then Orphay would burst into laughter at his own stupidities and sillinesses, seeing himself in her eyes. With a shout he'd pitched himself bodily into his mother's stomach, laughing and laughing with her, and they wrestled until they couldn't move any more on account of their aching joy. So then they only just held one another, and laughed.

When he grew older, the memory of Easter for him was never visual. He didn't look back and *see* his infant Easters. No, it was sound. And the sound of it was his mother's wonderful laughter.

When Orpheus finally had been left in the church alone, the meeting done, the people gone, the door bumped shut on Dolores's departure, he considered to himself that he would probably get up, now, and change clothes. But he didn't. He was sitting in the basement, the fellowship room. Strangely, his mind, emptied of every other thing, imagined the getting up, imagined his walking to the parsonage and pulling jeans from the dresser drawer and putting them on and, possibly, running a glass of water for himself. Water, yes. He was thirsty. But it was all in his head. For a moment he lost himself in an action that he hadn't performed. He hadn't moved. He kept sitting in the same chair.

Well, then he wondered what he was going to do—not just in this moment, but with his life. Here the imagination didn't work so well. He saw himself in a train, traveling somewhere; but he couldn't fix the destination, and he didn't know where. "All the world before me," he said aloud, but he didn't believe it, because he couldn't make one single part of the world real to his mind.

He thought about supper, wondering whether he could eat solid foods, now that his voice was back. He hadn't tried that. Maybe his stomach would reject it. But he could go to a restaurant, he thought, because he didn't have to worry about preaching tomorrow and he had the whole evening in which to be free.

*Not preach tomorrow.* There was a thought to think about. What would he do instead? For years his life had been composed of weeks, and the weeks divided by preaching. Preaching had clocked time for him, had ticked his experience into equal parts, the same way as the seasons of the church year had established years for him: Advent, Christmas, Epiphany, Lent, Easter, Pentecost and the long season thereafter. Without these things, time and the years were an indistinct blur—

No, he didn't feel like going to a restaurant. He didn't feel like eating at all.

Perhaps he should read.

Read what? That was a foolish thought.

He did nothing. He kept sitting in the basement with his hands thrust in his pockets. The furnace kicked on once or twice. The men's toilet was not properly closed in its tank; therefore it hissed water into itself sometimes, then shut with a thump, but continued to leak and so, when the tank level went down, hissed water again. This was the building he'd served in for—for how many years? Yet he'd never truly looked at the building as a living thing before nor listened to it. Neither was it speaking to him now. It was just maintaining itself—against the day, perhaps, when Mr. Arthur Williams would smash it to construct a new one. Old, old building. They'd dug out the basement space with a mule. That was the year of the flood. Once the hole was dug the water filled it and they had to dig it again. Same mule. There was a picture somewhere of the first members sitting out in front of the brand-new building, all dressed in a Sunday best, some smiling and some solemn, all of them preternaturally still and silent. They were dead now, though the building remained. Mrs. Story had been a Jaxson then. She was dead. She was dead. Yes, she was dead, now.

Orpheus sighed and stood up. Without thinking about it, he went upstairs into the sanctuary, walked up the narrow aisle, then stood facing the chancel, the little concave in which had been Holy Communion, into which had gone the communicants to be touched, out of which issued the Word, prayers, preaching. So he thought without much feeling. He turned and sat on the chancel steps, facing empty pews. *Sing to me, little church. Tell me all your stories—*

*How did your previous pastors leave? Were they given farewell dinners and speeches and gifts? Did they take love away with them? Was love a keepsake, and did you part with some of it—or did you keep it to yourself?*

*Hush, hush, little church. There is no blame on you.*

What Orpheus did, finally, was to lie back, his hands still in his pockets, his body stretched flat on the chancel floor.

He thought, staring at the ceiling, "I'll have to call Arthur and find out how much time I have to leave the parsonage. What? Two weeks? That's okay. I suppose I could leave to-morrow—if I knew where to go."

Which was to say: there was nowhere to go. This had been his whole life. He'd never considered another one. These had been his whole people. He knew no others. None.

All these thoughts moved through his mind like checkers pieces, mere facts and no emotion. Orpheus felt neither self-pity nor judgment nor anger at anyone. It was right. He did not dispute the exile at all. And that everyone had turned away from him was exactly what he'd expected; it was for this reason that he'd worn a suit that day—for dignity, somehow to approve their cutting him off, to make the sentence formal. He didn't want any one of them to feel guilty, because they had no guilt. Guilt was altogether his. It was right. Cain should always be named and marked and made a stranger.

Orpheus let his eyes close.

The floor beneath his back was hard, and his own flesh was no cushion since so much of it had melted away. His bones indicated the soreness to come. He didn't move. He kept his hands in his pockets for the warmth; the rest of him felt a little chilly; but he didn't get up. He fell asleep.

Orpheus dreamed.

Somewhere in his sleep he thought he heard a woman's laughter, laughing as though she were trying to repress it, but laughing and laughing nonetheless.

At first he felt very glad for the laughter—not just because it was a happy sound, but because it reminded him of his mother. Her spirit came and surrounded him. He appreciated that deeply, although he knew it wasn't real, but a tingling dream. Then it wasn't her spirit only, but her body; and the day was Easter. She was upstairs, laughing over the egg he had not found, and he was downstairs, a child desperate in the search.

He expected that he would feel glad to re-experience the Easters of his childhood. But he didn't. No, when the little boy Orphay heard his mother laughing upstairs, he immediately looked to the windows and saw that it was night. Her timing was way off. She had waited too long this time to reveal the egg to him. Day and daylight were altogether gone; Easter was over; and the poor child panicked.

Little Orphay screamed at the ceiling, "Mama! Mama! Come down!"

But his mother only kept on laughing, preciously, lightly

mindlessly laughing, and the boy was terrified for her because he loved her and she did not know the danger. It was his fault. He hadn't made her *believe* the danger. *Mama! Oh, Mama, come down!*

He went to the bottom of the attic stairs. There was only darkness up in his bedroom and the sound of her laughter, which jangled joyless now, like keys lifted up and shaken in the night. She wasn't coming down. He had to go up.

Step by step he ascended a very long staircase to the bedroom.

*Mama,* he called, trying not to cry. *You didn't know, but you should never hide the egg under my bed!*

Without ceasing the laughter, his mother asked sweetly, *Why not?*

*Oh, mama!* the poor boy wailed, overcome by knowledge too great for him to bear; he was so little to be privy to such evil. *Because the Robber is under there. The Robber will kill you!*

As soon as he said that, the laughter stopped, and he was in his bedroom, very sad. He was staring through darkness down at his bed. His mother lay on the bed, and she was dead. Too late. She was perfectly white, like an egg. It was moonlight through the window that made her so white.

For a long time the boy gazed on the form of his mother, struck to silence by her beauty. He had never taken notice of her beauty before. Then the sadness twisted deep in his stomach; it grew into his chest, and it swelled to aching into his throat, and then he couldn't help himself, but he burst into tears for the death of his mother. He hadn't warned her soon enough or well enough, and the Robber had killed her.

Orphay fell to his knees beside the bed, crying, *Mama, I'm sorry, I'm so sorry!* He folded his hands, gazing at her white profile, the perfect straightness of her nose, and sobbed: *Didn't you know that I loved you? Didn't I tell you that too? Didn't I tell you that I never wanted you to die?* He cried till his throat was sore. He was so lonely! He cried because he wanted to kill the Robber back for killing his mother, but the Robber was gone, having done the thing he came for. He cried because the whole world crawled with countless Robbers, everywhere in the night. But he cried most desperately because it was his Robber, under his bed, that had killed his mother—in the middle of her happiness.

She never moved. She never changed, his alabaster mother. She didn't so much as blink. The child slid down to the floor and lay on his back beside the bed. His tears subsided.

Then he had a thought; he had a memory. If he hadn't remembered the egg in time to find it, yet he could remember a certain healing, a charm that had worked in the past— and he tried it.

The child Orphay began to sing hymns. Toward the darkness near the ceiling, straight up, he sang in a pitiful voice, halting between the words to sob: *Rock of ages,* he sang, *cleft for me, let me hide myself in thee, in thee, in theeee—*

Then, as simply and as easily as time, his mother came to him in a whiteness that was light. She knelt down beside him and stroked his forehead and smiled. She said, *Does your head hurt? Here. Take my pillow.*

She nudged a pillow underneath his head so tenderly, whispering, *Orphay, my little Orphay.* And then she was gone.

And the dream was gone.

When Orpheus woke up again, it was the night indeed. Very dark. Some street light filtered through the stained-glass window; that was hard light on the right side of the church. And some moonlight, too: that was soft light on the left side. The sanctuary was quiet. The chancel in which he lay seemed a yawning mouth.

He woke without moving, by the mere opening of his eyes. He had been asleep for a long time. How long, he couldn't tell.

But when he did move, he felt something beneath his head. He turned and touched it, then his heart swelled up, and Orpheus started to cry.

"Who did this? Oh, who did this good thing?"

It was a pillow. Why should anyone have remembered him with such kindness, a pillow? He didn't deserve it. He deserved nothing. But his worthlessness made this little pillow as good as all the treasures of the world. That's why he was crying, for the pure kindness of the gift.

"Please," he wept into the darkness, "who would give me a pillow?"

Immediately he heard laughter in the church—light, tinkling, purely happy laughter, as if a wonderful joke had just come to its conclusion, familiar laughter. "We did," said a cheerful woman. "Ooo, Pastor, we fooled you!"

A softer, more hesitant voice whispered, "I thought your head hurt. I gave you my pillow"—and Orpheus felt such a flood of gratitude that he could not bear it. He covered his face to weep.

"Don't cry," said the man's soft voice.

But "Let him, let him," said the woman's delighted voice. "He got to get it out sometime. He been holdin' it in too long now. All God's child'en got to cry."

Orpheus felt a hand on his cheek, then looked and saw a dark form crouched beside him. He took the hand and held it, hard, as hard as he could. He whispered, "O my Corie Jones!"

"An' Arabelle Lee!" sang out Arabelle Lee.

"I don't," said Orpheus. "I don't deserve—"

"I love you," said Coral Jones swiftly, nervously. "An' God loves you too. He didn't never not love you. No, but he been waitin' for you, been waitin' ever' day of your life, to call you his chil'. And how do I know this?" said Corie. He was stroking Orpheus's hair. "On account of, you tol' me, an' I never forgot it. And then God gave me the proof—'cause look at me an' Arabelle Lee now." Corie of the great doe's eyes. Corie of the gentle hands. He said, "Me an' Arabelle, we doin' jus' fine. The baby's comin' soon, an' we ready, yes we are. We gon' take good care of that baby, 'cause we can—"

Orpheus could not talk, he could not talk.

Arabelle, the second dark form in church, crept to his side and chuckled low. "We heard you ain' the pastor no more. That right?"

Orpheus shook his head. He nodded. He was surrounded, and could not talk.

"Well, it's why we come," she said. "We checked the parsonage, but you wasn't there. So we come here, and here you was." She chuckled again. "Corie says, 'Go get him a pillow,' an' I do, quick's a bird-wing, gone and come again. Well, you needed somethin', and we know 'bout need. So we come. We been sittin' with you. Corie said, 'Le's sit till he wake.' Corie was very firm about that. An' then you woke up." Now she plain laughed at the wonder of it all. "Oh, Pastor!" she cried, delighted.

Slowly, Orpheus sat up between Corie and Arabelle. He put out his arms and gathered them against himself, Corie in his left arm, Arabelle in his right; and Corie buried his face in Orpheus's chest, and Arabelle pressed her cheek to his, and they held one another, all three.

"Pastor," murmured Arabelle, "you come live with us."

"No. No," said Corie, almost dreamy in the hug.

Arabelle pulled back and snapped: "What you mean, No? He cain't live with us?"

"No," said Corie. "I mean you can't say 'Pastor' no more. Not any more, no, 'cause he ain't a pastor."

"So," said the woman, understanding. Huge things were occurring, elemental changes. She rubbed her huge belly thoughtfully and said, "So. Then what do we call him? We got to call him somethin'."

Orpheus drew his knees to his chest and rocked slightly forward, utterly content to let these two decide his name, overwhelmed by the mere touch of their bodies against his. Had they no thought how he'd sinned against them in the past? No, none. He could not speak.

"Well, what's his name? It's Orpheus," said Arabelle, "ain' it? That's what I'll call him, plain Orpheus. Ex-pastor. Ex-man. Hey, Orpheus!" she chirped, and he managed a nod. "See? It works." She kissed him, and the tears rained down his cheeks.

*How can you kiss me?*

Corie, kneeling and gazing at his friend, said, "You call him Orpheus. Me," he whispered solemnly, hesitantly, "if he don't mind, I'll call him brother." As though testing the title, he said, "Why don' you get your stuff, brother, an' come home with us?" He stood up.

But Orpheus could only shake his head. Twice he lifted his hands, then dropped them helplessly onto his knees. Oh, he was no use: he couldn't stop his crying.

"Wait. Wait," said Corie Jones. "Jus' a minute." He turned

into a shadow again and slipped down the aisle, down the stairs. When he came back, he put a paper cup of water into Orpheus's hands. "Drink this," he said.

Orpheus took a sip, felt the pain of swallowing, and sighed profoundly.

"Brother," said Corie Jones of the soft doe's eyes. "what's the matter? Do you hurt?"

"No," whispered Orpheus. "No."

Arabelle said, "It ain' the beating Johnny gave you, is it?"

"Maybe what the church folk done to him," said Corie.

"No, no, no," whispered Orpheus.

"Well, but," said Corie, "why can't you stop cryin'?"

"O Corie Jones," said Orpheus. "Because I have seen the Lord."

All this took place in the first little hours of the Pentecost. Orpheus had slept a long time on the chancel floor before he woke, and Corie and Arabelle had given up their night at the Come-Back Inn to be with him. So they had crossed from Saturday into Sunday, together and unnoticing.

The grey light of dawn roused them, as it were, and persuaded them to get busy before the congregation began to arrive for worship.

Corie pointed at a great red car with a scrape down its side, missing the right head- and tail-lights, parked in front of the parsonage. "M' Buick," he said, solemnly and proud. "Two hun-derd and fifty dollars. Space enough for me an' Arabelle an' Tulip an' the baby—and you. And all your stuff."

Arabelle puffed out of the parsonage with foods and pots and pans. "I'm used to it," she laughed when Orpheus tried to take the load from her. "Me an' Tulip've moved often enough." And, as she crammed boxes into the trunk of the car: "Usually at night." She had such slender fingers, such a thin body to be carrying the great, bursting pod of her pregnancy before her. Orpheus was moved to see how, in fact, the street-wise woman took enormities in stride. "An' usually with my boyfriend's TV too—payment for hard times." She laughed.

"There," said Corie Jones, driving down Sycamore. He pointed at a restaurant. "That's where I work. Night-shift cook. Whady-a think a that?" Three heads turned as they drove by, three proud faces: yes, that's where Corie Jones earned his living.

And here's where Corie Jones lived, he and his family, a shotgun house with false brick on the front, three rooms in a dead-straight row and little privacy therein. The middle room served as a bedroom, the back room the kitchen. Orpheus would sleep on a sofa in the front room, and he would wake with Tulip staring in his eyes. That would be his future, then: Tulip in the mornings. "Brothah, did you dream last night?"

"Sister, kiss me, and all my dreams are gone."

"Hoo! Where did you get that breath?"

"Oh, Tulip. Sweet Tulip. Not everyone can smell like you."

"'Cause I'm so pretty."

"Kiss me, pretty Tulip."

When the family had gathered to eat on that evening of the Pentecost, Coral Jones, somewhat embarrassed, somewhat proud to be sitting at table with Orpheus in his own home—he the benefactor, finally, made good in giving—said, "Well." He said, "Well, then," and cleared his throat. "Well, do what you come here to do. Pray."

Orpheus prayed. He prayed in perfect peace, quietly, straight into the ear of Jesus. There were no distances any more between himself and his Lord, because this rental house was where Jesus lived and it had been granted unto Orpheus to live there too—the gift he had not asked, because it was something he hadn't to deserve.

> *Lord—let my shame*
> *Go where it doth deserve.*
> *And know you not, sayes Love, who bore the blame?*
> *My deare, then I will serve.*
> *You must sit down, sayes Love, and taste my meat:*
> *So I did sit and eat.*

Orpheus prayed. He said, "The eyes of all wait upon thee, O Lord, and thou givest them their meat in due season. Thou openest thine hand and satisfiest the desire of every living thing."

Tulip burst out laughing at such language from a white man.

Arabelle Lee said, "Oh!" and clutched at her stomach.

Corie Jones looked serious, because he took prayer and Orpheus, both, seriously.

But Arabelle had clutched her stomach because the contractions had begun.

*That which was from the beginning, which
we have heard, which we have seen with
our eyes, which we have looked upon and
touched with our hands, concerning the
word of life—the life was made manifest,
and we saw it, and testify to it, and proclaim to you the eternal life which was with
the Father and was made manifest to us—
that which we have seen and heard we proclaim also to you, so that you may have fellowship with us; and our fellowship is with
the Father and with his Son Jesus Christ.
And we are writing this that our joy may be
complete.*

We are, indeed.

—Walter Wangerin, Jr.